Advance Praise for *Playing The Game*

"Playing The Game *is a serious, straight-faced—and hilarious—account of the Maypole dance the coaches have to do every year in order to get even half-decent athletes into the Ivy League.*"
—Tom Wolfe, best-selling author of *The Bonfire of the Vanities* and *The Right Stuff*

"*The Ivy League's dirty, little athletic secrets are exposed by Chris Lincoln and Ivy presidents will be blinking and scrambling for safety.*"
—Paul Witteman, assistant managing editor, *Sports Illustrated* (ret.)

"*The Ivy League was created to provide the framework within which institutions sharing similar academic standards could offer their students a broad range of competitive intercollegiate athletic opportunities.* Playing The Game *offers many insights from a variety of perspectives on the difficulties and complexities involved (including the sometimes convoluted formulas that have been devised) in attempting to achieve the worthy but elusive goal of a "level playing field" among eight like-minded and well-intentioned colleges that otherwise vary in size, curricular requirements, resources, and traditions. There's informative reading here for everyone involved in intercollegiate athletics, from prospective student-athletes through to college presidents.*"
—Fred Hargadon, former dean of admission at Princeton University,
Stanford University, and Swarthmore College

"*As Chris Lincoln pulls back the curtain on Ivy League sports, he meets the two tests of a good book: He tells you stuff you don't know, and does so in an engrossing way. The voices in these pages—of coaches, prospective athletes, and administrators—are honest and heartfelt as they recount the pressure they feel to reconcile the Ivies' lofty ideals with a dodgier reality. Part explainer, part exposé, and part polemic,* Playing The Game *fills a huge gap in our knowledge of how college sports work.*"
—Alexander Wolff, *Sports Illustrated* senior writer, and author of
Big Game, Small World: A Basketball Adventure

"*Chris Lincoln has done an exceptional job of explaining a recruiting process that will surprise lots of folks who think they know all about the Ivy League. The interviews, stories, and analyses Lincoln presents may dismay non-athletes who'd like to attend the Ivy League schools when they realize the exceptional admissions advantages enjoyed by recruited youngsters. But* Playing the Game *should also help lead to the development of more open and fair systems of determining who plays (and studies) where.*"
—Bill Littlefield, host of National Public Radio's *"Only A Game"*

"Chris Lincoln hits the nail on the head regarding Ivy League and NESCAC athletic recruiting. It's rare to read such a daring and informative book that manages to walk the line between "exposing" hidden practices and representing the coaches' side of things. He points out all the unfair practices along with the games coaches and students play, but at the same time he is quick to suggest solutions that seem eminently feasible. The bottom line is that athletic recruiting at these top colleges is an incredibly complex and at times indecipherable system that Mr. Lincoln manages to make clear and logical."

—Dr. Michele Hernandez, author of *A is for Admission* and
former admissions officer at Dartmouth College

"Playing The Game offers a provocative look at athletics practices in the Ivy League. Chris Lincoln has contributed to a growing body of serious literature on the 'student-athlete' and challenges those who claim to lead by example to bring practice in line with philosophy. Corrective without being prescriptive, supportive but not sycophantic, Lincoln will prompt, and broaden, debate within the higher education community over the proper place of athletics in a student's total academic experience. This is a timely and compelling contribution to that debate."

—John McCardell, president of Middlebury College, 1991–2004

"Anyone interested in the connection between college athletics and academics should read Chris Lincoln's Playing The Game. *This is a well-researched and rigorous examination of the ways in which sports shape, for good and ill, the culture of higher education. Lincoln writes with verve, revealing the complexities of a subject at the center of our national discourse. Here is the story behind the story of what we see on the field. A fascinating look at the world of sports."*

—Christopher Merrill, author of *The Grass of Another Country: A Journey
Through the World of Soccer*

"Playing The Game is an insightful and candid look at the world of recruiting in some of the country's best academic institutions. On the heels of the works by William Bowen and his colleagues, Playing The Game *is an important response that will help balance the dialogue and hopefully lead to useful conversations."*

—Peter P. Roby, director of Sport in Society at Northeastern University

"Chris Lincoln takes us through the looking glass of Ivy League recruiting. As a former Ivy League athlete and someone who has followed the League for years, I think Playing The Game *is the most extensive look at the subject I've encountered in years. A must-read for anyone interested in the Ivy League in particular, and college sports in general."*

—Bill Reynolds, sports columnist, *Providence Journal,*
and author of *Fall River Dreams*

PLAYING THE GAME

Inside Athletic Recruiting in the Ivy League

Chris Lincoln

Foreword by Jay Fiedler

Dartmouth College and Miami Dolphins Quarterback

nomad press

Nomad Press
A division of Nomad Communications
10 9 8 7 6 5 4 3 2 1
Copyright © 2004 Nomad Press

The trademark "Nomad Press" and the Nomad Press logo are trademarks of
Nomad Communications, Inc.
Printed in the United States.

ISBN: 0-9722026-6-8

Questions regarding the ordering of this book should be addressed to
The Independent Publishers Group
814 N. Franklin St.
Chicago, IL 60610

Nomad Press
2456 Christian St.
White River Junction, VT 05001
802-649-1995
www.nomadpress.net

Dedication

For
Cecy, Nolan & Nick,
my dream home team

and for my parents,
John & Mary,
the ultimate academic and athletic duo.

About the Author

Chris Lincoln is a graduate of Middlebury College, where he played varsity soccer and hockey, studied art history and American literature, and was a dean's list student. His writing on sports and recreation has appeared in several New England–based magazines and newspapers. He lives in Vermont with his wife and two sons.

Contents

Foreword

When college coaches began to recruit me in high school, I had no intention of making it to the professional level in any sport. My goal was to use my athletic talent to help me get the best education possible while competing at the highest level possible. My recruiting process began during my junior year in high school when I received numerous letters from some of the top football programs in the country. Although I was also a standout athlete in basketball and track and field (and heard from a few college basketball and track and field programs), I received the most significant interest from colleges for my football abilities.

As my senior football season began, only about a quarter of the schools that had sent me letters continued to recruit me by making phone calls to my home. As my choices narrowed, I began to think about the criteria that I would use to evaluate each school. First, I wanted to go to a college that had a good engineering school and a top academic reputation. Second, I wanted to compete in both football and in track and field. And third, I didn't want to sit on the bench for two or three years, waiting for my chance to play. I wanted to go to a school where I could compete for a starting job as soon as possible.

By the end of my senior football season in high school, there were still a few major Division 1A football programs talking to me, but none of them were offering me a scholarship to play. These top schools had watched my performance suffer during my senior season due to a knee injury, and they also knew that I wanted to compete in track and field, which would conflict with their spring football practices. (This conflict eventually led me to turn down a track scholarship to Stanford.) Most of the scholarship offers I received came from Division 1AA football programs at schools in the Northeast. But the keenest interest in me came from schools in the Ivy League, where there are no athletic scholarships, only financial aid packages based on need. While many student-athletes would have chosen to take a scholarship offer and gone to college for free, I was fortunate enough to have great parents who allowed me to choose a college based solely on the criteria I had set at the beginning of the recruiting process. They did not force me to choose a school on the basis of its cost.

As the recruiting process unfolded, college coaches visited me at my home and my school. I learned more about what each institution had to offer, both from an academic and an athletic perspective. I discovered that the Ivy League schools recruiting me offered the best combination of football and track and field competition. Their football programs competed well against the scholarship programs that were offering me a free ride, and the Ivy track and field programs were actually better than the track and field programs at the scholarship schools. So when it came time for me to decide where I would make the five official visits I was allowed under NCAA recruiting rules, I decided to visit four Ivy League schools and Stanford. After deciding against the track scholarship at Stanford, I had to figure out which Ivy school was right for me.

I narrowed down my final list to Dartmouth, Harvard, Princeton, and Yale. These were the programs that had recruited me the hardest, and I felt they offered me the best chance of playing early in my college career. When I took my official visits, my goal was to discover where I would feel the most comfortable in terms of campus life. Based on my visits, I felt the students at Dartmouth and Yale were much more compatible with me than the students I met at Harvard and Princeton.

My final decision was a difficult one. I waited until the last day possible, May 1 of my senior year, to mail in my acceptance card. I sought advice from my parents, who had been through every step of the recruiting process with me (except on my official visits, which I made by myself). They believed that Dartmouth was the right place for me. I agreed. Dartmouth was the only school that offered me everything I wanted: a great engineering school, a campus I loved, students who felt right for me, a winning football tradition, and a good track program. It was also the only school that recruited me by having both the head football coach and the head track coach visit my home. It may have been a little thing, but the fact that the football coach had taken the time and effort to learn how much competing in track and field meant to me spoke volumes about how much he wanted me in his football program.

When I entered Dartmouth, I never imagined that I would eventually become a player in the NFL. Going to an Ivy League school not only provided me with an education that was second to none, it also provided me with a very competitive athletic environment where I was able to develop my skills on the football field. I certainly did not take the most popular road to the pros, but I have no doubt that it was the right road for me.

Today, hundreds of other high school athletes each year are making a similar choice and passing up an athletic scholarship to study and play at an Ivy League school. In the pages that follow, you will learn exactly how their Ivy League recruiting process works, and why it may be the toughest recruiting job for coaches in all of college sports. No other Division I conference in the country has such strict academic standards for its recruited athletes. And no other Division I conference competes without athletic scholarships. Athletic recruiting in the Ivy League is now a far more complex, time-consuming, pressure-filled, and controversial process than the one I went through nearly fifteen years ago.

This book takes you inside this fascinating game. The stories and voices, details and perspectives will both engage and inform you, leaving you the winner.

Jay Fiedler
Miami, Florida
June 2004

Preface

When my publisher approached me with the idea of writing a book on athletic recruiting at the highly selective schools of the Ivy League and the New England Small College Athletic Conference (NESCAC), I accepted immediately. I felt the project would be interesting and potentially helpful for my two sons, who show promise as athletes and as students. And I was excited because I have had direct experience with the subject. Years ago I was recruited by an Ivy and a NESCAC school, and more recently I have guided a number of high school soccer players through the college recruiting process, including two local boys whom I helped find spots at Cornell and Bates. As a result, I felt comfortable with the idea of writing about athletic recruiting at these selective schools, even though I knew I had a great deal to learn before sitting at the keyboard. At the start of my research, I had no agenda beyond learning everything I could about how the process works at these elite schools and focusing on its human rather than on its quantitative aspects. I had no idea just *how much* I would learn, or how broad and complex the subject would turn out to be. It has been a challenge to capture and to organize all the material I have found.

While conducting my research I sought stories and opinions of individual coaches, players, parents, athletic directors, admission officers, and even a few college presidents who are, or have been, involved in playing the athletic recruiting game in the Ivy League, and in its Division III soul mate, the NESCAC. I believed that the reader would quickly tire of too much straight factual reporting, and would instead prefer to hear more insightful, illuminating stories. I have been fortunate to hear many compelling personal accounts, thanks to the generosity of dozens of people, who kindly created a web of connections for me. I have acknowledged my debt to these generous contacts at the end of the book, but I wish to state now that any errors in my reporting, while wholly unintentional, are mine alone.

In addition to recording the stories, one of the most fascinating aspects of my research was having the opportunity to speak at length with a handful of Ivy League and NESCAC admission deans. With one son headed down the college application path within a year and another soon to follow, I was grateful for the rare opportunity to gain a better understanding of both the athletic recruiting process and the admission process in general. Any reader who is not necessarily a sports fan, but who is curious about the inner workings of admissions at these elite academic institutions will find the perspectives of these admission deans an insightful treat.

As wide ranging as this book is now, it was never intended to provide a comprehensive overview of recruiting for every single athletic program at every single Ivy League and NESCAC school. (That would be a job for ten people and take several years.) Rather, I have attempted to capture exactly what the recruiting process is like in a number of different men's and women's sports at several different Ivy League and NESCAC institutions. As you will discover, the schools share similar challenges and in certain sports share similar tests. One point that coaches and administrators emphasized, however, is that every school in these two leagues is also unique in having its own approach to athletics in general and to athletic recruiting in particular. Read the stories for what they are: detailed accounts of individual cases that reflect a greater picture.

Chapter One

Ground Rules

"There is no secret, and I have no qualms about saying it, but athletic talent makes a big difference in terms of our decisions. . . . The Ivy League principles always say that athletes should be treated like everyone else, but they are not. And that's what the presidents are sort of struggling with: 'Here's what the principles say, and here's what the practice is—and how to do we get them to match.'"

Michael Goldberger
Brown University
Director of Admission

Thirty years ago, as a senior at Hanover High School in Hanover, New Hampshire, I was recruited to play college soccer and hockey by a few schools in the Northeast. Coaches from Dartmouth, Middlebury, and the University of New Hampshire wrote me and called me and encouraged me to come to their schools. The UNH soccer coach offered me a full scholarship, the only one he had, saying he wanted to give it to an in-state player. I held him off for as long as I could, into March of my senior year, playing a game I'd been counseled to play by my next-door neighbor, the Dartmouth men's soccer coach, who was also recruiting me. Why, you might ask, would the Dartmouth coach have encouraged me to string the UNH coach along, when he wanted me at his school, on his team? Because he knew I might not get into Dartmouth, and he wanted me to keep all my options open. "You have to understand," he told me, "that the coaches are playing a game. They're telling you they want you, but they are telling twenty other kids they want them, too. They're doing this because they won't be able to get all of you into their schools. So you have to protect yourself. You should tell each one of them that their school is your first choice, so they will help you as much as possible. They're playing a game, and it's only fair that you play it back."

Much as I felt uncomfortable with the approach, I took his advice. It turned out to be a smart move. I did not get into Dartmouth in April, despite the coach's efforts to help me. My board scores, a combined 980, were just too low. But I did get into Middlebury, which had a better soccer team at the time, and I would never have been accepted had I not been recruited by the soccer coach and by the hockey coach, who had even more pull with Admissions. I told each of them that their school was my first choice. Along the way, I had been forced to pass up the UNH soccer scholarship in March, when the coach there forced my hand, saying he needed time to find another player if I wasn't going to accept his offer. I told him I wanted to wait on Dartmouth and Middlebury, and that I wanted to play both soccer and hockey, something I would not have been able to do on a full soccer scholarship. He proceeded to find a player from New Jersey, Bobby Black, who went on to be an All-American. You could say I did the UNH coach a favor.

Since then, the rules of the recruiting game in the Ivy League* and in the New England Small College Athletic Conference (NESCAC**), the league to which Middlebury belongs, have dramatically evolved into an increasingly complex procurement machine. Ivy League recruited athletes still enjoy a distinct advantage in the admission process much as they did in my day, and many continue to be admitted with lower academic credentials than their high school peers. But today athletic recruiting in the Ivy League has taken on a life of its own, threatening to destroy the Ivy image of adherence to the highest principles of academic

*The Ivy League includes Harvard, Princeton, Yale, Dartmouth, Brown, Cornell, Columbia, and the University of Pennsylvania.
**NESCAC includes Williams, Amherst, Middlebury, Colby, Bowdoin, Bates, Tufts, Wesleyan, Connecticut College, Trinity, and Hamilton.

excellence, untainted by the pursuit of athletic titles. As sports have become big business in many athletic conferences, so has the Ivy League succumbed to the temptation of glory in the winner's circle. When I socialize with graduates of these schools, they often say, "I would never get in now. It's so competitive." I always nod in agreement, but I don't say what I'm really thinking: that my chances of getting into one of these schools would probably be better, thanks to my ability to dribble a soccer ball and shoot a hockey puck. Today, my board scores (and yours, if you took them before 1996) would be one hundred points higher, thanks to the fact that the College Board "re-centered" SAT scores in 1996, raising math scores by an average of thirty points and verbal scores by an average of seventy. In the Ivy League, where only the highest combination of math and verbal scores from the SAT I *or* the SAT II tests are counted by Admissions when reviewing an athlete's application, I would now have a total score of 1190, because my Achievement scores (now called SAT IIs) were higher than my SATs. That total would be good enough, along with the right grades, teacher recommendations, and completed application, for a top recruited soccer or hockey player to be admitted to any Ivy school today, despite being 170 to 270 points lower than the average SAT scores of the general student body.

If you are being recruited today, you cannot play the game of telling every coach that his school is your first choice, as I did. Coaches talk to each other about players they are recruiting, and you will be called on your duplicity and rightly labeled a liar. I've never felt more uncomfortable than the night the Middlebury hockey coach called me, a week before the admission office was due to mail their letters, and told me that I had been accepted. "We're really looking forward to having you," he said. I was quiet for a moment before answering, "Yes . . . well . . . I'm waiting to hear what Dartmouth decides." After months of playing the game I'd been told to play by my neighbor, I couldn't lie to the Middlebury coach at crunch time. To his credit, my acceptance letter still arrived a week later. That phone call would never happen today, especially in the Ivy League, where coaches expect recruits to commit to a school months before April. Admission slots are now far too precious to risk having an accepted player enroll elsewhere. As a result, between 50 and 60 percent of recruited athletes in the Ivy League are now accepted through Early Decision or Early Action programs, and the rest, who apply regular decision, go through their own separate, accelerated admission timeframe, which results in nearly all of them knowing where they are likely to go to school by January or February, rarely as late as March. Unlike their high school peers, who wait and worry whether they'll be accepted at Harvard, Princeton, or Yale, recruited athletes are under pressure from coaches to *choose* between Harvard, Princeton, and Yale. Institutions with worldwide academic reputations usher athletes through their doors with special priority.

A player being recruited by an Ivy League school today would not be forced to pass up a full athletic scholarship, either, without knowing the likelihood of being admitted to that Ivy institution. This scenario, known as a "squeeze play," protects a college-bound athlete from winding up with nothing, no scholarship and no Ivy admission, as was my case in the spring of 1973. Back then the financial ramifications of such a scenario paled in comparison to those of today. I think UNH cost about $2,100 a year at the time, Dartmouth $4,600. The cost of attending UNH is seven times greater today, while the cost of attending Dartmouth has increased nearly ten-fold. In the past ten years alone the cost of attending a four-year college in the United States has doubled. I find this staggering, especially as a parent of two teenage boys who want to play college sports.

For many athletes, attending an Ivy school is a dream come true. The level of competition in many sports is extremely high, and the quality and reputation of the education is superb. There are those who argue that the Ivy League approach to college athletics offers the best of both worlds, and sets a shining example for Division I sports, where athletes in non-Ivy schools have been known to take separate classes, have special tutors and required study halls, live in athletic dorms, receive special treatment, and graduate at alarmingly low rates. In contrast, athletes in the Ivy League actually graduate at a *higher* rate than their classmates—all while balancing a year-round commitment to excelling in their chosen sport. This should all be celebrated, as should the remarkable accomplishments of the countless Ivy athletes who have gone on to achieve success in business, politics, medicine, law, education, the arts, and other careers following their graduation. A surprising number of heavy hitters in this country can boast of an Ivy League athletic career.

From my perspective, however, there are legitimate causes for concern with the Ivy League athletic system, and these are inextricably linked to its unique athletic recruiting and admission process. Because the Ivy League is intent on maintaining a balance between athletics and academics (a practice the schools affirmed nearly fifty years ago, when the League was formed), it now finds itself at the vortex of intense pressures unique to the Ivy League. These pressures include: demographic trends, such as the largest college applicant pool in history, which makes admission slots more precious than ever; athletic competition, where the level of play continues to rise across Division I, placing an ever greater premium on recruiting top athletic talent; and concern over the academic performance of Ivy athletes and their social interaction with their college classmates, both of which relate to the large amount of time Ivy athletes must now devote to their sport to remain competitive within the League and within Division I. These pressures will not diminish. If anything, they will only increase as Ivy League coaches, athletic directors, admission deans, and presidents struggle to maintain the precarious balance they seek between a proper emphasis on athletics and academics. In an era where many believe sports are out of control (and one can hardly argue with this view, looking around the country), the Ivy League struggles to keep a healthy perspective.

Unfortunately, this effort is sometimes accompanied by a superior attitude, the sort for which the Ivy League is notorious. Beneath the sanctimonious attitude, I found an all-too-human frailty. Too often the desire to excel in athletics betrays the principles on which Ivy athletics rests. The schools adopt rules to enforce their "Ivy principles" only to find ways to bend, or break them, in some cases by conspiring with each other. This hypocrisy is unsettling, as is the secrecy surrounding some of the League's admission standards for athletes and the exceptions they have made to their own rules over the years. The League is extremely competitive, and the pressure on kids to choose between schools can lead to ugly scenarios and outright lies on the part of both schools and applicants.

The Ivy League's unique approach to Division I college athletics differs vastly from the big-time schools. "It's not a matter of *degrees* of difference, it's just a different world," Princeton's long-time Dean of Admission, Fred Hargadon, told me just prior to his retirement in the summer of 2003. Hargadon should know. Before serving as Princeton's admission dean for fifteen years, he spent fifteen years in charge of admissions at Stanford, which has one of the nation's most successful big-time college athletic programs. To my surprise, Hargadon told me that he spent four times as many hours dealing with athletic recruits at Princeton than he had at Stanford.

Why is this the case? First and foremost, because the Ivy League is the only Division I athletic conference in the country that enforces its own set of academic standards for recruited athletes. Since 1984, the League has monitored and regulated the admission of every single athlete through what is known as the Academic Index (or A.I.), as a way to ensure that the academic capabilities of athletes are generally representative of each school's student body as a whole. Every Ivy institution has its own average, or "mean" A.I., and recruited athletes are screened for admission based on this average. The A.I. is calculated using a formula that includes an applicant's SAT or ACT scores and class rank or grade point average (GPA). While these scores, rank, and GPAs are all much higher than the minimum standard for Division I athletes set by the NCAA, within the Ivy League the academic criteria for as many as 40 to 50 percent of recruited athletes is lower than the credentials of their incoming classmates. This percentage varies by institution, and there are, as one Ivy admission dean told me, "gradations of exceptions." But this is the paradox of Ivy League athletics. In the larger, national context, the League's academic standards are exceptional, yet within its own universe, the Ivy League turns down other, more highly qualified students to admit some athletes. Big-time conferences would never dream of adopting Ivy recruiting standards; yet these very standards are exactly what stir much of the controversy within the Ivy League, causing headaches for coaches, athletic directors, admission deans, and presidents. As Brown Director of Athletics, Dave Roach, points out: "Look at the PAC 10. Stanford takes who they want. Oregon takes who they want. If somebody went to the PAC 10 athletic directors or presidents and said, 'Hey, we're gonna institute an Academic Index across the Conference,' they'd think they were nuts. They wouldn't even talk about it."

The PAC 10, Big 10, Big 12, Big East, ACC, SEC, and every other Division I athletic conference in the country wouldn't talk about compet-

ing without athletic scholarships either. But that is what the Ivy League ②
does. This is the League's second unique quality: financial aid is based on
need, not on athletic talent (or musical talent, academic talent, artistic talent, or any other kind of talent that might give a candidate for admission
an advantage over his or her peers.). As a result, recruited Ivy League athletes do not sign the NCAA's Letter of Intent, a formal commitment to
attend one school over another, as "signed" recruits by "State" do when
they accept a scholarship offer. As I discovered, and as you will see, the
League's reliance on a verbal commitment, rather than a written commitment, leads to lies, betrayals, and deception in the Ivy recruiting game. The
good news is that athletes in the Ivy League receive their need-based financial aid whether they are a leading scorer or a role player, a bench jockey or
someone who eventually decides to quit the team. No Ivy athlete is ever
forced to play to keep his or her financial aid.

The Ivy League is further distinguished by the fact that its member ③
institutions field many more intercollegiate teams than any other
Division I conference in the country, with an average of thirty-three
teams per school, versus a national D-I average of nineteen teams per
school. (Harvard, with forty-one, fields the most intercollegiate teams in
the nation.) Fielding such a large number of teams only exacerbates the
controversy over the number of admission slots awarded to athletes, and
yet the schools all value athletic participation and find it hard, if not
impossible, to eliminate teams (thanks in large part to active, vocal
alumni athletes who oppose cutting their programs). These Ivy teams
also compete for twenty-eight league championships, more than teams
in any other conference in the country. Yet, under league rules, Ivy athletes are subject to a far more stringent policy regarding "out-of-season"
participation in their sport, one that places greater restrictions on the
amount of time they can spend practicing and scrimmaging than their
Division I counterparts.

Despite this, the Ivy League has enjoyed a remarkable amount of
national success in a number of sports since 1990, including national
championships in men's and women's crew, men's and women's lacrosse,
men's and women's squash, and sailing, as well as high placement in softball, men's and women's ice hockey, and men's soccer. In the past decade,
individual Ivy athletes have won national titles in fencing, squash, skiing,

sailing, track and field, swimming, and wrestling, while others have competed for national championships in cross country and tennis.

Ivy schools compete fiercely with each other for the top student-athletes, because the pool of kids who qualify both academically and athletically is relatively small. "Let's face it," says Brown's Roach, "within the League, there's a pecking order." Perched on top is Harvard (though Princeton and Yale might argue about that), the nation's hardest school to get into, with its famous name and a long history of athletic success. "Harvard doesn't recruit," says Bruce Wood, author of the Ivy League history in the forthcoming *ESPN College Football Encyclopedia*, "they select." After Harvard has skimmed the cream, Princeton and Yale dip in, followed closely by Dartmouth, then a group of four schools, Penn, Brown, Columbia, and Cornell. This is not an absolute pecking order by any means, and it certainly does not apply to every sport. Each institution has its traditionally powerful teams, and coaches can, and do, recruit successfully against schools that are listed before theirs in the grouping above. What Dave Roach is referring to when he acknowledges a pecking order is the fact that coaches have to fight to overcome the status and prestige of Harvard, Princeton, and Yale when they are recruiting prospects.

There is also a financial aid pecking order in the League, whether some schools care to admit it or not. This is a fairly recent phenomenon, less than ten years old. For years, the financial aid packages at each school were tied into a larger league policy that sought to maintain financial equity between all eight Ivy institutions, and several other schools, including MIT, outside the League. Each spring, representatives from each of the group of nearly twenty schools gathered at what were known as "overlap meetings," where administrators sat down to review the financial aid packages of students who were about to receive "overlapping" acceptances to more than one institution. The administrators would compare the financial aid offers from the overlapping schools, and then make the awards uniform—with a general policy of meeting at the higher offer—so that the student would not have to base his or her final decision on which school to attend on the financial aid package. In the early 1990s, however, the League was taken to court by the Justice Department over this policy and sued for anti-trust violations, price fixing, and collusion, which put an end to this theoretically pure way of approaching and awarding financial aid.

What has followed is nothing less than a flexing of financial muscle, geared toward separating the most elite schools from the pack, in an intense competition to attract the best and the brightest students. Princeton revolutionized need-based financial aid in this country in the late 1990s by changing its policy to eliminate loans entirely and award only grants to students who qualified for financial aid. With a large (though not the League's largest) endowment, and the League's second smallest undergraduate student body (4,600, just above Dartmouth at 4,200), Princeton made a bold move to attract the best students possible across the board, not just athletes. Recruiting against Princeton today, when financial aid is part of the picture (as it is with many Ivy athletes, to one degree or another), is extremely hard. And it's not much easier to compete with the packages awarded by the massively endowed Harvard and Yale. Other schools will usually offer to match financial aid packages for recruited athletes, but, given the current timeframe of athletic admission decisions and commitments, getting two competing offers does not happen as often as you might think it would.

The financial aid picture for athletes is further compounded by differing policies on aid for international students. Dartmouth, for instance, gives virtually no aid to international students (Canada is exempt, much to the relief of the Big Green hockey coaches). As a result, Dartmouth will never compete with Harvard, Princeton, or Yale (all of whom award aid to international students) in squash, a sport now loaded with international talent. Ivy tennis rosters today also feature numerous international players, and Ivy soccer, basketball, and fencing teams have their share of international impact players as well.

The difference in the financial resources and priorities of each school also leads to differences in the size of each school's recruiting budget, the quality of its athletic facilities, the scope of its athletic budgets and payrolls (keeping top coaches can be a challenge), and the amount of fundraising required each year to support each school's athletic budget, including its recruiting efforts. In all these regards, every school in the League is different. There is no such thing as financial parity in the Ivy League.

Nor is there admissions parity. Some schools are simply harder to get into than others. Coaches and admission directors acknowledge that the toughest schools for athletes to gain admission to are Harvard (with the League's highest Academic Index) and Dartmouth (with a rising A.I. and the League's smallest student body). Princeton and Yale are close behind (they reject 90 percent of all their applicants), while Penn, Columbia, Brown, and Cornell all follow, each with varying degrees of admission difficulty for athletes, based on the size of their student body, their mean A.I., and their curriculum. Despite this general "ease of athletic admission" scale, it is not unheard-of for an athlete to be turned away by Cornell only to wind up at Harvard. The scale is a general guideline, not a hard and fast rule. Each year, when the League's admission deans get together for meetings, they will tease one another about the athletes they have each admitted, saying, "How could you have taken that kid? I saw his transcript. I saw his scores." The point being: they all make exceptions here and there, within the guidelines of the A.I., to support the sports that matter to their schools, the players they recruit from diverse backgrounds, and the local high school stars who will draw the interest of the hometown crowd.

The challenge facing the League's coaches is finding high school students with athletic talent who have the grades and tests scores to qualify for admission. It is, as I mentioned, a limited pool. The phrase I heard over and over around the League is, "You have to cast a wide net to make a small catch." That net now sprawls across the entire country, into Canada, and, for some schools, around the world. Ivy coaches manage recruiting lists that can be up to ten times larger than their non-Ivy, big-time athletic school counterparts. While a football coach at Notre Dame may manage a recruiting list of fifteen players, an Ivy football coach will start with a list of four hundred prospects; it's that much harder to find kids who qualify both on the field and in the classroom. For many years, Ivy coaches relied on a network of active, loyal alums interested in the success of their alma mater's athletic programs to help identify, evaluate, and interview prospects. But in 1987, the NCAA passed a rule that prohibits alumni from contacting potential recruits (in reaction to abuses by major college booster organizations and overzealous graduates, some of whom were suspected of offering bribes to athletes to attend their schools), and Ivy coaches were suddenly left to recruit entirely on their own. When league officials protested the NCAA ruling, which cut off their extensive and effective alumni network, Penn State's Joe Paterno, a Brown graduate, is reported to have accused the Ivy League of living in "a fairy tale world." The ruling was not a happy ending for coaches in the Ivies, whose alums are now limited to simply passing along the names of promising prospects.

The elimination of alums from the recruiting process, combined with the ever-increasing intensity of the recruiting taking place at most scholarship schools (many of which offer Ivy prospects money to come play), has raised the stakes higher than ever for Ivy League athletic programs and coaches. The cost of traveling across the country to watch players compete, visit their homes, meet their parents, and make a sales pitch has skyrocketed. And so has the amount of time Ivy coaches must now devote to their recruiting efforts, as much, some lament, as 75 percent of their time. The ultimate irony of the Ivy League is that it has succeeded in making the entire athletic recruiting process more time consuming, more complex, and more demanding than it is in any other league in the country—big-time or small-time—simply by virtue of enforcing its own set of academic standards for athletes. Special admission liaisons are assigned to every team at every school to help coaches gauge the academic qualifications of prospects, and every Ivy institution has an admission liaison based in the athletic department as well. An intense screening process takes place during the recruiting process, which eliminates many prospective athletes before an application is even filled out.

While Ivy League athletics may be held to ambitious academic standards, coaches remain under pressure to win. Livelihoods are at stake, just as they are at the big-time schools with low graduation rates. Ivy coaches get fired, or are forced to submit their resignations (the gentlemanly way of exiting a mired program). Losing seasons are tolerated for only so long. What's more, players in the League have also been known to revolt, leading to a coach's dismissal. Many schools will not award contracts to coaches that are longer than three years; in contrast, coaches at big-time schools can receive contracts for twice that length of time. These days, finding good players who are good students simply isn't enough. "There are plenty of kids out there who can play for us," Dartmouth men's soccer coach, Jeff Cook, told me. "The challenge is finding players who can make us better." Indeed, that is the goal of every coach, in every sport, in the League.

Thirty years ago, the recruiting game I played under the counsel of the Dartmouth soccer coach was a far simpler and less controversial game than the one being played today at these elite academic schools. Coaches are recruiting harder than ever today, parents are far more involved, kids are using every angle, and admission officers are balancing athletic recruiting within the context of the largest, most qualified college applicant pool in history. Getting into one of these schools, and playing a sport, is more challenging than ever. The level of academic and athletic talent is at an all-time high. As Russ Reilly, the Middlebury College athletic director, said to me one afternoon, "Chris, it's a lot more serious now. I'm not sure these kids today are having as much fun as you guys did back in the old days."

After what I've learned, I'm not sure, either.

Chapter Two

Big Time Player

"It's rare that anybody in our league will get a football kid of this stature. He's a big-time player."

John Lyons
Dartmouth College
Head Football Coach,
on prospect Matthew Slater

In mid-April 2003, Dartmouth head football coach John Lyons and his staff were anxiously waiting to hear if Matthew Slater would be attending Dartmouth in the fall. The son of NFL Hall of Fame lineman Jackie Slater had been through the entire recruiting process—receiving a visit from Lyons in his California home, making a visit to Hanover to see the Dartmouth campus with his parents, talking on the phone once a week with John Curry, the Dartmouth assistant who was his primary recruiting contact. Now it was time to decide. Slater had received his official letter of acceptance from Dartmouth Admissions. All he had to do was mail in the card, due by May 1, that confirmed he would be attending the school.

Slater had started out as a "million-to-one" shot for Dartmouth when Curry showed Lyons a videotape of the wide receiver with blazing speed back in December. Lyons had watched the tape and said, "Oh my god. He's like a man playing with boys. He's that much better." As a result of his exceptional ability, Matthew Slater's courtship had lasted far longer than usual for Ivy League football recruits, most of whom committed to Harvard, Yale, Dartmouth, Penn, and their Ivy counterparts by early February each year. "He was so good," says Lyons, "we just couldn't rush him. We said, 'Matthew, we'd love to have you, so whatever it takes we'll just do it.'"

Slater's football talents had attracted the attention of several other schools, including a number of Ivies. But he didn't like some of the Ivy coaches who had visited his home, and only Brown and Dartmouth made it through Slater's initial cut. The other suitors for his athletic talents were in another league altogether. They were all big-time football schools— UCLA, Oregon, Oregon State, Colorado, and Arizona State—and they were all offering him a full ride.

But Dartmouth had hung in there with the big-time schools, partly because Slater liked Curry, who was his initial contact with the school, and also because he really liked what he saw when he visited Hanover. "He was looking for a smaller school that had a quarter system, with three classes every semester," says Lyons. "He wanted to be in a smaller community, where he could interact with professors, because he's a bright kid. He liked the kids here. And he wanted an opportunity to play early."

Better still, a close friend and high school football teammate of Slater's had come to Dartmouth on a recruiting visit from California and loved what he found. He had committed early to attending the school, another plus for Slater.

"Matthew came here and wanted to really get it over," says Lyons. "And his parents said, 'No, no, we gotta take our time.'"

They took their son on a visit to Brown. "We were going, 'Oh no, he can't go to Brown,'" says Lyons, breaking into laughter. "'We don't want to play against this kid—we'd never be able to cover him!'"

Fortunately for Lyons, Brown did not have a quarter system, and Matthew was not wild about the school. He told Lyons he wasn't going to UCLA, either, because with 45,000 kids, it was too big. He wanted a small community. "I really like the idea of getting to know people," he said.

But Lyons sensed his parents didn't like the idea of having their son so far from home. "They're very nice people," says Lyons. "His father's a very sharp guy. Jackie's been around. He's very perceptive, he doesn't say a lot. He checks things out. He's very thorough."

Slater's parents continued to encourage their son to look at the big schools. Says Lyons, "His father was a longtime NFL player, he's in the Hall of Fame—so that's in the back of his head: can his son go to a school like this and get into the NFL?" Jackie Slater, however, didn't go to a big-time school. He was a college teammate of Walter Payton, another future NFL Hall of Famer, at a small school, Jackson State.

"If anybody would understand—'Hey, if you're good enough, it doesn't matter where you're coming from,'" says Lyons, it would be Jackie Slater. "I'm a little surprised that he got caught up in all that because he knows about Jay Fiedler and Jeff Kemp, who he played with, and Matt Burke from Harvard, who's with the Vikings. I mean, there are guys coming out of the Ivy League who are pretty damn good players in the NFL."

And, Lyons points out, there are also no guarantees when a player enters a big-time college football program. "My point to Matthew," says Lyons, "was that UCLA, Oregon—they have all underclass receivers. And those programs, at that level, it's a big business. Some of those guys don't even belong in college. They're borderline guys who should be in jail. They try to keep them in school and out of trouble. And they'll kill you, because their whole livelihood is being good enough in college to make money in the NFL. And this kid, you know, he's from a good family, he's got a lot of money, and he's been very sheltered. Personally, I think he could get eaten up at one of those places. Because it is so competitive at that highest level.

"I said, 'Matthew, come here, man. We're gonna get you on the field. You can run fast, and you're a good player. You can come in here, be an impact player, and play for four years, and have all kinds of numbers coming out of here. People are going to know who the hell you are. You go in there, you're fighting for your life with those guys. You're good—but so are all those guys.'"

For a while, the Dartmouth coaches thought Slater was going to Oregon because they kept recruiting him so hard. "Obviously," says Lyons, "when you go to Oregon and Oregon State and UCLA, you're getting wined and dined pretty good by these folks. It's a lot different than us taking them up to the Hanover Inn to eat dinner."

But despite the sales pitches from the big-time schools, Dartmouth remained Matthew Slater's first choice. Five days after receiving his official Dartmouth acceptance in early April, he spoke to Curry on the phone, who was pleased to tell Lyons that their dream prospect had said, "I've made my decision, I want to come to Dartmouth. I'm still working with my parents."

Lyons called him the next day. "He was waiting for my call," says Lyons. "He sounded really good. He said, 'Yeah, coach, I'm really excited, I just gotta work this out.'" Lyons told him, "Okay, if your parents have any questions, you give me a ring, and I'll be happy to talk to them. If not, we'll call you back at the end of the week."

Two days later, Lyons received a call from California. Only it wasn't the call he expected. Instead of one of Matthew Slater's parents on the line, it was the mother of Matthew Slater's high school teammate, the defensive back who was headed to Dartmouth. And she sounded delighted. "It's in the *LA Times*," she exclaimed. "I'm so happy Matthew committed to you guys."

It was news to Lyons. Apparently, the *Times* had written a short article about two baseball players, followed by a high school sports recap, which read: "Matthew Slater has decided to attend Dartmouth."

"Well," Lyons told the mother, "he hasn't." Slater still hadn't told him or Curry that he was coming.

And then, the very next day, the news was confirmed. The mail arrived in the Dartmouth football office containing a recruiting newsletter that Lyons and his staff subscribe to, and right there on the first page was a line reporting that Slater was headed to Hanover.

Still, Lyons and Curry had not heard a thing.

"John Curry has worked so hard on this," Lyons told me. "He's like the boxer Chuck Wepner in the fifteenth round of a fight. He's exhausted. I've never seen anything like this, that's gone on for this long. John's calling him up tonight to say, 'Hey Matthew, I see it's in the *LA Times*. You're coming to Dartmouth, huh?' He's just gonna start yelling at him: 'Yeah, you're coming, that's great!'" Lyons laughed.

Then, slowly his expression grew more somber. "I don't think his parents want him to go so far away. That's a factor. There's a war going on. And the war's going to be over in about three days."

The recruiting war in the Ivy League today is never over. Individuals and families make decisions, but the process of searching for players never ends for coaches. As Pat O'Leary, the Dartmouth assistant who recruited Jay Fiedler told me, "Our recruiting lasts fourteen months a year." For Dartmouth's storied football program, which has won more Ivy titles than any other school, the recruiting process became even more challenging back in 1996, immediately after they completed an undefeated season and captured the Ivy title outright.

"I'll never forget," John Lyons told me, "we came back from Princeton after we were undefeated in '96, and we were all happy. We came back here, and late that night I look and I've got something from Admissions, saying, 'Here are your new Academic Index bands.' And I thought, 'Oh my God, we're in trouble,' because it had changed dramatically."

What Lyons was referring to is a system unique to football recruiting in the Ivy League—the placement of recruits in stratified A.I. bands—and to the fact that the "mean," or average, A.I. of the Dartmouth student body had leapt significantly in 1996. The sharp rise in the mean A.I. of Dartmouth students was a direct result of President James Freedman's openly stated goal of lifting Dartmouth's overall academic reputation when he became president in 1988. But because the A.I. for each institution is based on a rolling four-year average for incoming classes, it took a while for Freedman's policy of admitting students with higher test scores (or, as one Big Green coach put it, "all the eggheads") to affect athletic recruiting at Dartmouth. But when it finally did, in 1996, it affected recruiting dramatically. Especially in football.

And the reason football stood out (and the reason it continues to stand out today as an Ivy League recruiting story) is because of the "banding" system that applies to the thirty football players who are allotted to each school's football program every year. Football is the most highly regulated of all Ivy League sports with regard to admissions. The bands vary from school to school (based on the school's "mean" A.I.), and they shift every year (almost always upward) as the A.I.s of each new incoming class are integrated into the A.I. calculations—so it is difficult to pinpoint exactly what each school's bands are at any given time. It is possible, however, to explain the formula that is used to establish the football bands, and to pass along John Lyons's opinion (echoed by a number of coaches and athletic directors around the League) about why the bands and the A.I. exist at all: "Because nobody trusts one another in this league."

Perhaps the best place to start is with the Academic Index formula itself. Unique to the Ivy League, the A.I. is a number that measures high school academic performance for the purposes of admission to an Ivy League school. It is calculated using a mathematical formula that relies heavily on applicants' test scores (66 percent of the "weight") and either their class rank or their GPA (the remaining 33 percent). A few specific examples will help to illustrate exactly how it works. Let's say a field hockey player, Kate, has SAT I scores of 650 Verbal, 680 Math; SAT II scores of 640 Literature, 680 Math, and 640 Chemistry; a GPA of 3.7; and a class rank in the top 20th percentile of her class. Because her high school provides class rank, that figure is used in her A.I. calculation, superseding her GPA. Kate's A.I. would be calculated by choosing her two best SAT or SAT II scores (they must be from two different subjects), and adding them together. (When the A.I. formula was established, the SAT IIs were optional at some Ivy institutions. As a result, it was decided that counting SAT II scores within the A.I. formula would also be optional. Hence, an SAT II score can never hurt a recruit's A.I. total, but only help it.) In Kate's case, her 650 Verbal from the SAT I and her 680 Math score from the SAT II are her two highest scores, totaling 1330. For the purposes of establishing an A.I., admission officers and coaches drop the zero on the SAT total and use 133 for the test score total. Now they are ready to add the number—59 points—assigned by the A.I. formula to a class rank in the top 20th percentile. The 59 points added to 133 give Kate an A.I. of 192.

Now let's take Rob, an ice hockey player, who has SAT I scores of 590 Verbal and 570 Math, SAT II scores of 630 Literature, 590 Math, and 600 Spanish, and a GPA of 3.5. Rob's prep school, like most private schools and an increasing number of better public high schools, no longer calculates class rank, because the college placement guidance counselor knows that it can hurt a student's chances of getting into a highly selective school (a truth that will be made very clear in a moment). Rob's calculations work as follows: 630 Literature, 600 Spanish (both taken from the SAT IIs, which are often higher scores for students than their regular SATs) for a test total of 1230, or 123. Add Rob's GPA of 3.5, which is awarded 69 points under the A.I. formula, and you get a total A.I. for Rob of 192.

As you can see from this exercise, Ivy coaches love recruiting players from high schools that do not calculate a class rank. Rob's 3.5 GPA is worth 69 points, while Kate's top 20th percentile class rank is worth 59 points. At a good high school, it's unlikely that Rob would be in the top 20th percentile with a 3.5 GPA, although it's certainly possible. Rob's test scores are also lower than Kate's, and yet his A.I. winds up being the same as hers. In either case, an A.I. of 192 is quite strong for a recruited athlete, well above the current league floor of 171 for athletes, though well below the 2003 average A.I. of 212 for Dartmouth students. But let's look at another example, and see how the difference in ten points can eliminate a prospect altogether. Joyce, a star point guard, attends a top high school that does not provide class rank. Her best combined board score is 1050, and she carries a 3.5 GPA (or 105 + 69) for a 174 A.I.—which puts her just above the League floor of 171. Andrea, on the other hand, is also a star point guard with 1050 boards and a 3.5 GPA. But her high school *does* provide class rank, and she falls into the 20th percentile. As a result, her A.I. (105 + 59 = 164) is calculated to be a full 10 points lower than Joyce's, and well below the League floor. This comparison of two very similar academic records illustrates how arbitrary the A.I. can be. The Council of Ivy Presidents established the current A.I. floor for athletes in June 2003. They voted to move it up from 169, where it had been since the inception of the A.I. in 1984, in an effort to bridge a widening A.I. gap between the general pool of applicants and the pool of recruited athletes in recent years, something we'll look at in greater detail later. For now, it's sufficient for you to know that the A.I. ranges from a perfect score of 240 (based on two 800 board scores and a number one class ranking or a 4.0 GPA) to 171 (which, as you've seen from the examples above, could be calculated based on any number of test score, class rank, and GPA scenarios). Below 171 an athlete cannot even be considered for admission to the Ivy League and coaches would be forced to cross him or her right off their list.

When Ivy League football teams recruit players, league rules require that they place each player into one of four A.I. bands. These bands are based on the mean (or average) A.I. of the school's student body as a whole, through what is referred to as "standard deviations" from the mean. Without getting too arcane and delving into math formulas, let's just say that standard deviation from the mean refers to the range above and below a school's given average A.I. According to Brown Director of Admission, Mike Goldberger, this constitutes an average of about fifteen points. "At some schools," he told me, "it's a little bigger. But that's the simple explanation." The football bands

bands

fall into four categories: mean to minus one standard deviation; minus one to minus two standard deviations; minus two to minus two and a half standard deviations; and minus two and a half down to the presumptive league-wide floor of 171. The rules state that schools must take eight players in the mean to minus one standard deviation band; twelve players in the minus one to minus two band; eight players in the minus two to minus two and a half band; and two players in the lowest band. Yet because the bands are all based on each individual institution's mean A.I., the bands for each Ivy football program vary. Hence, Harvard, with the League's highest A.I., recruits two players in a bottom band that actually never falls as low as the League's floor of 171—because a 2.5 standard deviation below Harvard's mean A.I. is about 180. (In fact, it's extremely rare for a Harvard athlete to be admitted with an A.I. below 180, and one coach at Brown, where the school's "mean" A.I. is lower, told me that he makes his living recruiting against the Crimson by finding great players with an A.I. between 171 and 175.) At the time this book was written, the A.I. hierarchy in the League read as follows: Harvard in first, Yale and Princeton neck-in-neck in second and/or third, Dartmouth a close fourth, then a gap, after which came Columbia, Penn, Brown, and Cornell.

What happened to John Lyons and his powerhouse Dartmouth football program in 1996, when his school's A.I. jumped dramatically, was simple and devastating. The Big Green's mean A.I. rose so sharply that Lyons could now recruit only two players in a range where he had previously been able to recruit eight. Worse, in the range where he had previously been able to recruit those eight players (which over four years amounts to thirty-two), Harvard had only been able to recruit two (or eight players over four years). Now, it was two for Dartmouth, two for Harvard. Even odds. And those are long odds when you're recruiting against Harvard.

That was partly why, in the spring of 2003, the possibility of landing Matthew Slater had Lyons and his staff jumping every time the phone rang. Yes, Slater was a big-time player, the best prospect Lyons had recruited during his eighteen-year tenure at Dartmouth. But more importantly, the youngster from California had the speed, running a 100-yard dash in 10.7 seconds under the scrutiny of an electronic timer, and the hands to put points on the scoreboard. Together with a group of good, young, returning players and a prized running back recruit, Slater could help lead the Big Green back to the pinnacle of Ivy football. Their once-dominant football program, which had slipped badly since the rise in Dartmouth's A.I. bands, was poised to dethrone Penn, who had just finished an undefeated Ivy season, and ready to even the score with Harvard and Yale, whose programs had improved in recent years, under the leadership of new head coaches.

Lyons sat in his office and held up the recruiting newsletter. He pointed to the line that reported Matthew Slater's intention to attend Dartmouth. "This is usually a pretty reliable thing. When the assistants saw this report they were ready to go to Murphy's, a local watering hole. I said, 'Wait a minute. Until Matthew tells us and I see the card in the mail. . . .'" His voice drifted off. He leaned back in his chair. "He would be the best player we've recruited since I've been here. They don't come here, kids who get a 1A offer from schools like Oregon, Oregon State, Colorado, Arizona State, and UCLA."

A week later, Lyons's prophecy proved correct. Matthew Slater did not come to Dartmouth. Apparently, he didn't work it out with his parents after all, and accepted an offer from UCLA instead.

As much as Lyons had sensed the news was coming, he was deeply disappointed to lose such a big-time player. Slater's blazing speed and sure hands would have made a huge impact on the fortunes of the Dartmouth program. Now, Lyons and his staff would have to find other ways to win following a 2002 season in which they had finished 2-5 in Ivy League games. In the weeks following that disastrous campaign, many had questioned Lyons' ability to carry on, but Dartmouth President Jim Wright stood by him, announcing the coach would be kept on.

"John Lyons is a good man, and he's also a good coach, and I've tried to be supportive of him," Wright told me. "I don't think that Ivy League schools sort of hire and fire coaches based on winning or losing. I think they've got coaches that are problems, that aren't good teachers. I regularly remind the coaches that they're teachers. If they're not good teachers, that's a different matter. I've tried to be supportive of John, absolutely, because he didn't suddenly become a bad coach."

Instead, the coach and his staff had suddenly faced a higher "mean" A.I., which radically altered their recruiting bands and the players they could pursue. Wright understood this, and he sympathized, but he downplayed his influence on the fortunes of the football or any other athletic program.

"I believe athletics are an important part of the Ivy and the Dartmouth experience," he explained to me in June 2003. "I think all things being more or less equal, I find winning more fun than losing. But the success of my presidency or these students' lives is not going to be determined by whether or not they win an Ivy championship. . . . I've urged Admissions and athletics to communicate and work together, but I would not want to exaggerate in any way a role that I've had there. I think Karl [Furstenberg, the Dartmouth dean of admission] knows how to communicate and talk with people, and he's eager to do that. Josie Harper [the Dartmouth athletic director] certainly knows how to do that. And the coaches do. I think that they work very well without my meddling or intervention, and that's the way it should be."

"Dartmouth has a pretty rich tradition of doing well in athletics," added the president. "Needless to say, there are some who would point out that in the last four or five years we have not done so well in some of our sports."

The most visible of those sports is football.

Says Lyons, "They've been good to me here. We had a lot of success, but then things went south. Fortunately, they're trying to change some of those things, but it takes a long time. Once it goes down, it's hard. . . . It's a level of commitment. They have a great history here in football, and they've let things slide. I kept telling them what they needed to do, but we kept winning and they wouldn't listen to me. And then all of a sudden it hits rock bottom, and they say, 'Maybe we should have paid attention to this stuff.' Now I see a president who's supportive, and now things are happening that never happened before. I think our Admissions relationship is good, but recruiting is just a hard job."

Especially when you're trying to climb back into contention, and you lose a big-time player like Matthew Slater. "Maybe he'll go to UCLA for a year and decide he wants to transfer," says Lyons, looking for the silver lining. "He really liked it here."

Chapter Three

Not Your Average Boosters

"Let's say there's a kid from Montpelier High School in Vermont. He may be a first-line player at Montpelier High School, but he's not good enough to play Division I hockey. He might have a 750 Verbal and 800 Math and be number one in his class. He comes in with a 230, 235 A.I., and he wants to go to Yale. He's a kid that the admission office is going to admit anyway, so we list him. It's a little bit of a hypocritical system. That kid never darkens my door, it's no loss to the hockey program, but he helps us be in compliance. . . . I think everybody does it."

Tim Taylor
Yale University
Head Men's Hockey Coach

Rob Chisholm was a first-line hockey player and captain at the Middlesex School, an exclusive, high-powered prep school in Concord, Massachusetts, when he applied to Harvard, Princeton, and Yale. The Nova Scotia native was also captain of the school's cross-country running and lacrosse teams, carried a 96 average, headed the school's environmental organization, performed in a singing group, acted in the theater, and was a member of a student-run organization called Sexual

Awareness for Everyone. In his junior year he won the junior class Student-Athlete Award, for excellence in both academics and athletics. At the end of his senior year, he received the Harvard Book Prize for outstanding character and citizenship. One faculty member described him as "the brightest kid on campus." He had excellent recommendations, and his chances of getting into Harvard, Princeton, and Yale were nothing short of outstanding.

His hockey skills, on the other hand, were not. At least they were not outstanding enough, coming out of a Division II prep school, for him to make the jump right into Division I college hockey. Despite being well aware of this, the hockey coaches at Harvard, Princeton, and Yale, when they learned of his interest in their schools, all added him to their lists of recruited players.

"I was admitted to Harvard, but was not heavily recruited at all," he says. "I didn't get a very promising vibe from the coach. I called Yale after I got in and they said, 'Oh yeah, why don't you come down and have a visit.' But they didn't sound enthusiastic to me, so I wasn't into it."

"I called the guys at Princeton," he continues, "and I said, 'Hey, I'm in and I'm interested.' And they said, 'All right, your plane leaves on Wednesday, get on it.'"

Interest from one out of the three programs was all he needed to make his final choice. He would attend Princeton. In the meantime, the Harvard and Yale hockey programs, which didn't really want him, had already used his high Academic Index to boost their team average and comply with league rules.

"I was an index booster," he told me. "You know about those, don't you?"

Academic Index boosters were around the Ivy League from the inception of the A.I. in the early 1980s until 2003. They began in football, where they spurred the creation of the football bands in the early '90s. And they spread into men's hockey and basketball, where they prompted more recent rule changes in 2003 aimed at eliminating them. The booster system, as Tim Taylor acknowledges, was hypocritical. And it illustrates how, in the highly politicized and competitive Ivy League, schools often act in the letter of the law, but certainly not in the spirit of the law. In the case of the boosters, the Ivy schools acted as a group, violating their own standards.

Here's what was wrong.

Until the 2003 rule changes, men's hockey and basketball programs in the League were using Academic Index boosters to comply with admission rules for incoming players in these two highly regulated sports. These rules required that each incoming class of male hockey and basketball players have an A.I. average within one standard deviation of the mean of the student body they were entering. Finding kids with higher A.I.s, who would never play for the team, was how many coaches and many admission deans balanced the lower A.I.s of recruited athletes who would play. The League's admission deans could be helpful, or not, depending on how they viewed the sport, the coach, and the idea of bending the rules. After making their acceptance decisions, many deans would comb through the records of the male students they had already admitted, searching to see if the students had a high A.I. and had listed ice hockey or basketball participation on their application. If so, they might be listed as an incoming hockey or basketball player, and help the "team" meet the A.I. average required under league rules. In contrast, Rob Chisholm was at least "lightly recruited" by Harvard before being included in their A.I. calculations, which makes his case look almost legitimate in comparison.

"We would joke about sitting around looking for some poor kid who once put on ice skates," says Fred Hargadon, the now retired Princeton dean of admission, in the spring of 2003. "It was on their application, and they'd already been admitted for other reasons . . . you would just look to see if there was anybody who'd been *near* an ice skating rink."

Some deans would argue that his description is a bit extreme, but it makes the point: the majority of these boosters were never on a coach's list, would never play a minute for the varsity team, and yet their higher A.I.s boosted the overall average of the incoming recruits, allowing the program to be in compliance with league rules. The vast majority of boosters were team players without ever knowing it, assuming a crucial role in enabling the real players to enter the school and put on a uniform.

Here's how this game was played in men's basketball. Under the Ivy rules in existence through the class admitted in 2003, programs were allowed to admit thirty-two players over four years (or eight players a year). Yet over four years, a basketball coach doesn't need thirty-two players, he needs twenty (as insurance against injuries and attrition), and he probably will only play eight or nine in most games, often fewer if the score is close. The admission deans, fully aware of this, knew the coaches really needed three, possibly four, talented players a year—with one or two real impact players in that mix—not the eight allowed under Ivy rules. And so, because Ivy admission spots are precious, the deans and the coaches would turn to the boosters—students who had already been admitted for other reasons—to lift the average A.I. of the incoming class of basketball players. A similar pattern was followed in men's hockey.

What's more, the A.I. averages for men's basketball and hockey were based on the players who were *admitted* to each school, not on those who actually *enrolled*. As a result, it was possible for a top student, such as Rob Chisholm, who was accepted at several Ivies, to be listed on the admitted "rosters" of three or four different men's basketball or hockey programs, even though, in the end, he would attend only one institution. The lukewarm reaction he received from the coaches at Harvard and Yale was part of a larger strategy: they didn't *want* to him come; they simply wanted to apply his higher A.I. to their team average. And they certainly didn't want him to count as one of their eight players a year; they wanted to reserve those for the recruits who would actually see ice time (thanks to Rob's and other boosters' higher A.I.s.)

"A key aspect to this game," one coach told me, "was accepting kids who you thought wouldn't actually come to your school, or to somehow discourage them from coming." In the process, unlike Rob Chisholm, most boosters never knew their A.I. had been used to help a hockey or basketball player get in.

In fairness, it should be pointed out that every player at the top of a coach's list in men's hockey or basketball is not necessarily a prospect with a low A.I. As Bob Ceplikas, an associate athletic director at Dartmouth, points out: "It's not always the case that our highest impact kid has the lowest credentials. Brian Van Abel, the hockey captain for the 2003–04 season, is a fantastic student. He could have gone anywhere in the country, if he wanted, without lifting a hockey stick."

Even so, everyone was aware of the flaw in the system that had been regulating men's hockey and basketball for nearly twenty years, and everyone agreed with the admission deans when they said the boosters had to go. "It was time," as Mike Goldberger of Brown puts it, "to stop using kids in a manipulative way."

"Averaging is one of the more ridiculous aspects of the admission process," said former Dartmouth men's basketball coach Dave Faucher in the summer of 2003, following the rule changes to eliminate the boosters. "Let's just say I needed three players. They're over the minimum A.I. They have good transcripts. Dartmouth believes in them as students and as people. And I believe in them as basketball players. And Dartmouth admits those three students. Now let's face it, some years those three students could average 210, other years they could average 182. To me, in the year that they average 182, that we put three or four more people on an admission list because we need their grades is ludicrous. Those admission slots should go to other needs, whether they're valedictorians for the professors, or whether they're musicians, or whether they're for other sports. Those extra people are not going to play, they're not a part of the basketball program, we don't have a jv team, there's no room, but we put their names down on a list so that our average looks impressive around the League. It's not.

"I've actually said, 'Yeah so-and-so's a 232, I think he watched a game on TV once.' He might show up on my list because he marked down basketball as something he might want to do, and he's this brilliant kid, probably on a high school team, but we have to put him on the list to average out the kids that we really want. Something's wrong with that.

"With Dartmouth our communication has gotten much better than it used to be," he added. "A few years ago, we had to find all our boosters. We'd have to almost call kids and say, 'Make sure you apply to Dartmouth,' because even if they didn't come, we needed their application and their high A.I. It's a step forward, eliminating the boosters."

Every year, the schools had shared data on incoming men's hockey and basketball players at annual meetings of the admission deans. The deans would know when boosters appeared on the list of two, three, or four different schools, paving the way for studs with low A.I.s to take the ice or the court. At those same meetings over the years, the deans always reported and informally talked to each other about whether any other team's cohort (in soccer, baseball, softball, field hockey, or another sport) fell below the "mean minus one" boundary, but this was never a requirement, and there was no punishment for failing to comply.

Under the 2003 rule amendments, however, this all changed. Men's hockey and basketball are now part of one large cohort that includes every other Ivy sport, and this group must have an average A.I. that falls within one standard deviation of the mean A.I. of the student body as a whole. (An "Ivy sport" is defined as one that competes for an Ivy championship. Excluded are skiing, sailing, equestrian, water polo, and men's volleyball.) There are twenty-eight Ivy sports, including football, but not every school sponsors a team in each Ivy sport, and football continues to be regulated separately, under its own A.I. band system. The other Ivy sports are now included in each school's cohort.

As an added insurance against boosters slipping into this new system, and in an effort to reduce the number of spots used for athletic recruits in each new class, the Ivy Presidents adopted a second rule in 2003. This rule limits the number of recruited athletes who may be admitted to each Ivy institution under a fairly arcane formula. The formula is based on the number of Ivy sports an institution fields and the size of the travel squad for each sport. Travel squads consist of the players who are included on team trips to away games. Travel squad sizes vary by sport (basketball requires fewer players than hockey, for instance), but the League enforces a uniform travel squad limit on every sport. (In other words, the size of every Ivy women's swimming travel squad is the same, the size of every Ivy men's squash travel squad is the same, the size of every Ivy women's lacrosse travel squad is the same, etc.) These travel squad numbers for each individual sport are then multiplied by a factor of 1.4 and added together to provide a grand total for all the Ivy sports the institution fields. This grand total is the number of athletic recruits a school may admit over a rolling four-year period. (Meaning, schools must stay within their limit over a rolling four-year average or they will be penalized.) Under this new formula, institutions are free to admit athletic recruits however they wish— meaning, one year the women's basketball team might get six players, the next year two, based on their needs, their status as a priority sport, and the needs and the priority status of other sports.

The final rule change instituted in 2003 raised the floor of the A.I. from 169 to 171. This change was made primarily to reflect the "re-centering" of SAT scores that took place in the mid-'90s, when sixty to seventy points were added to the combined math and verbal total by the College Board. (If you took the SATs prior to 1996, add one hundred points to your combined math and verbal score, and that's what you'd have today. See, you're not getting older, you're getting smarter. I've just broken 1000.) The two-point increase in the A.I. floor is hardly earth shattering, especially in light of mean A.I.s at most Ivies that are thirty to forty points higher. This seems like a lackluster effort on the part of the presidents, one that would get an athlete benched.

One idea that the deans and the presidents never considered originated with Dave Faucher, who had a gleam in his eye when he shared it with me in the spring of 2003: "Our average should be the people that are playing. That's why I've long said, if you want to talk about academic standing, take the Academic Index of the starters for every Ivy League team, and see where schools stand. That to me is an evaluation of where you are as an institution, much more than what the numbers say in the admission meetings, because the numbers are either the smartest jv players in the world, or kids that are walking around campus not playing."

He smiled when he said it, knowing that his team's average A.I., using this formula, would wind up at, or near, the League's top for men's basketball. Unfortunately for Faucher, over the past few years his teams had been at, or near, the League's bottom in the standings, and he was under fire as a result.

The A.I. system has been under fire since its inception in the early 1980s—and not just because of boosters. A number of coaches and administrators question whether the formula's heavy reliance on testing, which accounts for two-thirds of the index, discriminates against lower-income applicants, many of whom are minorities. Unlike their wealthier peers, the majority of these students have not attended top public or private schools or had access to expensive test-prep tutorials, and their test scores are often lower as a result. Ivy admission officers openly admit that the A.I. alone is not an accurate predictor of future academic performance. And yet their hands, and the hands of coaches, are tied by a mathematical formula that relies heavily on test scores.

"The index is skewed toward high testing," says Dartmouth football coach John Lyons, "and a lot of those kids that test high are well-to-do kids that have learned how to take those tests and have access to good schools. So it's becoming more difficult for the lower-end socioeconomic kids, whether they're white or black, to have the test scores that you need in this formula. But it doesn't mean that they're not smart kids who deserve a chance.

"They always come back to me and say, 'You don't have enough black kids.' I say, 'Wait a minute. I'm not the guy who's taking them, number one. You've created this system that to me is discriminatory—because it's placing all this reliance on these tests.' All I'm trying to do is figure out, 'Who are the best two guys in this band?' I don't care if they're white or black or purple. I mean, I gotta find some guys who can play and I can get to come here. I understand what they're trying to do, but if you truly want diversity, and you believe in that stuff, then there's got to be some flexibility. How can you truly want diversity and then you create this system: 'You only get two here, seven here, and so on?'"

It's an excellent question, one without a simple answer. But diversity does not appear to have been a driving force behind the creation and implementation of the A.I. two decades ago, when then–Princeton President William Bowen proposed establishing and enforcing a mathematical formula to regulate the admission of Ivy League athletes. Derek Bok, who was Harvard's president at the time, closely supported Bowen in his mission. (Ironically, the two later coauthored a book on minority admissions, *The Shape of the River*, in which they argued that SAT scores are not a valid way to measure the potential of minority applicants.) The strongest opponent of the Academic Index was A. Bartlett Giamatti, the president of Yale, who felt that every institution should retain its autonomy and responsibility to make its own admission decisions. If you listen to Tim Taylor, that feeling persists in the Yale admission office today: "The A.I. system, I don't think anybody likes it. Our admission office doesn't like it. . . . I don't think they like to be told who they should accept and who they shouldn't accept. Simple as that."

Not surprisingly, given the escalating booster abuse of the late '90s and early '00s, the origins of the A.I. are linked directly to concerns over the academic abilities of men's hockey and basketball players. "The A.I. came into play because the allegations were flying that Penn was taking dumb basketball players and Cornell was taking dumb hockey players," says Bob Ceplikas. "I mean, you can imagine. The Ivy presidents meet twice a year and tackle all these kinds of issues, and at the time—mid-'80s—they asked for the admission deans to come up with a mathematical means of measuring, 'Are our student-athletes representative of our student bodies or not?' Because until then, there was no mathematical device to either confirm or refute all these allegations that were flying all over the place, and they wanted something. So that's where it came from."

The mathematical means of establishing such representation, explains Ceplikas, is based on a statistical principle. "I've been told that if you have a population, and you have a subset of that population, the subset can be considered an overall part of that population if it has a statistical average that is within one standard deviation of the overall population. The normal standard deviation [for the A.I. at Ivy schools] is somewhere between twelve and sixteen points."

Or, just what a basketball coach would like to have his star forward score in the second half of a big game.

According to the League's executive director, Jeff Orleans, the eight Ivy institutions were reporting A.I.s and monitoring A.I.s starting in the fall of 1981—but without a final agreement as to what the rules would be for the classes admitted. A Yale graduate who also earned a Yale Law degree, Orleans helped to author the groundbreaking Title IX legislation before becoming the League's first (and only, as it has turned out) executive director in 1984. "They'd been collecting data for a few years before I arrived," he recalls, "and then they were monitoring the data. And in the '84–'85 year, they had some agreements to make about what the floor would be. Same floor for every school? Or would it relate to each school's own kind of A.I. distribution? Would there be exceptions below the floor if people had been admitting tangible numbers of folks below whatever the new floor would be? How would you transition them from whatever they were doing to zero? What should be the specific rules for football, basketball, and hockey? Those decisions all got made in the spring of '85. And the first class under the formal binding system was admitted in the fall of '86—the class of 1990."

"This all happened at a time when the presidents, as a group, were really looking at the Ivy League structure in a whole variety of ways,"

Orleans continues, never mentioning the controversy surrounding the Penn basketball or Cornell hockey players. "They had begun discussions with the presidents of what are now the Patriot League schools, about forming the Patriot League for football, so that we would have a common set of football opponents. They had just formed the ECAC Hockey League," he adds, explaining that the ECAC's back-to-back weekend games were designed to limit midweek travel and not interfere with classes. In both the ECAC Hockey League and the Patriot League, the other schools adopted some very general academic regulations that looked more like the Ivy League's.

Finally, around this same time, the Ivy presidents commissioned, received, and acted on a comprehensive report from the policy committee of the League's athletic directors. The Perry-Ryan Report, as it became known (for John Perry, the A.D. at Brown at the time, and Frank Ryan, the A.D. at Yale), helped put into place the current framework for season lengths and non-traditional practices (when practice starts, the numbers of contests, out-of-season practices, etc.)—in short, the boundaries of the Ivy athletic experience.

Orleans explains: "The presidents had done these four things—Patriot Football, ECAC Hockey, regulating the experience, and admissions—all at the same time because they had just become convinced, looking at what was happening nationally, that they needed to reapply the Ivy principles from the '50s to a changing world and give us some stability."

If that was their view in 1985, one can only imagine how the presidents felt as they revised their own rules in 2003—in an era when big-time college sports scandals are common occurrences. According to Orleans, "The theory [of the Ivy presidents] has always been that you look at the entire athletic experience. And it's not that you either are happy with *only* admissions or upset about *only* admissions, it's that you look at the whole athletic piece. So if you change admissions as a set of Ivy presidents, it's not because you're panicked, it's because you're looking at the whole picture. You do it all the time, and you've decided this piece needs to be updated a little bit. That's been an issue the last couple of years, where a focus that was building anyway, has been attributed in the popular press, in part because Bowen worked hard to get it attributed, to: *Yes, the Ivy presidents are admitting that their admissions are some-*

how out of whack. It just isn't true. It's part of a long, wide context of trying to make sure what we do stays right."

Many would argue that the system has never been right, that it has been filled with flaws from the start. And others agree with the popular press about William Bowen's continued influence over Ivy policy regarding the admission of athletes and their athletic experience. A number of these people point out that the Andrew G. Mellon Foundation, which Bowen now heads, awards millions of dollars in grants to Ivy League institutions each year. "There's no question that he has an agenda," says Bill Cleary, the retired athletic director at Harvard. Many athletic directors and coaches believe the A.I. rule changes in 2003 were indeed prompted by Bowen's book, *The Game of Life*, co-written with Richard Shulman, another officer of the Mellon Foundation. In their book, the authors argue, among other things, that recruited athletes at elite institutions take the place of other, more highly qualified academic candidates, and that the athletes then underperform in the classroom once they arrive on campus. We'll explore these and other claims the authors make later in this book, but for now, as we examine the 2003 reforms aimed at eliminating the boosters, it seems fair to say the rule changes came from a combination of pressure from Bowen and Shulman's book and a desire by the presidents to make sure things "stay right."

"We wanted to get rid of the boosters," James Wright, the president of Dartmouth and the current chair of the Council of Ivy Group Presidents, told me.

Strangely, for all their criticism of Ivy League athletic admissions, Bowen and Shulman never mention the boosters.

While the boosters may be gone in men's hockey and basketball, some coaches argue they still exist within men's football, despite the banding system that was created two decades ago to rid that sport of them.

When the number of football recruits fell in 2003 from thirty-five to thirty, says John Lyons, "My contention was, if you fellows really want to cut numbers, cut it to twenty-five—but give us twenty-five kids we can recruit that can *play*. Because a lot of these kids that we have to recruit in the higher-end band aren't good players. And we know it coming in, and we're doing it because we need bodies. You have to fill out your roster to run practices and everything. I don't think that's right. I'm recruiting you, but I'm not telling you: 'Hey, we're recruiting you because you're in this band that we need to fill up, and we have trouble filling it up.' Maybe the kid will turn out to be a great player, but not many of them do. And they're the first ones to quit. They're the first ones, when it gets tough, they're gonna bail out on you. I just don't think that's right."

A player such as Jay Fiedler, who led Dartmouth to an undefeated season and the outright Ivy title in 1996, is a rarity in the League—an impact player with a 780 math SAT score and an A.I. in the high band. Far more common are impact players in the lower A.I. bands. The presidents acknowledged this when they designed the A.I. system and added a provision whereby a school could petition for an exemption from the A.I. rules, something Columbia's football program did in the latter stages of its forty-four-game losing streak in the late 1980s.

The provision allowed an institution to come to the presidents and ask for relief from the A.I. structure if its team was in terrible competitive straights and the school had done everything they could think of to pull out of it, Jeff Orleans explains. "They had adequate recruiting. They had evaluated their coaching. They had a decent facility. And yet, somehow, they were still mired.

"Forty-four games," says Orleans, "is mired. It was mired even before that forty-four. The request came from Columbia to be able to admit a limited number of football players a couple of points below the [A.I.] floor level. And what that really meant was, 'These are players who by definition no one else in the League would be able to recruit.' And so, even if they might rather go to Harvard, they weren't going to have that chance."

The waiver lasted for two years. Several players were admitted under the A.I. floor, and Columbia was allowed to exceed the rolling four-year limit on the total number of recruits by an additional number of players. (Orleans refused to share specific numbers with me on this matter, which I found surprising, given that it had occurred more than a decade earlier. Bad memories lingered, apparently.)

"Columbia did that and it didn't really make much difference," says Orleans. "They came out of that for systemic reasons. A couple of these kids mattered athletically, a couple didn't. They all graduated. But when the word came out, the reaction was *so* unfavorable. *'Ending standards for athletics.'* The presidents basically said, 'We're never gonna do this again.' And they haven't."

For the most part, anyway. When freshmen became eligible in the early '90s, Columbia football was again in terrible straits, and for one year the program was given a waiver of the rolling four-year total and allowed to recruit five extra players. But the Lions did not receive a waiver of the A.I. floor level, which had been so controversial the first time.

Once, between those two events, Orleans recalls that the presidents were asked to provide a waiver for the men's hockey team at Brown. They said no. Since then, they have not granted any waivers, believing it is not the way to build a program, and certainly not a good idea for the rest of the League.

Today, Columbia's football program is under the guidance of a new head coach, Bob Shoop, who is described by Orleans as an "extremely passionate, organized, disciplined" coach. Shoop played at Yale, so he understands the League, and he was a successful assistant coach at BC, so he clearly understands football and recruiting.

"He and his coaches are all living in Columbia housing on campus," says Orleans. "When they entertain recruits and their families, they say, 'This is where I live. This is where I'm raising my kids. I have no second thoughts, Mr. and Mrs. Jones, why I'm here. If your son needs to talk to me, I'm going to be fifteen minutes away from his door. I'm not an absentee coach.'"

Orleans continues, "If anybody can do it, Bob will do it. He's got an admission office that is empathetic. He's got a financial aid director who is going to be as helpful as he can within the rules. So it will be a good test. And if Bob can't do it . . ." He pauses to consider the alternative. "Then maybe . . . then I would really be wondering if Columbia can do it."

One thing individual applicants can do—athletes and non-athletes alike—that individual athletic programs have not been able to do since the Columbia waiver backfired on the presidents, is to gain admission to an Ivy League institution with an A.I. that falls below the floor. The circumstances surrounding these rare exceptions must be highly compelling (almost always an extenuating social and/or economic circumstance), and for a recruited athlete, the admission dean at the institution is expected to give a "comparing, nonathletic justification" for that student's admission—that is, a reason why, beyond sports, the student should be admitted with an A.I. below the floor. This justification is shared with all the admission deans at their annual spring meeting, and reviewed by their policy committee. Each case with its supporting justification is then shared with the presidents. According to Orleans, the policy committee and the presidents "rarely, if ever" change an individual dean's admission decisions on these cases.

"There are very few athletes any more at any schools," he says, "who are proposed, who have A.I.s below the presumptive floor. Maybe it's a point or two or three in any event." Those who are admitted below the floor are often from backgrounds more harsh and challenging than any young person should have to endure.

"The level of the floor is certainly an issue because everybody is interested," Orleans concludes, "but I don't think admissions below the floor are a major issue. If you look at our All-Ivy teams, Players of the Year, Rookies of the Year, you won't find people below the floor on those. I mean, there are some very good athletes among that very small number of people [admitted below the floor], but coaches understand that they're not going to make a permanent living right on the edge [of the floor]."

Doing their job today is more complicated than ever for Ivy coaches, athletic directors, and admission deans, thanks to the new A.I. rules. The challenge they face is how to lump together the recruits for up to twenty-seven teams, and come up with an average A.I. within the "mean minus one" category. It's no longer primarily a matter of coaches managing their individual team A.I.s (although that will be a large part of the new system, as it was of the old one). A.D.s will now have the unenviable task of managing a "master" list for all sports, and sitting down with each of their coaches to determine how the impact players with lower A.I.s will be distributed. The admission deans don't want to make those calls. The athletic departments will have to decide which sports will receive the highest priority and get "extra" support.

According to Orleans, "Some A.D.s—Gary [Walters of Princeton] is one and Josie [Harper of Dartmouth] is another—are worried that people will load up in men's basketball and hockey, and that those kids will be unrepresentative, and that the schools that aren't willing to do that will not be competitive. The response of the other people is, 'My numbers are limited.

If that happens to us we're gonna get screamed at for being noncompetitive in twenty-five or thirty sports, including women's sports. And we just can't afford to do that.'"

Only time will tell how "favorite" programs with a winning tradition will fare at each school. But clearly Walters and Harper are concerned about others loading up in those two sports for two reasons. First, because Princeton has a winning tradition in basketball (as an undergraduate Walters played with Princeton star Bill Bradley) and Dartmouth has a winning tradition in hockey, neither school wants to lose its place among the League's elite in one of its priority sports. Second, because Princeton and Dartmouth have the League's two smallest undergraduate student bodies, they cannot admit as many men's hockey and basketball players—or athletes overall—as other schools in the League. In the words of Princeton's Fred Hargadon, "The problem for Dartmouth and for us is that two hundred athletes a year here is a much larger proportion of our freshman class than three hundred is at Penn or Cornell or Harvard." Even under the new recruiting limits (travel squad size x 1.4), Dartmouth and Princeton will never reach the ceiling, simply because they cannot devote that many places in a class to the admission of recruited athletes.

Don't cry for Princeton, however. They have a number of other assets, including the League's juiciest financial aid packages, to offset their limited recruiting numbers. As for Dartmouth, it still has one of the ten largest athletic programs in the country, in terms of the number of varsity sports, despite having the League's smallest enrollment. "It doesn't take a great mathematician to figure out that means we've got to stock a lot of teams with a minimal number of athletes," says Bob Ceplikas. "We've got to be incredibly efficient with what we get. That's a fact of life."

Another fact of life: according to some observers, there is a new generation of boosters. Only these boosters are real Ivy varsity athletes, on real lists, competing for real Ivy League championships. They compete in crew, cross country, track and field, swimming, squash, and tennis—Ivy sports that have traditionally had recruits with high A.I.s. Now their strong academic qualifications are helping to boost the large cohort's average A.I. and to balance the lower A.I.s of athletes in sports such as men's hockey and basketball, which have a tradition of impact players with lower A.I.s.

"That's one way to look at it," says Jeff Orleans, acknowledging the truth in this view. "Another way to look at it is that schools are going to say, 'We don't want to be competitive in only two or three sports, and we don't want to be accused of only trying to be competitive in two or three sports—especially men's sports. So we're going to have to figure something out where there are a few people from each sport at a high A.I. level and a few people from each sport at a low A.I. level. And one way to do that is if we see a kid who is a real player at 220 in any sport, we're gonna go after him or her—and build a team around the best athletes. Instead of locking up low A.I. kids and looking for boosters, we'll lock up the high A.I. kids, and then we'll look to see where we still need athletic help—further toward the bottom, where there is a bigger pool of good players.'"

It is an ideal scenario. And that dream-like vision may yet come true. For now, the immediate booster nightmare is over. But with averaging still a part of the rules, one wonders how long it will take for another strain of the booster virus to poison the Ivy system. No one will know how the overall team averaging is working for at least a few years. If, in the meantime, the new rules are compromised by the fierce athletic competition within the League, it may take several more years before another cure is sought. The League's health has been damaged by the boosters in men's basketball and hockey. One hopes the League can do a better job of protecting its own standing in the future. The manipulation and use of index boosters such as Rob Chisholm, who was accepted at Harvard, Princeton, and Yale on the basis of his outstanding academic and extracurricular record, and his exceptional leadership and personal qualities, is history.

And if Ivy League schools should value anything, it is history.

Chapter Four

On The Road

*"I went by a recruit's house at four o'clock in the afternoon
and Tim Murphy was coming in at eight. We're living
halfway across the country, and we're both there on the same
day for the same kid. It's unbelievable."*

Jack Siedlecki
Yale University
Head Football Coach

Every December, Yale head football coach Jack Siedlecki goes on a
fourteen-day, seventeen-city, whirlwind tour of the United States to
visit his top prospects in their homes. His counterpart at Harvard,
Tim Murphy, crisscrosses the country for three months every December,
January, and February, spending five days a week on airplanes, making
up to a hundred home visits to his top recruits. Together with their Ivy
football brethren, they blanket the entire country, venturing as far west
as Hawaii and even up into Canada, in search of what Murphy calls "a
rare breed"—talented football players who are good students. It's an
effort that makes recruiting for a big-time football school look like
picking cherries.

"People have no idea how hard it is," Siedlecki says. "I think an awful
lot of people think that a kid with a 3.5 GPA is automatically in. But he's
actually in the low band. And the two guys in the low band, those are

our number one draft picks. There are a thousand candidates for those two low-band spots. Where we have thirteen spots, in a higher band, we have fewer candidates because of how many kids are 200 A.I. or better. Not many kids in the country have those kinds of test scores and those kinds of grades. That's the pond that we're fishing in."

For Ivy League football programs, the fishing expeditions culminate each fall on the first Sunday after Thanksgiving, when head coaches and their assistants hit the road in droves, scattering to the four corners of the continental United States to finalize their list of recruits who will be invited onto campus for an official visit in January. The preparations for these recruiting trips are more than eleven months in the making, starting the previous January and February, when schools send high school juniors mass mailings that include a return questionnaire. At Harvard, this annual mailing is sent to every football-playing high school in the fifty states of America (over 13,000), to names culled from selected recruiting services, and to alumni referrals. It generates a return of 5,000 prospects. Dartmouth's annual football questionnaire is mailed to 12,000 prospects (also culled from every football-playing high school in America), an effort that produces 8,500 responses. At Yale, when the questionnaires come back, each coach is assigned a list of around four hundred prospects to manage, which they must narrow down to fifty by the time they hit the road in November. This is in contrast to the twelve to fifteen recruits being managed each year by the coaches at schools like USC and Notre Dame. The football programs in the Ivy League are the only programs in the country that search for prospects at every single football-playing high school in America, and the massive size of their mailings reflects two things: the challenge of finding good football players who are also good students and the paranoia coaches have that a great player will slip through the cracks, undiscovered.

"Guys at big-time schools like Notre Dame are pissing and moaning about recruiting a dozen kids," says John Lyons of Dartmouth. "I go, 'You're crazy.' Now, those twelve kids are being recruited by everybody, so it's very, very competitive. But it's an awful lot of work here. People will come up to me and say, 'What are you doing now that your season is over?' All we do is recruit. I wish we could spend as much time coaching and playing football as we do recruiting. 'Cause it's a very small part of the year that we're allowed to coach, and that's actually what we're hired to do here. Recruiting is the bulk of what we do."

"It's very labor intensive to comb through those 5,000 questionnaires to find a couple hundred who are really outstanding prospects," Harvard's Tim Murphy explains. "It takes a long time to do that. It takes us months and months of going through transcripts and video, to find in the end the thirty guys that we like *and* Admissions likes. It's no problem finding guys we like. It's hard finding guys we like and Admissions likes."

Murphy admits it took him two years to learn how to recruit in the Ivy League when he came to Cambridge in 1994. At thirty-seven, he was already a veteran head football coach with a winning record, who had run a successful program at Maine, and then reversed the fortunes of an ailing Cincinnati program, earning a lucrative six-year contract offer as a reward. But instead of signing that contract, Murphy opted to return to his native Massachusetts and take over an equally ailing Harvard program. In the process, he found himself playing an entirely different recruiting game than the one he had already mastered.

"My first two years here, I spun my wheels on a lot of great football players who just couldn't get in," Murphy says. "It was very frustrating. What Admissions was saying at that time was, 'Well, I'm sure he looks good to you, but I don't know if we'd be doing him a favor by taking him,' or, 'I don't think he really has a chance to get in here.' Now I don't waste Admissions' time because I know what their standards are.

"It's so much more demanding on the head coach and the assistant coaches than it was at the University of Cincinnati, where you had a smaller recruiting area, a little shorter timeframe, and basically didn't have to search so far and wide to satisfy such high standards. It takes up to 50 percent more time than it did at Cincinnati. It never ends."

According to Keith Clark, the offensive line and associate head football coach at Yale, recruiting has changed in the last ten years as the timeframe has accelerated. So much more of it is done early and pursued through the actual playing season that coaches are constantly exhausted. Indeed, when Ivy League football programs send out their first mailings to junior prospects every January and February, they are still wrapping up their recruiting of the current crop of high school seniors. When Pat O'Leary of Dartmouth says recruiting in the Ivies is a fourteen-month-a-year job, he is quite literally correct. As questionnaires return to offices in March and April, Ivy coaches begin the weeding-out process that takes so many hours and lasts through the summer, the fall, and into the next winter. Coaches hit the road for junior recruiting as early as May, traveling to Texas and California and other prime football states, but they are only allowed to watch video and read transcripts at this time, not meet with players.

Says Yale's Keith Clark, "You eliminate a lot of guys just on paper. For example, a lineman says he's a 5-foot-8-inch, 180-pound guard. Well, we're not going to recruit him. Or if he has a 2.8 GPA, then we're not going to go any further with the kid there, either. I think a big part of recruiting is actually just deleting. That's what you spend a ton of time on—trying to get official transcripts from guidance counselors at high schools, so you can actually look at them. I mean a kid could write on the questionnaire he's a 3.8. Honestly, that doesn't mean anything. Not until you see it confirmed from a school. But there are some schools where a kid could be a 3.8 and his class rank could still be in the 30th percentile. And that's going to hurt him. So you need to find out a little more specifically, but at least if you've got it on paper, you say, 'Okay, I know he's an offensive guard, he's 6 feet 4 inches, he's 260 pounds, and he's got a 3.8 GPA. Now I need to find out when he's taking the SATs or if he's taken them, and then I need to find out his class rank, what types of courses he's taken, and then find out if he fits into the parameters of what we're looking for. I need to get some videotape on the kid, talk to the coach, find out what kind of kid he is. . . .'"

"They cannot spend time with a kid; they cannot go visit a home," Murphy explains, citing NCAA rules governing junior-year recruiting. "This is an evaluation period, so they can only get the lay of the land. They can't begin to sell the kid."

At least not in person. The selling begins on the phone. During the month of May, NCAA rules allow football coaches to place one phone call to junior prospects. After July 1 coaches may call once a week. But in May, Murphy will call fifty to seventy-five juniors—based on lists of top prospects provided by his assistants—placing as many as fifteen calls in one night, often from his home. His assistants will call another fifty to seventy prospects over the course of the month.

Murphy says he gets right to the point when speaking to a prospect for the first time, explaining that his side of the conversation will go something like this: "The first thing is, I know you're getting a lot of these other phone calls, so I'm not going to keep you on all night—I know you've got a lot of homework to do. But I just wanted to make a connection. I'm Tim Murphy. I want you to remember that name. You're going to be getting a lot of literature from me and Harvard University over the coming months. I'd like to know a lot more about you, and this is why I'm interested in you, and this is why I think you might be interested in us. . . . " He then explains those reasons and asks the player if he has any questions.

"Some of them don't have a lot to say," Murphy says. "Other guys, you look up and you've been on the phone for forty-five minutes—and you've still got fourteen more calls to make, and your own kids to put to bed."

During the spring and summer, the recruiting process continues as coaches evaluate more videos and transcripts, meet with players and their parents on campus, and run summer football camps for high school players. The campus visits during this period are all made as "unofficial" visits, paid for by the player and his family. Under NCAA rules, recruited athletes are allowed to make an unlimited number of unofficial visits to as many schools as they wish, but they are limited to making only five "official" visits to schools that invite them in for a weekend and pay for their transportation, meals, and lodging. In the Ivy League, most of the official visits for football players take place in January, but for players who decide to apply Early Decision, or Early Action at Harvard and now Yale (under the encouragement of coaches), official visits will take place in the fall. Typically, about a third of the thirty football recruits admitted each year at Dartmouth, Harvard, and Yale are early applicants, and many of these have attended the school's summer football camp, where they have gotten a feel for the coaches, lived in a dorm, and developed a sense of what it would be like to attend the school. In turn, the coaches have gotten a chance to watch a player in action, and see what he's like on and off the field, and begin to seriously recruit any player who interests them.

By fall, the coaches are in season, and working seventy-five to eighty hours a week, running practices, watching game film, scouting opponents, meeting with players, traveling to and from games—and, of course, still recruiting.

"In season, it's brutal," says John Lyons. After arriving in the office at 7:15 on Monday through Thursday, and attending to a full day of football coaching duties, Lyons and his staff head home at 7:00 in the evening to make phone calls. "You're on the horn for a while. Some of the guys have to call the West Coast, which is a three-hour time difference. We come in a little later on Friday if it's a home game, but what we're trying to do is have each guy make twenty-five recruiting calls a week—ten guys getting to 250 kids a week."

Dartmouth has no real "back yard" for football recruiting, but Yale does, and on Thursday nights some assistants will go out to a local area high school to watch a practice.

"You want to tell the high school coach you're coming," says Keith Clark, the associate head coach at Yale, "so the coach can let the kid know you're going to be there watching the kid practice or play. You're going to wear a yellow jacket so the kid can see you in the stands. It's just an opportunity to show you're interested in a kid. But actually, seeing a kid live gives you a different perspective. Most of our recruiting and evaluation is done off of videotape. Sometimes high school videotapes are just brutal. Let's say he's a defensive back—he may not even be on the tape half the time. If you do have an opportunity to watch him play live, I think it gives you a much different perspective. You know how fast he is, and you see him outside the frames of the videotape, too. You can also see a lot of intangible things, like does he hustle? Is he willing to go up and whack somebody? What does his relationship look like with the other players and the coach? Is he somebody that has some leadership capabilities? All those types of things."

Once the Ivy football season ends, and Thanksgiving rolls around, the coaches have pared down their lists and are ready to hit the road. At this point, Murphy asks each of his six full-time coaches, who travel to different territories in December just like a door-to-door sales force, to give him a list of their top fifteen players. He then tries to visit all one hundred of these top recruits personally, which is how he winds up on an airplane five days a week for three straight months.

"I do that because, first, I don't think kids make cerebral decisions, I think they make emotional decisions," Murphy says. "They've got to feel that they're wanted and they've got to feel that they'll fit in. And second,

I've always gone on my instincts about what type of kid is going to be successful, and you can't get that from watching videos. You have to go out and meet a kid on his own turf, in his home with his parents, at his high school, and to me that's where you make your decision. A kid may look great on his questionnaire, he might look great on video, then you go meet him and somehow you just know: 'No, that's not the right kid for us.'"

Those one hundred home visits are more than twice as many as John Lyons or Jack Siedlecki will make. When Murphy took the Harvard job, he made it a goal that no other coach in the Ivy League would see as many kids in person as he does.

"Don't forget," he says, "when we got here, they hadn't had a winning season in a long time, so we just felt like this was the best approach. We were never going to take the premise that we're better than anybody. We knew we were going to have to outwork people, have to out-hustle people, and outsmart people, and if there's any reason that we've had success, it's that we've had excellent assistant coaches. And we've worked really hard at it. It's not magic."

But there is magic in the Harvard name, which Murphy admits is "obviously intriguing to people." And he acknowledges that his efforts require a "substantial" recruiting budget, although he cannot divulge a figure. "If you're going to recruit the entire nation actively, whether you're Stanford, Notre Dame, or Harvard, you've got to raise a lot of money to do it. We do it through the Friends of Harvard Football, a very supportive and enthusiastic alumni football base. They want to be successful—but not at all costs."

Nonetheless, the costs of recruiting football players the way Harvard does are greater than the costs of recruiting football players the way Dartmouth does, or even the way Yale does. That isn't to say Yale doesn't spend a "substantial" amount of money of its own, flying football coaches around the country to recruit players. "Everybody knows what a hotel room in Marin County costs," Jack Siedlecki says. "How much plane tickets to California and Texas cost. It's expensive to recruit all across the country." The odd thing is, given the sums being spent on travel, coaches receive a surprisingly low meal allowance while on the road—$25 a day.

"Even if you go to a MacDonald's and have a supersize for breakfast, that's still six bucks," says Dartmouth assistant coach Pat O'Leary, "so now you're down to $19. And if you have dinner and leave somebody a tip, 20 percent of the bill, you're eating crap. So I get to eat maybe one time a day. And then I've got to stay in a Red Roof Inn or a LaQuinta, while Princeton and Harvard, they're staying in a Marriott and Hilton. That's one thing that does get you down after a while."

Ivy football coaches compete with each other all across the country for players. "It is amazing how many overlap kids you have," Jack Siedlecki says. "You don't need to go head-to-head with Harvard on every kid, do or die. Or 'Oh, you didn't get him, he's gone to Dartmouth.' You certainly don't want to get into a one-out-of-three situation—Harvard, Yale, or Princeton. That's ninety kids. Recruit kids who you feel good about. As long as we're getting kids we want, we're doing pretty good."

Still, there are some unexpected turns along the way, due to the common criteria every Ivy coach is seeking. "I had been to California, and seen a kid in Sacramento," says Siedlecki, "and I had just enough time to fly up to Seattle and take a small flight over the Cascades to see this kid we had gotten involved with pretty late. The dad picked me up at the airport with the kid. And it turned out the dad was a Harvard grad. I had no idea going into it. The dad was very open. It was the kid's decision. But the kid was Harvard's. What are you gonna do?"

Usually a coach has forewarning. For Tim Murphy, the challenge comes when he looks across the line of scrimmage and sees players who were told they couldn't get into Harvard, and are now dying to kick some Crimson butt. "The good news about recruiting at Harvard is that a lot people are really interested. The bad news is that it's the hardest school to get into in America, and you have to give up on a lot of great kids that are going to play against you in our league. Obviously, they'll be ticked off if they didn't get in, or they may have a selective memory and think that you didn't really want 'em. That's the hard part."

For the assistant coaches who are recruiting fourteen months a year, the hardest part may be the three straight weeks they spend on the road, starting after Thanksgiving, looking for "the kids they feel good about"—players who will be invited to campus for an official visit in January. A typical day on the road during this period begins with a visit to the first of four high schools somewhere between 7:30 and 8:00 am. The recruit knows the coach is coming, and he's supposed to alert his high school coach so the coach can have the most recent videotape ready. Keith Clark explains the drill: "I want to see the coach, see the guidance counselor, and then I want to see the kid, in that order. I want to make sure if I haven't spoken to the coach about the kid yet, that I talk to him a little bit more. Find out about the kid's character and those types of things. Does he work hard? Most coaches by this point, and the kids you're dealing with, are pretty positive. Then I go see the guidance counselor. Any problems? Anything in the family I should know about? Those are questions I ask the coach, too. I ask the guidance counselor, 'Can you give me the transcript? SAT scores? Has he retaken the test?' And any other information I can find out about the kid."

While searching for athletes who are worth pursuing, some crazy things happen to coaches. Keith Clark describes driving 170 miles to a high school, the only school he was going to see in that area. "The coach had told me the kid was first team all-league and all-this and all-that, and I got there and I'm watching the videotape they had waiting for me and the kid wasn't even a starter. The coach flat out just lied to me." Clark had the composure to simply get up and walk out, but it was another name quickly crossed off his list.

After meetings with four kids a day in their high schools, a couple of home visits will complete a long day. "Basically, you're there to try to observe the family dynamics," explains Clark. "It's a big chance to talk to the parents. Cover financial aid. Is that an issue? Sometimes you can tell by walking in the house. If they live in a four- or five-thousand-square-foot house, then financial aid is probably not going to be a big deal. And if there are three Mercedes in the driveway. But those are the things that you really have to sit down with the parents and find out. And talk about what their interests are outside of football. I'll tell them we're looking for good football players who happen to be good students. Does he want to go to college and be involved in seven different types of organizations? I think that's great, but if that's what his focus is right from the start, I don't know how good a college football player he's going to be."

The home visit gives coaches a good opportunity to get a read on a player's commitment level. Coaches, as we have seen, have a limited number of admission spots, and they can't afford to waste any of them. "You want to make sure the kid's not going to come and decide that all of a sudden he'd rather spend his twenty hours a week playing piano as opposed to playing football. It's great, you can still play the piano, but make sure football is your number one priority." Another important reason for the home visit is the chance to identify the decision maker in the family. Is it mom, dad, or the kid? "I like to know the parents are involved, but some of them are just so overbearing, it's ridiculous. They really just dominate, and you're asking the kid a question and everybody else is answering for them."

It's not just a research mission, to get a complete picture of a recruit; at the same time, it's a sales call. Clark says, "You've gotta sell yourself a little bit, sell your staff, sell your facility, your football program—because the one common denominator is, whatever one of these schools a kid goes to, he's going to get a great education. I've never been able to sit there and look at a kid and say, 'Yale is better because of our math department,' or whatever. I mean, Yale has what's rated as the best history department in the country. I don't know. History doesn't change much from school to school. They still fought at Gettysburg. I think you're trying to sell the school itself. Not every kid's going to come here. You try to find the kids that want to be here, find the kids that you connect with. I don't connect with every kid. Some coach may connect with a kid that I don't connect with. Well, that's just the way it goes."

Fred Hargadon of Princeton says, "The part of the whole thing that dismays me is sitting here where a lot of people would give their right arm to go to a place like this—with all the resources—and I just really feel for coaches who have to go out and beg an eighteen-year old in any way to consider coming to a place like this. I think, quite frankly, a lot of these kids are put on too high a pedestal, and their parents put them high on a pedestal, and then they really expect too much special treatment. That's throughout the country; it's not just college admissions. They're spoiled. I don't know if that will be changed soon in any way . . . but I would make a lousy recruiter as a coach. I would no more sit in a living room and prostrate myself. I would simply tell him: 'Look, this is a great deal. If you like it, great, use it to your advantage. But I'm not gonna bend over backwards.' I think selling is okay a little bit. I'm sure I do it when I go out and wax warmly about what it is we offer here. But we don't have to put up with kids asking, 'Would I be able to start?' If I were a coach, boy, I'd sort 'em out pretty quickly, saying, 'I want the kid who knows this is an opportunity and that he wants it,' as opposed to, 'What will you do for me that Harvard won't, or that Duke or Stanford won't?'"

Hargadon is quick to add that parents of athletes are not the only ones guilty of placing their kids on a pedestal and making demands on colleges in today's admission game. "It's not only the parents of athletes, it's kids who are number one in their class. Their parents can't understand why they got letters inviting them to apply and they didn't get one from Princeton inviting them to apply. We don't do that. There are colleges buying names and sending the letters out, and the parents are sitting there feeling mad at us because they heard from lots of colleges sending them unsolicited mail and we didn't send them unsolicited mail. I'm thinking, 'It's a crazy world.' The first thing that would lead me to think you might be a good candidate is that you got up off your duff and wrote us and asked us for an application, and went and did it on your own. It's changing out there."

He concludes his point by saying, "It's like this girl in southern New Jersey who sued the school because they wanted to name co-valedictorians. I think there's always a danger of the tail wagging the dog, the candidate calling the shots, the applicant running the show, the schools and the coaches fawning over them."

Keith Clark has developed a healthy perspective over his years of Ivy recruiting. "My opinion is, you've got to check your ego at the door," he says. "The kid is going where he's going to go. Your job is to find out and make sure he's a good football player. You've got to sell your place as hard as you can, try to inject your personality into it. When the kid comes on the official visit, you don't have much control over whether he actually likes your school, likes your players, likes your coaching staff. I mean, it depends on whether his personality fits your situation. And if it does, great. And if it doesn't, that kid's going to go somewhere else and that's it. You can't take it personally. I know some coaches like to yell and scream at the kid when they make the decision. I'm just going to say, 'Hey, best of luck to you. Good luck.' I got ten other guys I gotta call.

"Recruiting these days," says Clark, "is a labor of love."

The labor is hardly unique to football coaches. Every man and woman who coaches a varsity sport in the Ivy League takes to the road at various points during the year to evaluate prospects, make home visits, invite kids to campus for official visits, and recruit talent for the next incoming class. Their travel schedules vary by sport, depending on when their team is in season, but the basic drill is universal for every coach: identify prospects as early as possible and qualify them based on their athletic ability, their grades, test scores, and financial situation. After that, coaches begin the process of selling their school and program.

"The process begins probably in November or December of the kids' junior year in terms of going out and seeing them play and getting an idea about them," says Julie Shackford, the Princeton women's soccer coach. "A lot of them will come on [unofficial] visits during their spring break, and we'll get an idea of the pool that we want to recruit based on just seeing them play by June or July, which can be late for some people, but I'm pretty conservative. And then usually by the time you start having conversations with kids July 1 [the legal date for coaches to initiate phone calls] and over the next three or four weeks, you have an idea of, number one, is this a kid that you want to recruit? And number two, are they interested in your school?"

Having her base in Princeton is ideal for Shackford, who is able to evaluate and recruit a large number of quality players right in her "back yard."

"The mid-Atlantic area is filled with great soccer, no question," she says. "And many of the premier tournaments are held on the East Coast, so it really is a perfect situation." Even so, she will still travel across the country several times a year to watch players compete in tournaments in other regions, attending a total of fifteen to twenty events each year. "You could do one every weekend, if you wanted to," she says of the number of soccer tournaments around the country and the lack of any black-out period on college soccer recruiting, beyond the one long weekend every year when the National Soccer Coaches Association of America holds its annual conference. "There's stuff going on all the time. . . . We go to Houston. We go to southern California. I was on the road in March and will be again in May, June, and July. Typically," she adds, addressing the issue of competing for players with other Ivy coaches, "we're all at the same places."

Yet unlike the recruiting in football, Shackford doesn't see the same competition between Ivy schools for players in women's soccer, at least not for the players she's been recruiting to Princeton. "We run into each other less and less," she says of her Ivy foes. "And I don't know if that's a result of the pool of players getting so large. This year [2003], I feel like

I competed with Duke. I lost my top two kids to Duke. And of the other three I have coming, one was looking at Penn, but other than that, none of them were looking at Ivy League schools. The year before, I actually got three kids from Stanford, who were offered money from Stanford. So it does vary from year to year, but I have noticed less and less competition with the Ivy League. And I think maybe that's just because there are so many players out there."

Shackford's view differs markedly from that of Jenny Graap, the head coach of women's lacrosse at Cornell.

"I find that the real struggle for me in recruiting is to win that top scholar-athlete over Harvard and Yale and Princeton and Dartmouth and Brown, and over all my Ivy League counterparts," she says. "That's my recruiting world. There are a set number of incredibly talented student-athletes, and all of the Ivies are going for them. I think our recruiting battle is certainly winning out over each other. And then you throw into that mix the top academic schools in the country that have women's lacrosse *and* offer scholarship money—the Stanfords, the Dukes, the Georgetowns, the Notre Dames—the schools that are perceived to be highly academic but also are able to pay the kid money to go there and play. That's become a reality for us, too, now. It's just not within our Ivy League that we're competing for these top scholars; it's with the prestigious universities that offer scholarship money. That for me is the recruiting war."

Roger Grillo, the head men's hockey coach at Brown, has yet a different point of view, based on recent developments in his sport. "There's a lot of options out there for kids now," he says. "Before there were only four major college hockey leagues. Now there are two additional leagues, each of which offers scholarships. And there are kids at all the schools that are Ivy League students. There's a ton of them."

During Brown's hockey season, "My two assistants are out [on the road] all the time," he says. "They're out and about and on the phone constantly. With a school like this, you can't just go running to games. You gotta know which kids are top students before you even spend time watching them play. Otherwise, you spin your wheels. You could fall in love with a guy and find out he got 900 on his SATs, or he's a C student, or a B student, and that's not gonna work, so you've gotta do your homework before you travel to watch a kid play."

Grillo recruits heavily in Canada, where he says the educational system is better than many Americans are aware. "I don't think people understand that. Kids coming out of Canada and high school there don't have much trouble coming to play for us. Their educational system is very, very solid. Those kids are pushed hard at the high school level. It allows us to have a bigger pool of kids and kids that are successful at Brown."

He competes with other Ivy schools for some players, but he says, "It's not as cutthroat or as crazy as people would think. We cross over, but we're not going to cross over with all five at one time. [Columbia and Penn do not have ice hockey teams.] Partly that's because we recruit all over. We go anywhere. So it depends on the territory. Some schools are stronger in certain areas. Cornell has a real stronghold in Ontario because of where they're located. For the prep school player, the top kid, we could compete with anybody—the Ivy League, BU, BC, other top scholarship schools."

"There are kids we miss," he admits, "Ivy League–caliber students, who wind up at NESCAC schools—the Middleburys, the Bowdoins, the Colbys, those kinds of schools. Kids that by the time they're a sophomore at those schools, you say, 'Gee, that kid would have been a pretty good player for us.'"

But the key for Grillo, beyond the academic criteria and athletic talent, is finding players with excellent character. "A big part of recruiting now is really finding out all about the kid. That's very critical to me, that the kids who are brought in are solid, solid character kids. Because those kids will work hard and get better." Playing over the Ivy League's longest, seven-month season, his team has far more practices than games. "We develop our kids through practice," he says.

But he is quick to add that any success his teams may have really begins with recruiting. "Recruiting is enormous. It's critical. It's your lifeline."

For Julie Shackford of Princeton, the lifeline begins with an extensive network of club team coaches, rather than the high school coaches her football-coaching colleagues rely on for information on promising players. She also attends regional development camps and tournaments run by the US Soccer Federation's Olympic Development Program (ODP) to find quality prospects. At these and other tournaments, she will sometimes spend $60 to $100 for a program listing information about each player, which can include the player's age, grade, high school, GPA, home address, phone number, email, and club coach's phone number. This information helps Shackford to evaluate and rate prospects and to follow up on players she has an interest in—either by calling the club coach or by mailing the player a letter with a questionnaire. Like every Ivy coach, she must confirm early in the process that a player's grades and test scores will meet her school's standards. And she must try to identify players that other coaches may be overlooking, or who, in her evaluation, show promise.

"Anyone can pick out the best players on the team," she says. "But can you find the next player who is gonna make a difference in a year or two? It's not like swimming or track, where you can get times. I've recruited from a videotape and that was a mistake, just because you can't see everything on a tape. So we literally do not make any decisions without seeing kids play in person."

As much as she keeps a sharp eye out for players who will blossom while at Princeton, she also seeks players who are already proven stars. "No kidding around," she adds, "I've also gotten some studs, too."

"If you have good kids on the team," says Fred Hargadon of Princeton, "they'll tend to attract good kids. I mean by good kids, ones who won't come in and be upset if they're not starting. Boy, do some of them make a difference. Some years you just get a great kid in terms of that program, because the next year kids come because that kid's here. I can name one, Kim Simons. Kim was the Class of '94. She's now the women's lacrosse coach at Georgetown. Kim came here from Pennsylvania, and I walked her around this campus, and I knew she was a big recruit to get. She came here and by her senior year that lacrosse team had gone from nowhere to national champion. And a lot of it was because the coach was able to tell the next group, 'Kim Simons is here.' And then Kim, who was an All-American, married an All-American on the men's team that won the national championship that year, Justin Tortolani, who's now a doctor. And Justin may have been the first big-time recruit for the men. It's a classic case where if you get the right kid, that's what you build with. And obviously in each case, an excellent coach—Chris Sailer [of women's lacrosse] and Bill Tierney [of men's lacrosse]. What was unusual about Kim: she's the epitome of the work ethic. It's easy to talk about team leadership, but real leadership is a person like Kim, who just set the example."

Roger Grillo has built a winning team in recent years around his star goaltender Yann Danis, widely regarded as the best college goalie in the country. "You can't just say, 'I'm going to bring in all these kids who are good kids and I'm gonna make them better.' It just doesn't work. You've still gotta bring in kids who are good hockey players. . . . I'd say 90 percent of the kids on our team were captains of their team when we recruited them. You want that type of person in your locker room."

Increasingly, Shackford finds herself spending more and more time with prospects during the recruiting process, even going so far as to visit their high schools and attend their classes, before heading home to say hello to their parents. "I do some of that. I've done more of that lately, and I feel that pressure just 'cause everybody else is doing it. That does give you a really good read of their family, you do get a good sense of what their deal is. But I don't do that too early, either. A lot of people do that July 1. I mean, there's too many things that go on between July and September, so usually I do those visits in early September, maybe late August, when you have a kid that's sincerely interested. Before that, they have too many options, and they haven't narrowed things down as much."

She reflects for a moment and adds: "I probably lose some kids because I'm not aggressive enough, but I just have to recruit within my personality. It's not that I'm not going after kids, but at the same time I don't feel like they need any more pressure than they're getting. And I kind of present to them what we have to offer, and they either take it or leave it."

Like Shackford, Jenny Graap of Cornell is ideally located for recruiting top players for her sport. "There's no doubt that coaches from all over the country are recruiting New York—particularly the enclaves in Syracuse, Long Island, and Westchester County," she says. "There are regions of very strong high school teams. Rochester is an up-and-coming region. I'm fortunate that New York is a hotbed for girls' lacrosse."

And she feels fortunate to be back coaching at her alma mater, after serving as the head coach at George Mason, a scholarship school with a new program. "When I came to Cornell in 1997, I was coming from four years of building a scholarship program at George Mason, so I had knowledge of the recruiting process and also how the scholarship world operated. I think what really benefited me as a recruiter—not only being an alum of Cornell and really having a firm understanding of the different colleges and the nuances of the largest Ivy—was that I also had the perspective of coming from the scholarship world, where things really were, in my mind, somewhat corrupt. Women's lacrosse is not a big-time sport, it's not a revenue sport, and even in that small world, I felt enormous pressure giving out the scholarships at George Mason—having to deal with families who potentially didn't even need the money. It was all about the ego, it was all about their daughter getting signed into a program. That alone kind of made my stomach turn—that you're giving money to people who don't need it. And then others need the money, but their daughter hasn't gotten all the accolades or is somewhere lower on the recruiting list, so they don't get the big bucks. For me, philosophically, I had a lot of problems with the scholarship world, and when I say some corruption, I guess what I mean is I'd have athletes play for me in the scholarship setting and they would play the first season, and then they would come into my office and basically say, 'Well, coach, I'm not coming back unless you give me more money.' That happened continually, and so you're constantly feeling like, 'Oh my God, the love of the game and all the positives of playing are just lost a lot of the time, unfortunately, because of the scholarships.'

"The bottom line for me is I learned a ton in that setting," Graap continues. "I was compromising my own beliefs. I don't really want to slam my previous institution, but as a scholarship coach, you really don't have to take into account their academics. All they need to be is a qualifier [under NCAA academic guidelines]. That's their minimum. And so I would obviously know that some of these players really are borderline students. I mean, some never even aspired to go to college, or really didn't do the work necessary to be a collegiate student-athlete. I knew all of this when I was recruiting them: I could tell, based on their transcripts and based on speaking with them and having a sense of their intelligence. That's a tough situation, too, because I would see women fail. I'd see them come in and actually fail out. Or women would come in and just have no work ethic, no ability to do their course work without tons of supervision. You'd force them to sit down in study hall. You'd have to oversee that study hall. You'd be constantly worried every semester when the grades came out. You were in a panic. Every semester my eligibility was impacted—I would lose kids midway through the year based on their grades. As a coach in that setting, you are so hampered by all of these factors that really affect your team and your ability to keep a cohesive squad. It was really a lot of work. Now, yes, I recognize if I had just recruited better students, I wouldn't have put myself in that situation, so I'm not trying to generalize and say that every scholarship kid is going to be in that situation. I'm just saying that where I was at that point in time, building a program that had no clout at all because it was brand new, I was definitely recruiting some of the left-overs, some of the women who weren't picked up by the top-notch scholarship schools."

When Graap had the opportunity to return to Cornell, where she had been a captain of the field hockey and lacrosse teams and earned a degree from Cornell's College of Human Ecology in 1986, she jumped at the chance to coach in the Ivy League.

"The difference for me, philosophically, is that I really fit in the Ivy League," she explains. "I just feel so strongly that athletics have so much to offer as far as education. And I really feel that women playing these team sports should be free of all that mess and all that nonsense of putting labels and price tags on each other's heads. I just feel the Ivy League allows the players to participate on equal ground instead of feeling like, 'Oh, she thinks she's great because she's on a $10,000 scholarship,' or, 'Oh, she's really lazy—she's not doing her workouts, but she's on a full ride.' You're constantly measuring yourself against some monetary factor. In the Ivy League you're free of all that. You're on need-based financial aid, or you're paying your own way, and there's just no problem looking at your teammates and knowing that you're all making the same sacrifices and you all have the same commitment. To me, it's a lot freer of all that excess baggage. You always have to earn your way into the school. I think the outside world may assume coaches have all this power in the Ivy recruiting process, and I really find that laughable. Because the women in my experience that gain admission to an Ivy League institution deserve to be here. There's just no question about it. I've not experienced a situation where as a coach I've been able to pull some woman into Cornell who doesn't belong here. The rigorous admission standards are tough, and they're certainly frustrating. I would love to go out there and just pick the best lacrosse players and not necessarily have all this hassle with their SAT I and SAT IIs and their GPA and their

class rank and all the other factors, but the truth is I think it really protects us, and I think it's valid. And so I embrace it versus fight it. I think
it's really special."

So special that each summer she spends 80 percent of her time out on
the road recruiting, watching tournaments, visiting homes, looking for
new players who fit the Ivy mold. And then she spends hours during the
fall making phone calls, talking with prospects each night, and arranging
and hosting weekend after weekend of official visits for her most promising recruits.

"It's gotta be a passion," says Roger Grillo of the ever-increasing
demands on coaches' time and energy in today's Ivy recruiting game. "It's
gotta be something that you love to do. I think the key is you have to have
good people around you. I'm fortunate now. I have assistant coaches who
are really into it, really driven. It's definitely not like it used to be. There are
people getting out of coaching all the time now. There used to be guys who
would stay in it just for the lifestyle—you know, go play golf, be their own
boss, have their own hours. But the demands now are greater."

Spending twelve-hour days in the office, followed by another hour or
two at home each night calling players on the phone, can lose its luster
and lead to problems. "As the president of the College Hockey Coaches
Association, I see a level of divorce and stress-related issues," says Grillo.
"What we've tried to do the last couple of years down at the annual con-
vention is bring in people to speak about that—how to balance everything. We brought in a guy last year and he's coming back this year—a
guy named Dr. Jack Stark, who's a sports psychologist, only he doesn't
deal with athletes, he deals with coaches. He talks about how to make
yourself a better coach. More effective. He talks about nutrition. He talks
about exercise. He talks about finding hobbies, other interests. . . ."

Where are coaches meant to find the time for hobbies and other interests?

"You have to make it," says Grillo, who each winter slips into a work-
induced rut and gains twenty pounds. He sheds the weight by playing
noontime basketball in the off-season. "I don't do it as much during the
season because it takes an hour and a half out of your day. But I love it. You
need a release, you really do. If you don't have one, you're screwed."

Having a release is just one part of Grillo's formula for success, which
has lifted Brown from the bottom of the Ivy League standings to a top

regular season finish in 2003–04, alongside perennial men's hockey power, Cornell.

"You've gotta do your homework," says the coach, of how he has succeeded in the Ivy recruiting game. "You've gotta get on the phone. You've gotta get on a plane and watch kids play. You've gotta use your radar during home visits. You've gotta be visible. You've gotta work."

He pauses, then puts it simply: "If you're digging a hole and I'm digging a hole and I work harder than you do, then I'm gonna get done before you."

He smiles. "And the more you win, the easier it is. That's the way it works."

Chapter Five
Lists & Liaisons

"For us to go forward with a recruit, three things have to happen. We have to love the kid. The kid has to love us. And Admissions has to bless the marriage."

Tim Taylor
Yale University
Head Men's Hockey Coach

The courtships are not always smooth. Some end abruptly, early on. Some last for months, only to end in disappointment. Others move forward in fits and starts, gaining momentum or losing steam, depending on circumstances and revelations. At times, money and pressure wreak havoc. Now and then, a new infatuation interferes. And sometimes, no matter how hard the parties may work at it—and they often work their hearts out, hoping to reach the altar—the marriage is just not meant to be. The chaperone overseeing their dance waves a finger, "No, no," and that's the end of that.

Time to move on to the next best thing.

There is nothing like athletic recruiting in the Ivy League to make coaches cry, prospects pout, and admission officers shake their heads. The process of evaluating recruits academically is so stringent and exacting that every Ivy institution has adopted a special process to monitor and facilitate the transfer of information between the athletic department and the admission office, and to provide feedback for coaches about where players stand in terms of their potential for eventual admission—feedback that starts long before an application is ever filed. This collaborative effort varies slightly from school to school, but every institution has what are known as "liaisons" in both the athletic department and the admission office, and their role, in general terms, is to interact with each other and with coaches so everyone's time and the coaches' recruiting dollars are used as efficiently as possible.

The model on the athletic side usually looks like this: there is an athletic department liaison who interacts with coaches and admission officers to facilitate the flow of information between the two departments, who makes sure forms and documents find their proper home in a prospect's admission file, and who offers advice and perspective to coaches who have questions about an athlete's academic qualifications, including whether it even makes sense to pursue a player. Usually, this athletic department liaison has an admissions background. Often, he or she has other, nonadmission-related duties within the athletic department, for the role of admission liaison, while critical to the recruiting process, is rarely a full-time job.

Partly, this is because the support system is even greater on the Admissions side, where as many as six or seven admission officers serve as liaisons to the athletic department. Usually, one of these officers acts as the primary department liaison to athletics. Working with his or her counterpart in the athletic department, the officer assumes the responsibility for making sure that all of a recruit's transcripts, recommendations, essays, test scores, and other paperwork are complete and in the admission file. The four or five additional admission officers who serve as athletic department liaisons are each assigned to specific sports, and they work directly with the coaches in those sports to offer feedback and advice as, over many months, the coaches finalize their list of prospects.

This list, in the end, is as precious as gold, the result of months of careful sifting, aimed at one thing: finding outstanding players who look good to Admissions.

Says Peter Lasagna, the former men's coach of lacrosse at Brown, who now coaches at Bates: "In the Ivy League you're almost as successful as your liaison is good at his or her job."

There is not another athletic conference in the country that requires its member schools to answer to the admission office the way the Ivy League does, which is why (apologies to Linda Ronstadt) in the Ivy League recruiting game, "It's not easy to fall in love."

Tim Taylor has been wooing Ivy League recruits for over thirty years, twenty-four of them as the head coach of the Yale men's hockey team. A Harvard graduate, Taylor was a star forward for the Crimson in the early 1960s, during an era when legendary coach Cooney Weiland did virtually no recruiting at all and still won 315 games and eight Ivy titles in twenty-one years. Taylor, who played for the US National Team in 1965 and 1967 and served as the head coach of the 1994 US Olympic team at Lillehammer, is highly regarded in hockey circles as a master strategist and a brilliant teacher. He also has a sharp eye for talent, and the singular ability to convince players to come to Yale, attributes that have helped him to win more games than any other Yale hockey coach in history and to lead the Bulldogs to six of their nine Ivy titles in men's hockey.

A number of Taylor's players have gone on to play hockey in the Olympics, and a few have had careers in the NHL, which is the goal of nearly every Ivy League hockey player today. It's not a fantasy, either. A surprising number of Ivy League hockey players do go on to play professionally at some level after graduation (as many as 75 percent from some programs, far more than players from any other sport in the League), but most will play for just a few years before leveraging their Ivy degrees and connections to launch other careers, often on Wall Street. Even so, up to a dozen NHL scouts attend every Ivy hockey game, looking for talent, and they find it often enough to make their visits pay.

In May 2003, Taylor lost his (and the League's) best offensive player, sophomore center Chris Higgins, when the Long Island native decided to leave school and sign a reported $1.3 million contract with the Montreal Canadiens. Taylor and Yale's Athletic Director, Tom Beckett, had advised Higgins to wait at least one more year before making the decision to turn pro, believing the odds were much greater that Higgins would eventually earn his Yale degree if he had just one year to complete rather than two. Taylor also felt strongly that no college player had ever "come out too late," but that a number had definitely left the collegiate game too early, only to languish in the minors. The nineteen-year-old Higgins felt, however, that he was ready to play at the next level. After being chosen as a finalist for the Hobey Baker Award (named for the Princeton star who died young in World War I, and given annually to college hockey's top player), and being honored as college hockey's top forward in the East, the sophomore wanted a new challenge. Higgins was a rarity in Ivy League and in Division I men's ice hockey, an extremely talented player who was also young—just eighteen as a freshman, compared to an average freshman age of nearly twenty. The vast majority of Ivy League and Division I hockey players spend a year (or two) playing junior hockey in the Midwest or Canada before entering the college game. In contrast, Higgins had come straight out of prep school to compete against players four and five years older, and he wound up leading the League in scoring as a freshman. The Canadiens, who had drafted him in the first round following that stunning freshman year, were now reinforcing his sense that it was time for a new challenge and encouraging him to jump. After weighing the pros and cons for weeks (and changing his mind almost daily), Higgins finally decided to leave Yale to pursue his dream of an NHL career.

For Taylor, the decision was bittersweet. Landing Higgins two years earlier, over archrival Harvard and scholarship powerhouses Boston College and Boston University, had been a tremendous coup. Losing him would be equally devastating. He wished Higgins every success, even as he wished his star would stay. It was extremely rare for an Ivy athlete to leave school to turn pro, and extremely hard to see a recruiting process that had worked to such perfection lead to such a loss.

It was Taylor's associate head coach, C.J. Marottolo, who had identified Higgins as a top prospect early on, when the player was just a sophomore at Avon Old Farms School in Connecticut.

"It was the semifinals of the New England Prep School championship," Taylor recalls, "and the game went into overtime. Chris had a great play at the end of the game, and created an opportunity to win the game. . . . C.J. came back and said, 'I saw a really good sophomore at Avon.' So we sent him the form letter and questionnaire that we're legally allowed to send sophomores and got some information back that he was doing pretty well in school."

The questionnaire was just one of several Higgins received that year, and he filled Yale's out without thinking too much about it. "I just thought they sent them to everyone," Higgins says. "I just filled them out and sent them back. I don't think Yale was the first school to send me a questionnaire, but they were the first school to send me a letter saying, 'We want you. We want you to play. We think you're a good player.'"

The letter arrived via FedEx on the first day it was legal for Higgins to receive a personal letter from a college coach, September 1 of his junior year.

"It was pretty exciting to be recruited by such a good program," he says. "The letter made a pretty big impact because I knew they were obviously watching me before my junior year. I didn't really receive too much interest from the top college programs around that time. They only started contacting me after I had a good junior year. Yale showed their interest early, and I really liked that."

Taylor really liked Higgins' academic record at Avon, where the three-sport athlete (soccer, hockey, and lacrosse) carried a 4.0 average. "I've been at this quite a while," Taylor says of his experience recruiting in the Ivy League, "and I've got a pretty good sense and feel for what might float and what might not float in the admission office. Obviously, it's very important that I have credibility with the admission office, and it's very important that I trust and understand their perspective and know when to defer to them and when to stand up and be counted from my perspective. After all the giving and taking, we usually end up with a solid class."

Each year, Taylor and his staff correspond with three hundred to four hundred prospects. "We are certainly contacted by that many as well," he says. "Some of the contact is very brief—we get an academic report that just rules a kid out.

"Essentially," Taylor continues, "we look for a qualification that will give us one of three reads: green light, yellow light, red light. It's pretty easy for me and my staff to pick out the red-light kids and just excuse them. The yellow-light kids can be kids we have to wait and see what their SAT scores might be. Or they may have high SATs but lousy grades, and they may just be waking up. There are a lot of circumstances that can lead a kid to being a yellow-light kid. And a green light would be a kid that's got real strong academics, high class rank, and good test scores. We would feel comfortable that if he materializes as one of the very few kids that we want to put all our support behind, he would be a pretty admissible kid."

Taylor explains, "The way it works now, I don't think very many programs or coaches use a shotgun approach. I don't think we throw thirty names at the admission office and say, 'You pick.' At one point, they used to ask you for a list of top kids, and you would rank kids one through twenty, and they'd try hard to take your first guy. Then they might take your sixth guy, then your thirteenth and fourteenth. And the credentials were all there."

Today the list is far more refined for every coach at every school, and Admissions is in the loop early and often, even with a player of Chris Higgins' talent, who had top grades at a good prep school and board scores in the mid-1200s. "We essentially target," says Taylor. "We need to get good players. In each class, we need to get about six kids who are good hockey players, so that at any one time we have twenty-four to twenty-eight kids in the school that are dedicated to being very good hockey players, who love the game, and are pretty good at it."

Bob Ceplikas, the liaison to the admission office for the Dartmouth College athletic department since 1990, says, "There's always a significant amount of direct communication between coaches and admission officers. Things are divided up different ways at different schools, in terms of how many different admission officers are involved in working with different coaches." Using the feedback of admission officers, Ivy coaches will eliminate prospects or continue to pursue them, eventually inviting only those players who appear likely of gaining admission onto campus for an official visit.

"What we do," says Ceplikas, "and what most Ivies do, is to have each coach put together a list . . . it's a rank-ordered priority list—and that's a coach's way of conveying to the admission office their assessment of these prospective students' projected impact in terms of athletic ability. They generally do write-ups of each one as well, a fairly concise one—because the admission office has to wade through enough stuff as it is—that basically articulates the student's athletic credentials and projected impact. Sometimes they include comparisons to student-athletes currently at Dartmouth as frames of reference. It's all intended to give the admission office a piece of expert testimony of that particular dimension, athletic talent."

"Then," he adds, "it is Admissions' job to factor it in to all the different elements that are in the file in order to reach a decision. In the Ivy League, we may have this famous formula, called the Academic Index, but there's still nothing cut-and-dried about whether a particular A.I. number gets a student admitted or not admitted."

Tim Murphy of Harvard echoes a sentiment expressed by coaches around the League when he says, "You always scratch your head once in a while when you have a kid you really like, who you think looks great on paper, who doesn't get in. But in the end, the tail doesn't wag the dog here."

Hence, coaches bite their tongues (most of the time), because they know that maintaining good relations with Admissions is crucial to their success.

"In our system, if you are a supported athlete—which means you're on the list that the coach brings to the admission office—you count," says Jeff Orleans, the Executive Director of the Council of Ivy Group Presidents (which is Ivy-speak for their sports commissioner). "And no coach in our league takes the risk that even a double legacy, minority female with a 240 A.I. will get in without being on the list. If you really want the student, you put them on the list. Or you can never tell."

In plain language what Orleans is saying is that Ivy coaches take nothing for granted when it comes to submitting their lists to Admissions. The girl he describes—with two parents who graduated from the Ivy institution to which she is applying, the highest possible A.I. (based on a 4.0 GPA and 800 board scores), and status as a member of an "underrepresented" group—is stacked to succeed in the Ivy admission game. Yet a coach would be playing with fire if he should choose to leave her off a final list.

"If she turns out to be an All-Ivy player," Orleans explains, "the admission dean will come down to you and say, 'Well, you know, when you were asking me for field hockey admits, you told me you needed five players and I gave you five players. You didn't tell me that Christine Peeler was coming. Don't ever do that to me again. Oh, and don't worry about it next year 'cause next year your list is zero.'"

During his tenure at Princeton, Fred Hargadon says, "I would meet with the coaches at the beginning of every year and say, 'Look, just because your top candidate has 1600 SATs, I don't want you listing him less than the top. I'm trusting you to rank them by their athletic ability. So don't try to save the top for somebody else, because I can sniff that out faster than. . . .'" He laughs. "So they trusted me. I always reminded them: If you promise not to tell me who to admit, I promise not to call your plays."

"There is a game within the game," says Karl Furstenberg, Dartmouth's dean of admission. "And that is coaches dealing with and getting along with Admissions."

Orleans sums up this delicate Ivy League dynamic with a smile: "No one wants to piss off their admission office."

No one wants to piss off the Ivy presidents, either. But the way the list system works was doing just that, as Jeff Orleans explains: "We had a long review of this about four or five years ago. The [admission] deans went to the presidents and said, 'You know, our book says that if you're an athlete you have until May 1 along with everybody else to make a commitment . . . but we know that our coaches are telling these kids *if you want to be on my list, you have to tell me early in the process that you're gonna come because I don't have any admits to waste.'* So the presidents said to the athletic people, 'Is this true?' The athletic people said, 'Of course, it's true. The deans are telling us that we don't have any admission spots to waste.' The presidents said to the deans, 'Is that true?' The deans said, 'Yes. You're telling us that we have numerical limits.' So the presidents said, 'We'll study this.'"

A committee of coaches, athletic directors, admission deans, and Orleans spent several months studying the nature of the system, and, he says, "Eventually we came back to the presidents and said, 'If you want to have limited numbers, high academic standards, more financial aid, internal competitive equity of some sort, and the chance to be real Division I programs—and you're gonna limit numbers substantially—something has to give. And what has to give is that just as you are pushing kids to make choices for early decision, kids are being pushed to make choices in athletics. And we ought to stop pretending that isn't true.'"

According to Orleans, "The presidents said, 'That's awful.' And the group said, 'We agree. See if you can find a better solution.' And so the presidents had a couple of discussions and decided that that is, in fact, the price to pay for all the other things that we hope they're getting right in terms of admissions and financial aid—that we do ask kids for commitments. What we did was to open—make a little more obvious—the way the process works. We now tell kids explicitly in an Ivy admission statement, 'You can be asked for a commitment in return for the issuance of a Likely Letter. And you don't have to make a commitment before May 1 if you don't want to, but the [admission] dean is free in deciding to issue a Likely Letter to consider your degree of commitment.'"

In other words, if you don't tell a coach you're coming, you're not getting the letter, and the coach is moving on to other prospects. The pressure to make a decision will bear down on you, in one form or another.

Tim Taylor says he doesn't believe in giving kids deadlines. "I've pretty much stayed away from that. I do believe in the official visit process, and it's important that they get to see the campuses and meet the coaching staffs and familiarize themselves with the academic product they're buying. When we've done everything, and the kid's done everything, they know they have to decide."

Having said that, Taylor admits that a kid who has trouble making up his mind can get dropped from his list. "He's going to make four or five other visits, and in the meantime other guys are going by the wayside while we're waiting for this kid to make up his mind—and he hasn't given us a strong indication that he is going to make Yale his first choice." Well, that's the end of that courtship.

For recruits who apply Early Decision, as Chris Higgins did, their first choice is obvious. "I made my decision in August before my senior year," he says, admitting it was hard to choose Yale over Harvard. "I just felt more comfortable here, and I felt more accepted, which gave the edge over Harvard. I applied Early Decision to Yale. I had to officially get accepted, but they told me I'd have no problem." Around the Ivy League, between 50 and 60 percent of all recruited athletes are now accepted under early decision programs, compared to 30 to 40 percent of the general applicant pool. This is a trend that reflects both the increasing popularity of Early Decision as an option for all applicants, and the pressure on kids to commit to a coach, get on the list, and take their best shot at getting in.

This pressure from coaches on recruits to apply early raises concerns from Bruce Bailey of the Lakeside School in Seattle. "Quite frankly, as the director of our college placement, I've gotten pretty sensitive to coaches over the years in terms of 'promises, promises' and the games that get played and the squeeze kids get in terms of apply early, because that's the real game. They all want these kids to apply early so they can wrap them up. And you know sometimes I think it's credible, and sometimes I just think they're just trying to get a big pool of athletes."

Julie Shackford, the women's soccer coach at Princeton says, "Ninety percent of my recruits go early and I don't think that's me. I really think that that's being pushed in all the high schools. Certainly there are coaches out there who will say, 'You have to apply early or you're not going to get in, or I'm going to move on to somebody else.' But my feeling is if you want a kid, you'll let them make the choice about what process they want to apply in. It's just turned out that I get so many early, and I think it's a combination of pressure from their schools and kids wanting to have the decision done, because their senior years are so packed now, and obviously from a coaching perspective it is nice to know that your class is done early."

For recruits who apply in the regular decision admission pool, Taylor says, "I don't find it difficult to tell a kid at some point in the process, 'I gotta know if you're going to come. If it isn't going to be you, I can't waste an admission spot on you and have you go to Harvard.'"

There is no set time, he says, for making this statement to a prospect. "My assistant coaches and I meet every two days [all year round] and share progress. We recruit night and day. This year, we had two defensemen and one forward admitted early. Since that time, we've gotten one more defenseman, another forward, and a goaltender. And those three were all committed—and in the bank, so to speak—by the end of January."

The Division I scholarship signing date in early February is partly responsible for this accelerated admission timeframe for athletes in the Ivy League. The need to address "squeeze play" scenarios—the offers athletes receive from scholarship schools—was the original impetus behind Likely Letters and admission decisions prior to mid-April. But, the far bigger factor in the accelerated timeframe is the precious nature of the admission slots, and the need for coaches to manage their lists precisely—all of which leads to more pressure on kids and to some ugly games.

"Sometimes coaches say to a kid, 'You're at the top of my list,' which is a blatant lie," says Taylor. "We know he's got twenty forwards at the top of his list. He's said that to each one of them—several have come back and told us. A lot of people do that. They're probably fancy in the way they word it, so they don't feel like they're lying."

Then there are the kids in Taylor's program who were turned off by another Ivy coach who put pressure on them to make a commitment by September of their senior year. According to Taylor, the coach told one of them, "If you don't let me know by the first of September for Early Decision, we'll probably go on to another defenseman." The player had made an unofficial visit to the school, but he had not yet visited any of the other Ivies he was interested in. "So," Taylor says, "he told the coach, 'I'm not ready to commit to you.' There's nothing illegal about that. The coach is just saying, 'Look it, we need to recruit kids who want to go to our school, and we need to know by this timetable or else we have to go on.'"

Taylor leans forward and continues, "We would all like to have our recruiting done yesterday. Nobody likes to have it drag on. If you're involved with good kids, there's going to be a lot of competition for those kids. Every phone call we make to a kid in limbo, every contact we have with him, it comes up: 'How are you coming with your decision? Have you got a timetable? Have you visited all the schools? Have you met all the coaches? Have you listened to what Coach Mazzoleni [of Harvard] is saying? What Coach Gaudet [of Dartmouth] is saying? Do you know where you stand with them? We want you to be our number one defenseman, and we need to know sometime soon where you're gonna go.'"

"We're all doing that," Taylor admits. "So the issue is getting forced by the coaches. It's also sometimes forced by the families. The families come in and say, 'We love ya.' I've got a kid right now, he's actually got a two-year plan. He's a junior in high school, and he's trying to decide whether to go to prep school or go out to play junior hockey. In the course of trying to make that decision, his father said to me, 'Can you tell me now that my son would be a kid you'd want?' And my answer was, 'Look, we want your son now. I don't know what he's going to look like on paper to the Yale admission office. We've gotta see his transcript at the end of his junior year, and his SAT scores. Then I will walk his academic paperwork over to my liaison in the admission office and we'll discuss him.' Sometimes the parents are pushing this timetable. Everybody's pushing it forward."

Looking for love in the Ivy League recruiting game is an increasingly fast-paced affair.

Chris Higgins' love affair with Yale almost ended when his early acceptance letter arrived in mid-December of his senior year, and he reviewed the school's financial aid package with his parents.

"Their first estimate was, to quote my parents, 'Nowhere near what we expected,'" he says. "So we called up Coach Taylor and told him, 'Hey, it's not gonna work. We need more money if we're going to come here, and we really want to come here, so see what you can do.'"

Any applicant who receives an Ivy League financial aid package has the right to ask for a review of the package and to try to negotiate an increase in their aid, if possible, whether it is through a grant, a loan, or a work-study job on campus. In Higgins' case, he sent word back through the hockey coaches, who were his primary contacts at the school, because he knew they had a vested interest in having him come to Yale. It was an advantage the average student would never enjoy.

BC and BU were still dangling scholarships in front of Higgins, in the event things turned sour with the Bulldogs. As a result, he had leverage with Yale, a precious commodity in any negotiation, but especially vital in the Ivy League recruiting game, where financial aid is need-based. Having a scholarship offer from another school in your back pocket can prompt a coach, and a financial aid office to "Find a way (to repeat an Ivy refrain) to make it work."

It did not take long for Yale to respond to the request. Chris' father, a Brooklyn firefighter who had played college soccer at St. Bonaventure, and his mother, a homemaker, had four children to educate and limited resources to expend on one son—especially one who could attend college at no cost.

"They did a little work and got us back a reasonable number," says Higgins, "and I was willing to pay money . . . so I could come to Yale."

Like many other Ivy athletes, he chose to invest in his education, solving the problem by taking on what he characterizes as, "a lot of student loans. It's pretty tempting to take the full scholarships. I don't really think too many guys would turn down those offers. But like I said, I felt really comfortable here. Obviously, this is a better academic school than most. I felt I should receive an education like this. I had done well at Avon—I had always done well in school—so I wanted to continue to do well and challenge myself, not only in the hockey rink but in the classroom."

This is a common refrain from Ivy athletes. They want the best of both worlds, athletically and academically. As a result, many have lists of their own, filled with their goals for school, sports, and life. In the case of Chris Higgins, the chance to pursue his goal of playing in the NHL came sooner than expected. And so, in spite of his love for Yale, which had led him to choose student loans over a free ride, he left school early to chase his dream. Yes, he broke Tim Taylor's heart in the process. But the coach, who wished him well, could not afford to linger over a sad good-bye. He was too busy looking for other talented prospects to lead to the altar.

Chapter Six

The Closing

"The whole process is really stressful. Especially as it started to get into January, all the stress just hit. We had exams, and then everyone at school's asking, 'Where you going? Where you going?' every day."

Carl Morris
Harvard University & Miami Dolphins wide receiver

A
t one point in the fall of his senior year at Episcopal High School, a private boarding school in Alexandria, Virginia, Carl Morris was being recruited by eight of the top twenty-five college football programs in the country. Virginia, Virginia Tech, North Carolina, Stanford, University of Washington, Northwestern, and other universities were all after the athletic wide receiver, despite the fact that his senior year was just his second season playing football. Until his junior year Morris had been a soccer player, following in the footsteps of his maternal grandfather, who had been a defender for England's most storied professional club, Manchester United. But toward the end of his sophomore year, when he led the Episcopal team in scoring, the 6-foot-1-inch, 180-pound center forward started to feel "burned out" on soccer, and by spring he had decided to switch from British football to American football, a dream he had cherished since childhood, when his parents had refused to allow him to play Pop Warner for safety concerns.

"I decided that I didn't want to look back and say, 'I should have played football,'" Morris says of his decision. "I always thought I could be good at football."

He was right. He was so good and so heavily recruited by the fall of his senior year that phone calls from college coaches were getting in the way of his schoolwork and affecting his grades.

"My pager was going off all the time in study hall," Morris recalls, "and it got to the point where I was tired of calling people back, so I forwarded all my calls to my parents, and I let them narrow it down for me."

The recruiting process was familiar to Jane and Verne Morris, whose older child, Jemma, had been recruited to play college basketball a few years earlier. That recruiting process, however, had been a disaster, and they swore that if they'd only known how the game was played, their daughter would have gone to her first choice, instead of having to scramble at the last minute to find a school that still had a full scholarship available and wanted her in their program. Early on, Jemma had been offered full rides to a couple of schools she liked; coaches had told her, "Take your time," as she was deciding. But then the schools turned around and pulled their offers without warning and awarded the scholarships to other girls. It had been a rude awakening for the Morris household. Jemma's disappointment was matched only by her parents' anxiety; they needed the scholarship money in order to send their daughter to college. The family found themselves searching for another school with a scholarship to offer, but scholarships were scarce that late in the process.

The manager of a restaurant in northern Virginia, Verne Morris had started working at the age of thirteen to help his parents put bread on his family's table. The oldest of eight children, he had been forced to give up sports, including his favorite, running track. Instead of playing after school, he worked, and as soon as he graduated from high school he worked full-time. His wife, Jane, who grew up in England, had also been a good athlete, running track and serving as the captain of her secondary school netball team, the British equivalent of basketball without the hoop. She now worked as a receiving clerk for Saab aircraft in the family's hometown, Sterling, Virginia. Both parents wanted their children to get the best education possible, so when Jemma finally got another full-scholarship offer in the spring of her senior year from Wagner College on Staten Island, the Morris family jumped at it. In the end, they were fortunate, but they had learned a number of harsh lessons along the way. They promised themselves the process would work differently for Carl, if he were ever offered a similar opportunity.

And there was every indication he would be recruited. He was an outstanding soccer player in a youth league and a star basketball player. In fact, basketball had been his ticket into the exclusive Episcopal High School. In eighth grade, when he had played in a three-on-three basketball tournament at the school and his team had won, the Episcopal varsity coach, who had played at Georgetown and knew talent when he saw it, invited Morris to consider attending the school. Since Carl liked the coach, he had an interview and his parents went for a tour. Going to Episcopal would mean four years of living away from home at a boarding school and a sizeable chunk of student loan debt as part of Carl's financial aid package. But it would also mean a top-flight education, excellent athletics, and the best preparation for a bright future. The Morrises decided that enrolling in Espicopal would be in Carl's best interests.

They were right. He earned a B+ average through four years, in a competitive academic environment, and scored in the mid-1200s on his SATs. He starred on three straight state championship basketball teams, and made the highly successful switch from soccer to football his junior year, a move that arguably changed his life. He showed such raw promise in his first football season that college recruiters began mailing him letters that winter and spring. Within the first few weeks of his senior year, they were calling him so often that he handed his pager over to his dad.

Within a couple of weeks, Verne Morris had cut the number of recruiting calls in half, eliminating the schools his son wasn't really interested in while maintaining relationships with the schools Carl did like, including several big-time Division 1A programs, and three 1AA schools—Harvard, William & Mary, and Princeton. The big-time schools had discovered Morris by virtue of following his Episcopal quarterback, a high school All-American who lured college recruiters to games in bunches. When the coaches saw Morris catching the star quarterback's passes, they added him to their hot prospect list. Harvard, on the other hand, had joined the recruiting fray months earlier, in the spring of his junior year, using their favorite proven method—a direct-mail piece featuring the magical Harvard name.

"I got a questionnaire from them," Morris says. "I just thought it was pretty funny, *'Wow, Harvard.'* It never even crossed my mind that Harvard would be a consideration. I was on the phone with my parents one day, and I was telling them about it, and my dad got really excited: 'You gotta fill it out! You gotta fill it out!" I was like, 'I don't know about that.' So I just filled it out to appease him." Morris shakes his head and smiles. "It just seems like a mythical place to a lot of high school students."

"Carl Morris was one of those five thousand," Tim Murphy says, referring to the annual list of prospects generated by Harvard's direct mailer. "Until I saw his video. His video was absolutely knock your socks off. He was very raw—he hadn't played much football—but we just don't see many kids who can do what he can do naturally. He became our top recruiting priority at a very early point in time."

Harvard assistant Bruce Tall was assigned the primary responsibility for recruiting Morris, and as soon as it was legal under NCAA rules, he began calling the wide receiver once a week. He also traveled down to Episcopal High School every week he was allowed to be there under NCAA rules. (Division I coaches must take an annual exam on NCAA recruiting rules, and the manual they study in preparation is two inches thick, containing nearly five hundred pages of bylaws covering everything from telephone calls to number of visits, sports camps to entertainment, and a mind-boggling array of other categories. "If you can think of another rule that's not in here," says Pat O'Leary, holding up the hefty manual, "you're probably a lawyer who should be working for the NCAA." It is, indeed, a daunting volume.) Under NCAA rules, head coaches are allowed to visit a prospect at home up to three times. Tim Murphy visited Carl Morris three times.

And Bruce Tall called every week, along with twenty other coaches.

"It was basically every night of the week," Carl Morris says of the recruiting calls. "Different schools every night, 'cause they can only call you once a week, and I didn't want to talk to twenty schools in one night. I talked to three schools every night, one the same night each week. If they wanted to call you that much, it would pretty much be every week at the same time.

"Some guys would talk about anything just to keep you on the phone," Morris recalls. "Some of them, they were either too pushy or you could tell they really weren't sincere, they really didn't care, they were just making the call. They really could have cared less about you."

Morris got a different feeling from Bruce Tall.

"Coach Tall would ask me about how I did, and we'd talk about my games, and then we'd talk about how they did that week, and then he'd ask me about my family. We just talked for about twenty minutes each time. He was one of my favorites. I think there were maybe three guys in the whole process that I *really* liked. He was one of them."

The others were the wide receiver coach at Princeton and the head coach at Virginia, which was Morris's top choice, despite the fact that it didn't have any scholarships left for wide receivers by the time it showed an interest in him.

"Even when Harvard was in the picture, Virginia was still my number one choice," Morris recalls. "It was my home state. Our quarterback, who was one of my good friends, signed with them the first day you could. I knew students who went there, and everyone loved the school and was having a good time, and I just felt it was the place for me."

Morris decided to visit the schools with the three coaches he liked— Virginia, Harvard, and Princeton—as well as the University of Washington, and William & Mary, another Virginia-based school that had offered him a full scholarship the summer before and still had it on the table, ready for him to sign. After making the visits, he decided, he would make his final decision. The real stress and pressure lay ahead.

In the Ivy League, official visits for football recruits occur every January, when schools fly in anywhere from fifty to seventy players (depending on the program and its resources) over three or four weekends to close the deal. The players' travel, meals, lodging, and (modest) entertainment expenses are all paid for by the host institution. Parents, who are encouraged to join their sons on these visits, must pay for their own airfare, but NCAA rules allow them to receive lodging and meals compliments of the host institution once they arrive. The players and their families are waltzed through a carefully orchestrated forty-eight hours designed to show off the school and its football program in the best light. The recruits stay on campus with current players, who show them around, answer their questions, and give them a feel for their school and program, while the parents are put up in hotels, taken out to dinner by the coaches, and encouraged to bond with each other during the day. The players meet with their future position coach (if he is a different coach than the one who has been recruiting him), and many are required to have an admission interview. (At some schools, including Harvard, all football recruits are interviewed by Admissions when they visit the campus.) While the details of these official visit football weekends vary slightly from school to school, the intention is the same at each Ivy institution: roll out the red carpet and, in a final meeting with the head coach, get the player to commit to coming.

"I always warn kids who are not going to visit Harvard first," says Tim Murphy. "'Listen, understand, they're still gonna knock your socks off. Why? Because you've never really been to a college campus where someone really, really wants you. It's a very *powerful* weekend. It's kinda like the first pretty girl you ever see—you think that's the one. Life doesn't work like that.'"

Naturally, Murphy doesn't give kids who visit Harvard first the same words of warning. But that's all part of the recruiting game in the Ivy League, where football coaches are after the same players: you play every angle to make your school seem more attractive, and once kids are on your campus, you put the pressure on them to choose you.

"What's happening now," says John Lyons, "is these kids are rolling around making all these Ivy League visits in January, and some coaches won't let them out of their office. They're saying, 'You don't commit, you're not getting a spot.'"

Yale's Jack Siedlecki admits, "I'll say to people all the time, 'If we're your number one choice, you're an absolute fool not to say yes.' I'll sit right here and say that to parents. 'You go out and test the waters and go check it out. There might not be any spots left. We've got thirty spots now. They go fast. It's just reality.'"

Years ago, admission spots for football players were not as precious. In the 1960s and early 1970s, before co-education, women's sports, and Title IX, Dartmouth head coach Bob Blackman created a football dynasty, thanks to his innovative recruiting techniques (among other things, he was the first college football coach in the country to send weekly newsletters to recruits), and the large number of admitted athletes in each new class. Back then, says current Big Green coach, John Lyons, "The whole school was made up of athletes. Blackman had a Freshman A team, a Freshman B team. There were five hundred football players, and whoever shook out played." And they played well. Dartmouth was undefeated in 1970 and won the Lambert Trophy as the East's top team, finishing ahead of Penn State in the voting.

Lyons, who played at the University of Pennsylvania in the late 1960s, recalls having 116 teammates on his freshman team. (Freshmen did not become eligible for varsity competition in the Ivy League until 1993.) When he played in his final varsity game, Lyons says, "There were seventeen of us left."

"It used to be, you dealt with so many numbers," he continues. "But then it went from one hundred in the entering class, down to fifty. The League had it at fifty when I came here with Buddy [Buddy Teevens, now the head coach at Stanford] in 1988. Then it went to forty-five. And at some point in the '90s, it went to thirty-five. Now, this was our first year [2003's entering class] at thirty."

"You've got to be careful with thirty spots," he says. "There's no margin for error now because there's always going to be attrition at these schools. They don't have a scholarship hanging over your head. What they're asking us to do is hit that number right on the head. 'Cause if you go over, you're penalized, and you get caught short by not having enough."

People need to understand how hard, how selective, and how quick the process is now, says Yale's Siedlecki. "Three or four years ago, I would have high school coaches say to me in January, 'Wow, you've got 'til May 1 [for an admitted student to send in his official enrollment confirmation]—you're trying to pressure this kid for no reason.' And then, a week later they'd call back and say, 'He went to whatever school and didn't really like it; now he's ready to commit to you.' And I would say, 'Hey, I don't have any spots left.' The word's out that's how the system works. More and more, kids understand that if you're ready to make a decision, you better make it."

During these official visits, coaches will tell a prospect—let's say a tight end—exactly where things stand. The basic pitch goes like this: "We have two spots for tight ends this year, and we think you're great. We'd love to have you. That spot is available right now, and we hope you'll take it. If you wait too long to make your decision, though, we can't promise that spot will be available. We understand if you want to make other visits. But you need to understand the spot may not be around." If the kid cannot commit then and there, he probably has until the following Thursday (or possibly into the following week, in some cases), to call and say, "Coach, I've thought about what you said, and I'd like to accept that spot. I want to commit to coming to x." Once the next weekend arrives, there are no guarantees. The coaches claim they are just being honest with their prospects, and in a very real sense they are—thirty spots do go quickly. But the Ivy League system puts a tremendous amount of pressure on seventeen- and eighteen-year-old kids to make a decision, and the League's reliance on verbal commitments can lead to some ugly situations, and not just in football recruiting, either, but in other sports as well.

All the pressure and stress occurs in January because the official Letter of Intent signing date for scholarship schools lands each year on the first Wednesday in February. (The Ivy League does not use the NCAA Letter of Intent because of the scholarship overtones associated with it.) While every other student who has applied to an Ivy institution under regular decision must wait until April to learn whether he or she will have a spot in the next incoming class, Ivy athletes who do not apply under an early decision program have their own, separate admission timeframe. An athlete who must decide whether or not to accept a scholarship offer, the Ivies have decided, has the right to know before making that decision whether they are likely to be admitted to the Ivy League school of their choice. Known as a "squeeze play," the scenario requires written confirmation from the prospect's guidance counselor that the scholarship offer is, indeed, legitimate. The Ivy admission office will mail the prospect what is known as a "Likely Letter," stating his or her chances of admission, with an answer of "highly likely" meaning "yes"—providing the kid doesn't rob a bank or blow up the high school.

In the case of football, Likely Letters confirming a prospect's future admission are sent in January and February to every recruit who has been offered a spot and told the coach he is coming—regardless of whether or not the player has been offered a scholarship to a non-Ivy school. These football Likely Letters are, in essence, the Ivy League's version of an NCAA Letter of Intent. Only the process is backwards. Instead of having the prospect sign the letter saying he or she will come, as is the case with an NCAA Letter of Intent, the Ivy schools sign a letter saying they will admit the player. Some football prospects collect Likely Letters like all-star awards, securing two or three of them before making their final choice. Clearly, coaches don't appreciate this deception, and they have been known to take some drastic measures (including a few that flaunt the rules) to try to stop it from happening. But these are smart kids, in some cases with equally conniving and dishonest parents, and they can outfox even the most diligent coaches and the most selective Ivy admission officers. We'll delve into this unfortunate aspect of the Ivy recruiting game in more detail later on. For now, it's January, when the heat comes on for everyone involved in the Ivy football recruiting game—from players to parents to coaches.

According to Tim Murphy of Harvard, the dramatic acceleration of the recruiting process in the past few years is really driven by the parents and the student-athletes. "It's not driven by the coaches," he says. "It just seems like people want to know earlier and earlier. They want to make decisions earlier and earlier. You get kids making decisions after their junior year to go to Notre Dame or Stanford, and it's just a trickle-down effect that's reached all of us."

In the case of Ivy League football recruiting, the acceleration takes on a few added dimensions. The first and most critical has been identified by Yale's Jack Siedlecki: "The big thing is you don't want to drop from your best pool to the bottom. You want to go from the first guy to the second guy, not from the first guy to the tenth guy. As long as you have enough guys in the pool, and you are doing the process properly, you'll get that. If you start letting a lot of kids wait, and kids are falling off, all of a sudden you go from the first guy to the tenth guy—and chances are, you got a guy who can't play."

Hence, Yale tries to get their best prospects to visit on the first weekend in January. This gives the recruits the greatest amount of time to make their decision, and it allows Siedlecki to offer prospects a place in the class without having to worry whether he will have any spots left. At Harvard,

Murphy has kids visit "whenever they can" in January. But in recent years both schools have wrapped up recruiting their thirty football players within days of each other, before anyone else in the League, usually after just two weeks of visits. Most schools will have a third weekend of visits and some, lower in the pecking order, will have a fourth.

The second factor affecting Ivy football recruiting is tied directly into the first: the League's Academic Index bands—which every coaching staff must consider when weighing a prospect's relative value.

"You can't just say, 'Let's list the linemen and rate 'em one through ten. Let's list the backs and rate 'em one through ten,'" says Siedlecki. "Because if one, two, and three are all in one band, guess what? You can't recruit 'em." The athletic talent has to be distributed along with the academic talent (at least as it is measured by the A.I.). "You can't have a bunch of low-band guys on your board. You have to eliminate kids; they might be great players, but you gotta eliminate them."

Because Ivy League institutions have different "mean" A.I.s, a player can fall into two different bands at two different schools, potentially increasing or decreasing his odds of being offered a spot. "The problem in all this," says Dartmouth's Lyons, "is that you're going to recruit a player who could be in somebody's low band, where they got seven spots, or somebody else's middle band, where they got thirteen, and it's just confusing as hell. What we try to do is juggle, or we look at it and say, 'Okay, how many guys are we graduating at wide receiver or quarterback? How many guys do we need to bring in at a certain position?' And then we have to juggle that with the whole Academic Index thing, and set priorities."

When players come for their official visits to Hanover, Lyons may review the whole index system with them. "Our admission people don't like us talking about the Index. But how can we do our job without telling people, 'Hey, this is how it works'? I'm gonna tell them the truth: 'This is what we can work with here. And this is where you fall. This is how many we can take. You better find out what band you're in at these other schools.'"

What can frustrate coaches further is to recruit a player for nine months, under the assumption that he has 195 A.I. and falls into one band, only to have Admissions inform them in late December, as the player is about to be invited for his official visit in January, that the prospect's A.I. is actually 181 and is actually in a lower band. This can occur when a player comes from a high school that does not calculate class rank, or when the coach has received incomplete or inaccurate information from a high school guidance counselor, or when a guidance counselor has completed a form and, unbeknown to the coach, put down a class rank, even when the school does not calculate class rank (something that is often done for Ivy schools and the US military academies). In the first case, an Ivy admission officer may call a guidance counselor at a school that does not rank and ask him or her to provide an estimated class rank for a player. The guidance counselor, not wanting to offend an Ivy League school, will provide a best-guess ranking, sometimes on the spot, and that ranking will, in turn, lower the prospect's A.I. As we saw earlier, class rank, when compared to the GPA that establishes that rank, will generate a lower A.I. total. Suddenly, a player who has been recruited for six months in an A.I. band with thirteen spots will have dropped into a band with only seven—or, worse, from a band with seven spots into the low band with only two. And, just to compound the problem even further, he may play the same position as two other prospects already in that band. So much for nine months of evaluation and recruiting. Coaches have to scramble to find another kid to invite for a visit.

Carl Morris, who had an A.I. close to 190, almost didn't get to Harvard for his official visit. Six inches of snow delayed his Friday evening flight from Washington's Reagan National Airport, and cancelled his mother's flight from Dulles. Jane Morris drove through the driving snow and managed to get on the last flight out of National with her son. Verne Morris had to work and could not make the trip. "He works all the time," Carl says. "It was tough for him to get out. He was dying to get up there, he wanted to come so badly."

The next morning, Morris woke early for a series of interviews and meetings—first with Admissions, then with his position coach, then with Coach Murphy. "It was pretty hectic," he says. But he was well prepared, thanks in part to his sister, Jemma.

"My sister helped me out a lot," Morris says. "She told me how to present myself to the coaches, how the visits work, what you can do, what you can't do. She said, 'Look people in the eye when you speak with them, just be yourself, and don't try to be who you think they want you to be. If they like you, they like you—if not, then you're not going to go there.' She just told me basic stuff, but when you're in high school, and you're visiting a school like Harvard on a recruiting trip, you obviously want to put your best foot forward and try to do the best you can. It was good advice."

Another person easing the stress was his on-campus host, strong safety Mike Brooks, who just happened to be Carl's cousin.

"The best part of the whole recruiting process," says Morris, "happened early on. My dad called me one day and said, 'Your cousin goes to Harvard, and he's playing football.' Our family's huge and there are people everywhere, people I haven't even met. I ended up calling Mike and we talked for a bit. When we were both home for Christmas, we all went out to eat, and that was the first time we met. We became best friends."

"My cousin made me feel comfortable about the whole situation," says Morris. "Obviously, coaches don't go to the school. They can tell you what they know from recruiting. They can tell you the sunnier side of everything. I wanted to know about things from a student's perspective, and when I got here, Mike showed me a good time, introduced me to some good people, and that's when I kind of realized it was a regular school, just like any other school. And from then on I was, like, 'This is a great situation, great education, great place, great people, great area, and good football on top of that.'"

"People think that Harvard is a bunch of geniuses and millionaires," says Murphy. "That if you're a public high school kid, you won't get in. In reality, most of the kids here are on financial aid and most of the kids here are from public high schools."

But what really shocks people, says Murphy, is that Harvard has the largest Division I athletic program in America. "They never know that. They think that athletics aren't important here, and that you have to be a rich boarding school kid to get in. They go zero for three on their perceptions. When you tell them the facts, they're disarmed."

On Sunday, Morris and his mother were invited into Tim Murphy's office for a final meeting—the closing. "Coach Murphy asked me if I wanted to come to Harvard," Morris recalls. "He tried to push it a little bit, 'cause that's what they all do. He asked me how my trip went, how I liked my time, asked me how I liked the school, how I felt about things. I told him it was looking pretty good, but I still had some issues to settle with Virginia, and I was still considering it. He was pressing it, saying, 'This is a program where you'll be able to come in and play freshman year, where at Virginia you'll be sitting out as a red-shirt. We really want you here and Virginia seems like they're jerking you around.' And he looked at my mom and said, 'How would you like your son to graduate from Harvard? How would you like him to have that degree?' My mom is always the most relaxed and laid back. My dad gets excited about certain things. She said, 'It's up to my son. We just help him when he wants us to.' I told Coach Murphy I had to wait a little bit longer. I wasn't going to be pressured into making my decision just before I was going home on the plane."

The game was in full swing, and Carl Morris was playing it well.

"I think the hardest thing about recruiting," says Jack Siedlecki, "is when you go through a recruiting process for seven, eight, nine months, bring a kid on a visit, kid has a bad visit, you're done. In two days, after all you went through."

A bad visit for one school, however, can be good news for another.

"The only reason we got our quarterback, Brian Mann," says John Lyons of his star, who graduated in 2003, "was because Harvard screwed it up. They had him, and they told him he was the only quarterback they were recruiting. But then on his visit, they brought in a transfer kid from BU. The head coach spent all of his time with the transfer, and Brian got pissed and started shopping around. He was all set to go there. He got in. But we got Brian because they didn't spend any time with him or his parents on his visit."

While some prospects (in football and other sports) who are invited on an official Ivy visit have been prescreened by Admissions as a "likely" admit (and may have also gotten a preread from the financial aid office), not every recruit who makes an official visit is guaranteed to be accepted.

"One of the things that I pushed for when I first came up here," says Lyons, "is we're going out recruiting and we're bringing all these kids on campus, and then Admissions turns around and rejects them. Or we don't know what their financial aid is, so these kids want to come, but then they don't get enough financial aid. I said, 'Hey, this doesn't make any sense at all.'"

Every athletic department's "paper trail" with Admissions varies slightly from school to school, but most admission departments require the prospect to have submitted a complete application and to have a complete file—including their transcript, SAT I and SAT II scores, teacher recommendations, essays—prior to coming on an official visit. As Lyons says, it makes no sense to pay to bring a kid to campus only to have Admissions turn him or her down, and yet that does happen.

Harvard requires every football player to have an admission interview while on campus, just to be sure they are up to snuff, and the Yale admission office will ask to interview as many as a third of Siedlecki's recruits when they visit.

"When you start talking about kids who are in the first and second band," says Siedlecki, "which is nine kids out of the thirty—you can poke holes in every one of those kids in terms of being an Ivy League admit, just because of where they are on the scale. There's some reason that they're not 200 or 210 or whatever—so what is it? Test scores? Usually we won't get whacked with the test score kids. Not every kid in the country has an equal opportunity in terms of getting in here, in terms of where they go to high school. If your high school doesn't have a lot of A.P. [Advanced Placement] courses, it automatically raises a flag with our admission people. It's not your fault. It's not your fault that you're at whatever high school out in Nebraska or Iowa or wherever. If you're taking the best courses the school has available, then what else can you do? But if you don't have A.P. English, A.P. Chemistry, A.P. Calculus, our admission people want to talk to you and see if they really think you can compete with all these kids who come here who did take A.P. courses."

"On the other side of that," Siedlecki continues, "is the kid, particularly in big public high schools, who's a real good student, he's a football player—he's playing two or three sports—he's got a guidance counselor telling him, 'Hey, just take the good college level courses, you don't need to take the A.P. courses.' And all of a sudden our admission people look at the kid's transcript and say, 'How come he hasn't taken

A.P. courses? They offer them. He didn't take them.' So they're gonna want to interview that kid, too."

Siedlecki smiles. "I say this to our admission liaison: there should be a label on the door, 'Office of Rejection,' not 'Office of Admission.' We reject 90 percent of the kids who apply here. We have tremendous kids that get in here, but the reality is if you're an admission person here, you're looking to eliminate kids."

Bruce Bailey, the director of college counseling at the Lakeside School in Seattle, where Bill Gates prepped for Harvard, addresses this highly competitive process and the need for an Ivy League applicant today to have some kind of "hook" to help him or her get in. "There are 100,000 more high school graduates every year," he says of the current college applicant pool, which is the largest in history. "Not all of them will apply to college, but that's the statistic each year from 1998 to 2006 [or a staggering 900,000 more potential applicants in the pool over the course of a decade]. And they're applying to more schools. I get a little cynical because Harvard calls me and tells me they've got 20,000 applicants in regular admission, and they're taking 1,000 of them. That's a 5 percent admit rate. Then they moan and groan that there isn't enough staff to read them all. That tells me even more that if you don't have a hook . . . they can't read the applications as well anymore, so they don't. They just look for specific kids, and fill their slots. We need a football team. We need a hockey team. . . ."

As Bailey says of his exclusive private school, "We play in a unique league. I'm not aware of another around like it on a national level. We play in what's called the Seattle Metropolitan League, which is made up of our independent school, several Catholic schools, and the Seattle inner-city public schools—so it's an incredible mix of schools. It's quite a competitive, demanding sports program. We've had a long tradition here of athletic involvement and achievement, so it's a big deal at this school. We tend to have very few Division I, non–Ivy League type of athletes, but we get enough of the Ivy type of athlete, where they can get in and they're good enough to compete there. I'm looking at our senior class right now, and I can see three or four kids who will be significant factors at significant Ivy League schools. And pretty clearly the hook that got them in was their athletic ability.

"There are a variety of hooks," Bailey continues. "There's the super, super academic—not just a kid who gets the grades and has the numbers, but a kid who has reflected in his or her own writing and his or her teacher recommendations: 'This is a unique, academic, intellectual person.' We had two of them in the class this year [2003] and they got in everywhere. That's an academic hook. There's the athletic hook. To some extent, there's the artistic hook, particularly in music. Kids are sending in tapes of their musical ability, and I think the orchestra and band leaders are coming to Admissions saying, 'Hey, I need a first violin.' I don't think it's as big as athletics, but it's there. I think there is a little bit of a geographic hook. Colleges certainly like to have kids from every part of the country. Then, of course, you have the underrepresented groups—still huge—and the connected family hook, particularly an alum who's had a past record of involvement, perhaps even financial support. Those are real hooks. Kids can't make them up. If they have them, they got 'em, and they might as well play 'em. I think they're more relevant than they've ever been. Because the acceptance rates are so low now that all those teams and orchestras and underrepresented group interests, there's only a few spots left so you've almost got to have one."

"I do worry about all the people that we don't take," admits Karl Furstenberg, the dean of admission at Dartmouth. "And how fair is that to the hard-working, really bright kid who doesn't have a hook. The athletic recruiting model does creep into other aspects of college admission—for example, with our arts department. We get ratings from music, theater, and dance and they follow the athletic model.

"At least as we experience it at highly selective colleges," he continues, "I think there is pressure on all students to specialize. In fairness to athletics, it's not just in athletics. People like to criticize athletics because it's so visible, but it's also kids who play an instrument, who are involved in drama or in writing, and they go to Bread Loaf when they're twelve years old. There's a great deal of specialization outside athletics. They go to summer science camp and math camp and what have you. So there's a real premium on defining one's interests early on and then developing those interests to a high degree. That's part of the misunderstood message from selective colleges: That a lot of people feel, 'Gosh, to get accepted at

Dartmouth I really need to be world class in something.' In fact, the common denominator for most of the students we admit is that they're really bright and they like to learn. And they define that learning in a lot of different ways, not just necessarily academic. Most of the students we admit are really quite talented academically, but they're not all finished products. Part of my job is to look for potential."

"We don't take any shortcuts," says Fred Hargadon of Princeton, describing how his office reviews every application. "We really try to get a sense of the kid. We all do it differently. No one school is the model for other schools. I happen to think that's the best point about college admissions in this country: that we don't all end up agreeing on the same thousand people to attend. Just think what chaos it would be. I think the saving grace of college admissions is that we don't do it all the same way."

In Ivy League football recruiting, however, the schools *do* all do it in a similar fashion. The student's hook is clear and obvious. And the admission process begins with prospects who apply early, which is anywhere from seven to ten football players a year (or almost a third of the thirty) in the Ivy football programs discussed here. While other Ivies offer Early Decision, a binding early admission program, in recent years Harvard has been the only school to offer Early Action, which is nonbinding and allows a student to continue to apply to other schools if they choose to after they have been accepted by Harvard.

"In terms of how we market that," says Tim Murphy, "We say, 'Great, if you're going to apply early someplace, apply to our place because in the best scenario you can be accepted early, but if you decide it's not for you, you still have all your options open. And kids say, 'Yeah, that makes a lot of sense.'"

According to Dartmouth's Pat O'Leary, that scenario doesn't always play out in the kid's favor. "Harvard tells all the kids that they recruit, 'Apply Early Action and let's see what happens.' But then, the Harvard coaches will go as far as to tell the kids, 'Well, don't tell any other Ivy League coaches that you applied Early Action. Don't be forthcoming with that information.' So it's up to us, we've got to be detectives. We've got to grill kids: 'You apply Early Action anywhere?' Because if a kid applies Early Action to Harvard, we have to be smart. We know that 90–95 percent of the kids that get accepted at Harvard and were recruited for football, that's where they go. So if I find out, now I'm backing off. I'm going to the next guy on my list.

"Harvard knows that everybody else will back off, including Princeton and Yale. And they don't want to get the reputation of leaving kids out in the cold—which they kind of already do if a kid doesn't get in through Early Action and other schools have backed off in the meantime. But it doesn't matter, it's Harvard—people don't care. The stories about this don't get handed down to the kids because as soon as somebody sees the light flashing *'Harvard'* well, you know. . . . I don't know if I can sit here and say I blame them, 'cause everybody in the country, every time you see a movie, every time somebody talks about the Ivy League, it's 'Harvard.'"

O'Leary leans forward to make his final point. "Harvard, in my mind, they can legitimately go head to head with Notre Dame, Duke, Penn State on a kid. They can legitimately do that. Can we? Not at places like that."

For the class matriculating in the fall of 2004, Yale joined Harvard, changing from Early Decision to Early Action. "If you're accepted Early Action," says Jack Siedlecki, "you've got Yale in your pocket, and you can go out and pursue other schools if you want to. The reality of it is that Harvard football yields over 90 percent of their EA kids. So even though a kid might say he's looking around, in the end he's going. You're wasting time and money if you fool around with kids who are EA at Harvard. And I think people will look at us the same way."

This is certainly good news for the coaches at Yale and Harvard, who reap the benefits of having their Early Action pool of applicants protected from the pitches of other Ivy recruiters, but as O'Leary points out it can backfire on the recruits if they are not accepted under Early Action, and other schools have backed off in the meantime.

"Certainly, for a very selfish reason, we want them to apply early," says Tim Murphy. "They have everything to gain and nothing to lose. Whereas, if you apply early to other schools, you have a lot to lose. I make the analogy that if you go Early Decision somewhere, boy, you better be doggone sure that's the person you want to marry because that's a lifetime decision. I think when people see it in that light they say, 'Yeah.' It's like anything else, there's no substitute for experience or research."

If you are seventeen, and being recruited by Harvard, which point of view are you going to take?

Carl Morris had applied to Harvard under their Early Action program, which was the main reason he made his visit to Princeton unofficially and why the Tigers eventually stopped chasing him. This was fine with Morris, who wanted to attend a college where the coaching staff really wanted him—and after his visit to Harvard, he began to doubt how much Virginia cared. Like all big football schools, Virginia made its recruiting decisions based on where players stood at the end of their junior year, and at that time Morris had played only one year of football. He didn't have great statistics, just great potential. The Cavaliers had made all of their offers to receivers going into their senior year, before Morris blossomed.

"They didn't have a scholarship for me," he says, "so I was supposed to wait until they heard back from some of the guys, and it was getting to the point where I wanted to do something where I was the top guy. That was the main reason why I lost interest in Virginia."

He also lost interest in the University of Washington after returning from Cambridge, and cancelled his visit to Seattle. Only William & Mary remained on his list, running neck and neck with Harvard.

The full scholarship that William & Mary had waiting for Morris was a significant factor in its favor. He would graduate from Episcopal with sizeable student loans, and he would incur even more student loans if he attended Harvard. His visit to William & Mary had gone well, and there was no doubt the coaching staff there wanted him. As he struggled to make his final decision, he sought advice from his parents, his friends, and his high school coach.

Tim Murphy called him to follow up in mid-January. He informed the coach that he had decided to stop pursuing Virginia, and was leaning toward Harvard. "Well," said Murphy, "you've been accepted, so congratulations."

A few days later, Morris went to breakfast with Mark Gowin, his Episcopal football and baseball coach, and a trusted advisor. Gowin took out a piece of paper in an effort to help his star decide between Harvard and William & Mary. "We wrote down all the things that we thought were most important," says Morris, "and it came it out five to four. It went to Harvard by one."

Among the factors in Harvard's favor: a worldwide academic reputation, an urban environment, the feeling Morris got from the players on the team, and the social scene. He actually felt the style of football played by William & Mary favored him more, as did the chance to major in business (unlike Harvard, which offers economics). The full ride was also very hard to pass up. On the one hand, it was an odd decision, one that illustrated how unpredictable seventeen-year-old kids can be when forced to make a choice. On the other hand, it made perfect sense. "I decided," says Morris, "that Harvard is something you can't turn down."

That night, he called Tim Murphy and told him he was headed to Harvard. Then he called the coach who had been recruiting him at William & Mary, and told him the same thing. The coach lost it.

"He flipped out," says Morris. "He started screaming at me. *'What are you doing!'* He just lost it. I hung up on him. I hung up the phone and called my dad, and my dad—he doesn't take anything from anyone—he was not happy. He was ready to call the coach up and tell him what he thought." But Morris's father collected himself and did not call the coach.

"Ten minutes later," Morris recalls, "the coach called me back and said, 'Sorry, I shouldn't have done that.' But I was like, 'I'm pretty set on this decision, so there's really not a lot that you can do.'"

The next morning at nine o'clock, the William & Mary coach walked into Mark Gowin's office and said, "I just want to talk to Carl one more time before he makes this final."

"I had talked to my coach the night before," says Morris. "I'd called him and told him what happened, and he wasn't happy about it, either. He came down to me at breakfast and said, 'The coach is in my office. He wants to talk to you one more time. You don't have to if you don't want to. I understand that you don't want to.' And I said, 'I really don't.' My coach said, 'That's understandable, but I think you should, just to lay it to rest.' So, I spoke to him for about ten minutes and told him, 'Thanks for everything, but I've made my decision. It's nothing against you or your school.' He didn't get angry. He kind of accepted it. But it was pretty intense."

Mark Gowin appeared in the door, just as Carl had requested, after ten minutes. The game was over. The seventeen-year-old had survived a nightmare, and dodged a disaster. As his father said, "I'm really glad you didn't choose William & Mary, only to find out about this when you got there."

For Tim Murphy, the hard work of Bruce Tall, the Harvard name, his own closing arguments, and good fortune had all combined to deliver a prize. "Our saving grace," he says, "was his lack of football experience. If that kid had played football since freshman year, in my opinion he would have ended up at Stanford, Notre Dame, or Virginia."

Instead, Carl Morris wound up earning a Harvard degree and winning the Ivy League Player of the Year award in his junior and senior seasons. He made his parents and his sister proud. And then he set off to become an NFL wide receiver. He was waived by the Indianapolis Colts in June 2003 after three weeks of preseason. Head coach Tony Dungy said he liked the way he played and felt he had the talent to make it in the NFL, but the Colts' roster was full of gifted wide receivers and the team needed help in other areas. There was no room on the roster for a promising player in his position. Dungy wished him well, and told him he was sure he would find a team. The Philadelphia Eagles picked him up off waivers, but only for a week, which left Morris puzzled. Why would the Eagles bring him in for a week of practice, have him sit through an entire preseason game without playing a down, only to release him again on Monday? Other teams had expressed an interest in him prior to the Eagles' action, including the San Diego Chargers, whose receiving corps was thin. Did the Eagles want to keep the Chargers, another NFC team, from picking him up? His agent wondered about the Eagles' motivation. Morris hoped that wasn't the case. This was an entirely different recruiting game than he had been through with William & Mary and Harvard, with higher stakes and more ruthless players. It was impossible to predict what the final result might be.

Morris returned to Cambridge, discouraged but still determined to sign with an NFL team. Through a Harvard connection he found a job with a Boston law firm. Every day after work, he raced over to Cambridge to watch the end of Crimson football practice and catch balls from the younger quarterbacks. For three months he also worked out with the Harvard strength coaches and stood on the sidelines for Harvard home games.

In early December, he received the call he'd been waiting for. The Miami Dolphins invited him to try out for their practice squad. Impressed by his performance, they signed him to a contract through the end of the season. In January, they offered him a two-year practice squad extension. By mid-February he was preparing to depart for Cologne, Germany, to play in NFL Europe, where he would gain some valuable game experience. Seven months after his graduation from Harvard, Carl Morris was part of an NFL team and hoping to make his mark on a professional playing field. His law career could wait.

Chapter Seven

Performance Anxiety

"The A.I. is derived in order to give every recruited athlete a number. But the A.I. itself doesn't tell me a whole lot about whether that kid should be admitted or not. . . . I can tell you there are kids with high A.I.s I wouldn't go near with a ten-foot pole. And there are others that have low A.I.s, and they'd be the first ones I'd want in the class."

Fred Hargadon
Princeton University
Dean of Admission, 1988–2003

Pretend for a moment that you are the dean of admission at Princeton. A high school basketball star who has accepted a full athletic scholarship to play for Duke in the fall contacts your office weeks before school is scheduled to begin, and expresses an interest in coming to Princeton instead. Why? Because during a summer tour of Europe a senior professor at Oxford University has asked where he intends to go to college. When he proudly answers, "Duke," the professor says he has never heard of the school, and insists the young man must mean Princeton, the source of many Rhodes Scholars. Surprised by the Oxford don's reaction, the player is convinced that Princeton has more caché in educational circles, and he wants to switch schools. The Tiger basketball coach, delirious over his good fortune, begins telling you that this kid is a slam-dunk—not only a great player, but a great young man from a good midwestern family: Father's a banker, mother's a homemaker, kid's a real solid citizen, a hard worker, and a team player. The whole town loves him. What's more, he's the best high school player in America! Okay, coach, okay. Calm down. You look over the player's high school transcript, which is solid, but when you review his SAT scores, you see a red flag. A 485 Verbal? That's trouble. What should you do? Turn down Bill Bradley?

Back in 1961, Princeton accepted Bill Bradley under this exact scenario, 485 Verbal and all. And then the admission office watched as he nearly flunked freshman French. To lift himself out of his early academic trouble at Princeton, Bradley did what came naturally. He used his exceptional drive and discipline, the same drive and discipline that he had cultivated as an athlete, practicing jump shot after jump shot over endless solitary hours, to boost his grades. He simply studied harder, applying himself in the Princeton library until it closed each night. Soon his work habits and native intelligence had him thriving in the classroom as well as on the basketball court. By the time he was senior, he had won an Olympic gold medal in Tokyo. He then led Princeton to the Final Four in the NCAA basketball tournament, and on the plane ride home celebrated the accomplishment by working on his history thesis. He graduated magna cum laude in history, earned a Rhodes Scholarship, won an NBA title with the New York Knicks, served as a United States Senator, ran for President, and launched a successful career in the private sector. Not bad for a kid with a 485 Verbal, who would never have gotten into Princeton without his exceptional basketball skills. He has, to put it mildly, made the most of his talents. And in the process, he has demonstrated just how fallible an SAT score is in measuring intelligence, drive, a hunger for knowledge, and eventual success.

Looking at Bradley's case, and the cases of hundreds of other Ivy athletes, one can see why A. Bartlett Giamatti, the president of Yale, was opposed to implementing an Academic Index when William Bowen, then-president of Princeton proposed the idea back in the early 1980s. As Fred Hargadon points out, the A.I. itself does not tell Ivy admission officers much about a recruited athlete's study habits, curiosity, motivation, character, or career goals, thanks to its heavy emphasis on test scores. "It can tell me who—if they're a recruited athlete—would be below the floor, who we can't touch," says Hargadon of the A.I. But beyond that, the A.I. does not provide any Ivy admission officer with any information to make an informed decision on any individual candidate.

"It is so shortsighted to reduce admission to statistics in terms of Academic Index, and I don't think anybody who uses it sees as a good predictor of success in college," says Michael Goldberger, director of admission at Brown.

And yet, over the past fifteen years, as the mean A.I. of students in the Ivy League has continued to rise steadily, compressing by 20 percent the one standard deviation from the mean formula for recruited athletes, the A.I. has taken on a greater role than ever in shaping the nature of every Ivy incoming class. As strictly academic criteria gain more and more importance, the danger increases that personal qualities and other forms of intelligence lose their value.

"In this country, in this day and age, it's a battle to keep people from according numbers more respect than they deserve," says Hargadon. "In admissions—I think in life in general now—the biggest problem we run into is when you can't measure precisely, or quantify precisely, the things you really value most, you end up running the risk that you're going to place *too* much value on the things that you can measure precisely, or quantify, like SAT scores."

Driven by a personal interest in the ways in which people learn, Michael Goldberger has studied standardized testing in some detail. "After the birth of my son, Kenneth, who is now twenty-three and has multihandicaps, I started taking classes at Rhode Island College in special education," he explains "I was the [athletic department] liaison to the admission office, studying about testing and assessments, and I got a sense that maybe Brown's admission office could do a better job using tests than they were doing. What intrigued me about testing was trying to figure out what it was all about—why people have some remarkable strengths, but also some real deficiencies in certain areas—and starting to understand that testing devices are not as accurate as everybody believes they are. There is a standard error of measurement, and there are standard deviations. To believe that a 590 SAT is stronger than 580 is absurd as you start learning about testing and the ranges."

"We have done studies here and our rating system is a better predictor of success than SATs," he continues. "SATs are not as good as the judgment of admission officers. We look at quality of writing, we look at SATs, we look at classroom performance, we look at teacher recommendations—that allows us to give an academic rating for each student. It only makes sense: more factors will be a better predictor than a single factor."

Ivy admission officers across the league agree: SAT scores are only one factor among many in appraising the application of any candidate. The high school transcript, completed application, essays, teacher and guidance counselor recommendations, interview, leadership skills, extra curricular activities, community service, work internships, and paying jobs are all factored into the review of each candidate, which is why some decisions to reject athletes, who do qualify strictly on the basis of A.I. numbers, can drive coaches crazy.

"We get so much more information on kids than coaches do," says Goldberger, "from teacher recommendations and things, and we have so much in the file to look at that coaches never see. And most of that is confidential, and most of that we will never share. We will never get those types of recommendations if the word gets out. A teacher in the math class says, 'You know, I just don't like the way this kid's attitude surfaces in class,' or, 'He thinks everything is owed him.' Teachers will say things sometimes—about everybody, not just athletes. We'll see it about everyone. And if you see it, you have to act on it. If it seems out of character with everything else in the file, you'll make a phone call. You'll talk to the teacher, but you can never share that with anyone. You can only say to the coach, 'Look, this is just a bad kid and you don't want him on your team.' Generally we'll just say, 'We simply can't do this one.'"

This thorough evaluation of every individual athlete's application is in sharp contrast to the process at most big-time schools, even those with high academic reputations. One Ivy League lacrosse player I interviewed was offered a spot at Virginia by the head coach in July between his junior and senior year of high school. The coach had seen him play in an All-Star showcase, and made him an offer immediately afterward, one that included scholarship money. "You can apply later," the coach told him. "But I need to know now if you want to take a place in the class." The later application was a mere formality. This scenario could not occur in the Ivy League, where almost every coach has seen a highly ranked player turned down by Admissions, due to some red flag in the file.

"My advice to recruits is *meet us halfway*," says Fred Hargadon. "If you give us one-sentence answers to questions that should be a half page, then I can tell you right away this isn't a kid we want. He's not meeting us halfway. You try to figure out if they know what they'd be getting into if they came to Princeton—and if they want that badly enough to do the hard work. In a way, it's a case of false sincerity on their part. What happens is, in the case of some athletes, they've been put on such a pedestal at such an early age that they almost figure, 'Why should you make me fill out this application?' and they just do a very cursory job of it. They don't have a chance of getting by me. And I don't have any hesitation turning them down. I won't tell the coach what was in the application. I never do that. I basically say, 'Trust me, that's my judgment.' The other day, the squash coach said that over the years, he didn't know how I did it, but when I would turn down prospects he really wanted, he'd find out a year later that they went somewhere and either gave up the sport or bottomed out for some other reason. So he trusted my judgment, which is not perfect by any means. I think every place here is valuable, and I'll be damned if I'm going to give it to someone who thinks we owe it to them because they've been recruited."

"We really do call each kid as a kid," Hargadon adds of the individualized Ivy admission process, "knowing the sport is interested in him or her."

But selecting which recruits to admit or which applicants to take from the general pool is hardly an exact science. All kinds of students get into academic trouble, athletes and nonathletes alike. "There are some kids who have come in here, and everywhere else," says Hargadon, "with really eye-popping credentials—and goof off and not do well. I sit on the Examination In Standing Committee, so all through the year I have a vote on this committee about whether somebody who's flunked a course, we ask them to leave or not. . . . Well, you talk about immediate feedback every year on what I've done in Admissions." He laughs. "The other faculty sit there, and this kid'll show up, and they'll look down the table at me and you can see that bubble above their head, saying, 'What did you have in mind when you admitted this one?' But in fact, the majority of them that are in difficulty have test scores and grades that are no different. You know, they're eighteen to twenty-two. Things happen in their lives."

After thirty-five years spent in elite college admissions, Hargadon has accumulated wisdom. "If we wanted to pick exactly the wrong age to admit kids to college," he says with a smile, "we have it nailed down pat."

A number of coaches told me that they have more academic problems with high A.I. kids than with low A.I. kids (such as the industrious Bill Bradley would have been). "Some of these guys with the high scores," says John Lyons, "they have zero common sense. I'm going to be honest with you—they give me more trouble than these other guys with low scores. Some of the obviously smart kids never really worked, never applied themselves, and think they can keep screwing around here, and they get all distracted with a lot of stuff. They let things slide and all of a sudden, they haven't done anything and they're way behind the eight ball. It goes fast. And there's no excuse for these guys screwing up because obviously they're smart enough kids."

The basic rule of thumb for athletes, according to Dave Roach, the Brown athletic director who was a successful women's swimming coach before he became an administrator, is to prioritize their lives as follows: schoolwork first, athletics second, and social life third. "If the social life becomes number one or two," he says, "that's when you have trouble."

In Lyons' view, the recruits with lower A.I.s understand the challenge and the opportunity in front of them, and they focus on doing the hard work in the classroom, sometimes out of a fear of failure, but often out of sheer drive.

"In my experience," he says, citing over twenty years in the Ivy League, "there's no correlation to what a kid comes in index-wise and what he grad-uates with for a GPA. I got a kid right now who came in with a 172 [A.I.], and he has the highest GPA on the team. Mike Giles. He's a 3.7, 3.8. He was at a good high school, he had decent SATs, good grades, but his class rank was down. The kid's got some smarts to him. Not everybody tests well, but there are a lot of savvy kids who are sharp enough to figure it out." Under the current Ivy system, however, many of these savvy prospects are elimi-nated in the Ivy screening process, thanks to carrying an A.I. that is too low. Their A.I. can be above the floor (sometimes by twenty points or more), but because it falls below the one standard deviation of the mean formula, the coach will drop the kid from his list, based purely on the numbers.

I interviewed Mike Giles. I don't know if he will become a senator or a presidential candidate like Bill Bradley, but his work ethic, intelligence, drive, and genuine courtesy are all extremely impressive, as is his 3.7 GPA at Dartmouth. Like Bradley, he is making the most of his talents. And like Bradley, athletic talent was his ticket into the Ivy League.

Today that ticket into the Ivy League and NESCAC is under greater scrutiny than ever, as the academic worthiness of athletes such as Mike Giles to take a spot in the class at an Ivy League or a NESCAC institution is being questioned, both on campus and off. The public debate and controversy have been driven largely by William Bowen, the creator of the Academic Index and the author of two recent books filled with negative profiles of college athletes. In *The Game of Life,* written with Richard Shulman, and *Reclaiming the Game,* written with Sarah Levin, Bowen argues that, among other things, Ivy and NESCAC athletes underperform in the classroom as measured by their incoming SAT scores and their final college GPAs and class rank. He and his coauthors criticize Admissions at these elite schools for awarding places to athletes over other, more academically qualified candidates according to board scores, high school rank, and GPA. And they claim that athletes in the 1950s and 1960s more closely resembled their fellow classmates in their academic profile than do athletes today, arguing that athletes' academic criteria are slipping from one generation to the next. In addition, the authors contend that athletes on these elite campuses are now increasingly isolated from their classmates because of their highly specialized talents and the amount of time they spend playing and practicing with their teammates.

The books, dense with statistics and charts, each carry the subtitle, *College Sports and Educational Values.* But, as Gary Walters, the Princeton athletic director points out, "*The Game of Life* is a book about admissions, it is not a book about the value of athletics. It was a book written to influence admission decisions at selective schools. It's a political document. It's not a sociological treatise. Bowen makes the claim that his conclusions are data driven, but he conveniently fails to mention that the political philosophy of the author is actually driving the data. As one wag put it, 'Bowen uses statistics as a drunken man uses lampposts . . . for support rather than illumination.'"

Bowen and his coauthors could never make the same accusations against any other group on campus, employing the same standards, data, and arguments, and get away with it. But because we live in a time when admission slots at these elite schools are more scarce and precious than ever, the work of Bowen and his partners has been accepted at face value because it touches a nerve: athletes are being favored while most nonathletes have to compete for spots without an advantage. For parents whose children are not recruited athletes, the Bowen books are proof positive that the admission process is unjust. For academics and critics of "big-time" sports, who feel that athletics are out of control and in danger of warping the educational values at schools in the Ivy League and NESCAC, the books reinforce a bias against athletes, who now walk around campus with a great big bull's eye on their jerseys.

Which viewpoint is reasonable? Are athletes being unfairly singled out? Or is their gig finally up? Do they belong on these elite campuses, in some cases gaining admission with lower academic criteria? Or should their spots be taken by others with higher test scores and grades? What should be the ultimate measure for admission?

For those actively involved in the admission process, the Bowen books are filled with flaws.

"I found *The Game of Life* very disappointing, to be blunt about it, and they tried to make admissions far more simplistic than it is," says Michael Goldberger, the director of admission at Brown. "I think sometimes they used some data in misleading ways and that was disappointing. There was one section where they talked about the number of spots that were being used in the class by athletes. And I remember at Columbia, they counted one-hundred-plus kids playing track. And I looked in the last four years leading up to that, and I think the total was, in fact, fifty recruited athletes in track and field. Then I discovered what the authors had done was they had counted the kid that ran cross-country, indoor track, and outdoor track as three athletes. That is just such a misuse of statistics, and to not say that that is what they were doing. . . ."

Goldberger shakes his head. "There would be certain charts where they would say for the group it would be this percentage, and, in fact, there was only one school that had reported data—but they didn't say it was one school," he continues. "They said it was for the group that was thirty-one schools. It is the type of thing that I think somebody would be failed for if they turned it into the authors."

Drew Hyland, the chairman of the philosophy department at Trinity College, who played basketball at Princeton, wrote in a note to Walters: "The biases of the book are not confirmed by the evidence. Rather, the biases are the criteria by which the evidence is interpreted."

Few have questioned Bowen in the media, where his findings have been reported without an examination of his biases or his use of statistics. His status as a former president of Princeton and the current president of the Mellon Foundation (which just happens to award millions in grants each year to Ivy and NESCAC institutions) gives him a credibility and an influence that have gone largely unquestioned in the popular press. Certainly no Ivy League or NESCAC president wants to alienate a source of millions in grant money by publicly questioning his thesis or his data. (Between March and December 2002, for instance, Ivy League and NESCAC institutions received a total of $22,503,000 in grants from the Mellon Foundation.) Apparently compromised by these funds, the presidents in both leagues adopted new athletic admission standards and athletic policies in 2003 in what could be characterized as knee-jerk reactions to *The Game of Life*. Eager to diffuse any negative p.r. in the wake of the Bowen campaign, the presidents have raised the A.I. in the Ivy League by two points, and limited the number of athletic recruits in both the Ivy League and NESCAC. The presidents may deny that they have reacted in response to Bowen's campaign, saying merely that his books have "informed our discussions," but he has clearly been hugely influential in shaping the policy on athletic admissions in each league. Outsiders who have been paying attention to his crusade may not realize how Bowen has shaped his data to support his arguments or how he has contradicted himself in the process in a politically correct form of hypocrisy.

The hypocrisy has to do with his use of test scores and grades in both *The Game of Life* and *Reclaiming the Game* to determine the merit of a given applicant to college. In his earlier book on minority admissions, *The Shape of the River*, co-written with then–Harvard president, Derek Bok, Bowen argued exactly the opposite—that test scores and grades alone were not accurate predictors of a minority student's potential or merit, and should not be used to determine a student's worthiness for admission. Bowen and Bok wrote: "Test scores and grades are useful measures of the ability to do work, but they are no more than that. They are far from infallible indicators of other qualities some might regard as intrinsic, such as a deep love of learning or a capacity for high academic achievement. Taken together, grades and test scores predict only 15–20 percent of the variance among all students in academic performance and a smaller percentage among black students. Moreover, such quantitative measures are even less useful in answering other questions in the admission process, such as predicting which applicants will contribute most in later life to their professions and communities." What's more, they add: "... it is not clear that students with higher grades and scores have necessarily worked harder."

When it comes to the admission of athletes, however, Bowen simply discards this thesis, choosing to enact a double standard. In *The Game of Life* he argues that athletes are taking the place of other, more qualified candidates, based on test scores and grades. In *Reclaiming the Game*, he states that athletes "underperform" in the classroom, based on test scores and grades. He ignores his earlier thesis that test scores and grades "predict only 15–20 percent of the variance among all students in academic performance." Interestingly, the state of California college system has completely abandoned using the SAT I and SAT II because they have such a low level of predictability, 13 percent, as to be almost useless in any significant way. While it is not politically correct to criticize students of color, athletes seem to be fair game for Bowen and his associates. Both are the beneficiaries of what could arguably be considered a form of affirmative action in the admission process at these elite schools (in that both are sometimes admitted with lower test scores and grades), but in Bowen's world, athletes are held to a different standard. Such bias is alarming.

(Dr. Bowen did not make himself available to talk to me on these issues. I offered to meet with him at his convenience over a three-month period while I was conducting research for this book in the late spring and summer of 2003, and I tried again to arrange an interview with him in February 2004, prior to the publication of this book. He was never able to speak with me.)

"You might be admitted if you are a student of color," says Mike Schoenfeld, the dean of enrollment planning at Middlebury, discussing acceptances below a certain academic level. "But nobody wants to hear that. You might be admitted if you are a legacy. But that's preference for white people, and nobody wants to hear that, either."

Indeed, Steven Cornish, now a freshman dean at Brown, but for many years a freshman dean at Dartmouth (where I interviewed him), told me that when he reviewed the files of incoming Dartmouth freshmen prior to his first meeting with them, if he saw SAT scores that were "well below" the school's average, he knew immediately that the student was either a minority, a legacy, or an athlete.

"What struck me most having read both *The Shape of the River* and *The Game of Life*," says Fred Hargadon, "is the absence in the first book of a term that is used frequently in the second book. I think the term is *opportunity cost*. The fact is, it's spread throughout the second book about athletes—in talking about the place that an athlete takes up of a student that might have otherwise been admitted. And it is never used in the first book about minorities, where it would seem to me, in both situations, you're talking about the same thing: who didn't get the place because you're doing this. I think they would argue that there is a social value to minority admissions in the first book, while there isn't to athletic admissions. But I think that question is complicated for athletic admissions. I think there is some social value. Not all sports, but certainly some sports are still more likely an avenue for kids from working-class families into college than would otherwise be the case. That's not going to be the case for sports like squash or crew, but for sports like baseball and football and basketball and wrestling and so forth, you still get a socio-economic mix there that often you wouldn't have otherwise."

Mike Goldberger of Brown agrees. "There are kids that have come to Brown that have been great for Brown, but never would have come but for the athletic department getting involved. There is a kid named Nate Woods who played football here, who lived five miles from the nearest paved road. You know, just a rural nowhere in Florida. We had a football coach who found him. But he had never heard of Brown and he did a great job for us. He was a wonderful student and a great kid. The diversity that type of background brings to Brown is so valuable to all young kids. Not everyone goes to Sidwell Friends or Phillips Andover. There is an America out there, and these opportunities should be shared with other people. I've always felt that our athletes actually have the best experience here in terms of experiencing diversity: the most different types of kids in terms of race, and economic background, and academic interests, you tend to find in athletics. And I think that's great."

When I asked admission deans at Princeton, Dartmouth, Brown, Middlebury, Williams, and Amherst how they predict a student's academic performance, I was told that each school's admission office takes into account not just test scores and grades but numerous other factors from a student's application file to create a prediction of how well he or she will perform in college. Fred Hargadon wrote, "In assessing the academic abilities and preparation of applicants, those of us in Admissions take into account not just a student's SAT I scores or grade point average, but also three SAT II scores, a recalculated GPA counting only core academic subjects, the number and kind of honors or advanced courses, the quality and the nature of the school, and the quality and depth of the curriculum it offers, how well the student has taken advantage of the academic resources provided by the school, however limited those resources may be, and the student's self-presentation in his or her application. We then assign an academic rating of one to five (one being the highest). On the whole, these ratings turn out to be reasonably good predictors for where most students who enroll end up finishing in their graduating classes four years later, whether or not such students are also athletes or not. We don't attempt to predict precise GPAs four years later."

If admission officers do not attempt such a prediction, based on all the factors present in an applicant's file, one wonders how Bowen and his coauthors can claim to be able to do so, based solely on SAT scores? (Which in *The Shape of the River* he admitted were not enough on their own.)

"At a place like this," says Karl Furstenberg, the dean of admission at Dartmouth, "we are dealing with such a rarefied slice of the national population that they should all be successful, quite frankly." Furstenberg believes that Bowen and his coauthors "got it basically right" with their criticisms of athletics at elite academic schools, but he points out that there is a danger in defining a student's success in terms of where they finish in their college class, as Bowen and his coauthors do. "Ninety percent of our freshman class has been in the top 10 percent of their high school class," he explains. "When they get here, 90 percent of them are *not* going to be in the top 10 percent. . . . That's one of the problems with *The Game of Life*. They say athletes are more likely to be in the bottom half of the class academically. Well, somebody's got to be in the bottom half, and they went through a highly, highly, highly selective process to begin with. So it's a little unfair to single them out. There are other kids in the bottom half of the class."

Says Fred Hargadon, "I would be interested to see how many students in an entire graduating class 'underperformed' using the Bowen-Shulman-

Levin calculus for determining 'underperformance.' For instance, if we enrolled a freshman class comprised entirely of Academic 1 rated students, four years later at least half of them would graduate in the bottom half of the class, and at least a quarter of them in the bottom quarter."

Pointing out another significant flaw in *The Game of Life*, Mike Goldberger discusses the intense screening of athletes that takes place long before an admission decision is ever made. As we have seen, Ivy coaches eliminate hundreds, even thousands, of potential candidates during the recruiting process, only to wind up with a final list of academically and athletically qualified prospects that can range from two golfers to four baseball players, six soccer players to eight hockey players, five swimmers to four basketball players.

"When the authors talk about admit rates," says Goldberger, "and say the admit rate for athletes is so much higher now than it is for African Americans, the fact that they don't talk about is that there is always a series of meetings that takes place before athletic finalists are identified. Last year, I think we had seven hundred males who were brought to Brown who wanted to play intercollegiate tennis and put that on the application where we list it. And I think our coach gave us a list with three names on it. So if you look at the admit rate for three kids—if we took two out of the three— that is 67 percent of the recruited tennis players were admitted last year. But if you said, 'Well, here are the seven hundred that would be comparable to African Americans,' then the admit rate is very, very different. To not compare apples to apples or oranges to oranges, and to pick different steps along the way and then make the comparisons, is misleading."

"I think the book could lead people to believe that the only measure of the value of an education and what you've gotten out of it is your GPA at the end of it, and I don't think that's reasonable," says Fred Hargadon. "I think some kids trade a decimal point on their GPA because they also want the rewards of some activity while they're here. That can be as true for people in the orchestra or in student government. I've known kids involved in student government who have just let their GPA slip because they're so active. I don't think it's an adequate measure just to look at GPA. I mean, let's face it, I talk to a lot of kids here. And there's no doubt in my mind some of the most valuable things they will have gained is from their experience on the team, their experience with kids not on teams—in their dorms or eating clubs.

"It's not to make light of every college having some students who are not making good uses of the academic resources at the institution," Hargadon continues. "But that is not limited to athletes. All kinds of kids don't make good use of the resources—but the majority do, as do the majority of athletes. What you don't find out by reading that book is what it is like to be a student-athlete, or why on earth these kids would have opted to go to the Ivy League—knowing they're going to have to work much harder—than to a scholarship school, or a less competitive academic school. It seems to me too much of a fault-finding book for kids engaged in athletics. That's my sense of it. My sense is that if you're talking about college athletics to have *nothing* from the student-athletes about their experiences, or why they chose to take the path to go to the Ivy League, it makes you wonder if this is meant to be a complete story or a one-sided story."

Says Mike Goldberger, "I thought they were pretty disingenuous in terms of saying that they really liked athletics, and, in fact, it was so clear from the tone of the book that they don't like athletics. You ought to just say it."

Nevertheless, Goldberger believes the Bowen books have value despite their bias. "I actually thought *The Game of Life* was a good book to come out, and it was good to look at those issues. What roles should athletics play? And how much time should be dedicated to it? And what type of commitment should be required? It brought issues out, and it's important to talk about these things, to make people think, 'What are the benefits of it? Why do you have athletics in the Ivy League? Why do you have them in college? Look what is happening with Alabama in terms of coaches and the scandals. How important is it? Is this better? Is the Middlebury and NESCAC system better?' I think you just need to revisit those things every once in a while, and not get locked into, 'Well, this is the way that we've always done it and this is the right way to do it.'"

"In order to differentiate Harvard from Yale, or Yale from Dartmouth, people want to point out that they have the most 'distinguished' academic class," says Gary Walters. "You get to the point where the law of diminishing returns sets in. Because if you start to define yourself more and more narrowly by your academic credentials, you begin to change the very makeup and construction of that class in some fundamental ways, where academic credentials now all of a sudden become the end all and be all for admittance." Lost in such an evaluation process, Walters argues, are issues related to drive, ambition, and passion that become differentiating factors in success in life. "I think in the process selective colleges can become so narrowly academic in their focus that they compromise their commitment to social justice, to diversity in all its various forms, and to the development of the total person," Walters adds. "The short-sighted pursuit of academic elitism will only be achieved at the cost of producing well-rounded leaders."

Why? Because some of the potential leaders can no longer get in.

"Let me tell you a story," he says. "This is going to be one of the sad outcomes of the continuing trend to rely increasingly on standardized test scores for admission decisions at schools like Princeton.

"Calvin Johnson was a guard I recruited when I was coaching basketball at Dartmouth in the 1970s. He was the other Johnson guard in Michigan that year—the one not named Magic. They were both All-State. Magic was 6 feet 9 inches. Calvin was 5 feet 9 inches. So I get a call from Calvin's freshman dean during his freshman week at Dartmouth, and she says, 'Gary, Mr. Johnson wants to major in pre-med.' Let me tell you that Calvin had marginal academic credentials for Dartmouth, but he had a competitive heart that you could almost see pounding through his chest. You don't need to know anything more than that. I said to the dean, 'He didn't mention pre-med to me when we recruited him.'

"'Yeah, well he wants to major in pre-med.' I said, 'Send him down.'

"So he comes down. 'Calvin,' I said, 'what's this story about pre-med?'

"'Coach,' he said, 'I want to be a doctor.'

"'You never said anything to me about that when we were recruiting you.'

"He said, 'Yeah, I know, but . . . I want to be a doctor.'

"I said, 'Look, you're coming to us from Oak High School in Muskegon, Michigan, and haven't had the academic preparation or the benefit of taking some of the advanced courses required for pre-med. I just want you to *survive* your freshman year and maintain your athletic eligibility, 'cause this is going to be a rough transition for you. You don't have the academic foundation of the kids from prep school that you'll be competing against. I don't question your motivation, but you're going to have to develop some of your primary skills, taking some fundamental courses to prepare you to become a doctor, or to prepare you to become anything else.'

"'Well,' he said, 'I'm pretty set on what I want to do. I really want to be a doctor.'

"'Okay,' I said. I called the dean. 'Mr. Johnson wants to be a doctor. That's his dream. Let's see how it goes.'

"So now we're in the heart of the basketball season. And the team is on the bus, driving from Columbia to Cornell on a Friday or a Saturday—you know, that bus trip you make in the middle of winter—and you turn around and it's 1:30 in the morning, and you've got one light on back there, and it's Calvin's.

"At the end of his junior year, he was accepted Early Decision to Dartmouth Medical School, one of two or three Dartmouth students who were accepted Early Decision. He ended up going to Mass General after he got out of Dartmouth Medical School, and ended up with a triple specialty. He started out in anesthesiology, then he went to pediatric anesthesiology, and then he went to pediatric cardio-anesthesiology.

"In addition to that, he ended up becoming an assistant professor and the youngest chief of anesthesiology in the United States when he took the job at Wayne State. And now he is a professor of anesthesiology and chief of the department at Charles Drew/Martin Luther King Hospital in Los Angeles, while he's also practicing his medical specialty.

"A year and a half ago, we had a reunion of the basketball team, but Calvin couldn't make it. I talked to him on the phone. He was telling me he was coaching his kid's team.

"I said, 'Hold it a second. You're practicing your specialty. You're running the department and teaching at Charles Drew/MLK. You're coaching your kid's team. Let me just ask you a question: When do you do the administrative work?'

"He said, 'Yeah, I do that between twelve and two in the morning.'

"I said, 'When do you sleep?'

"He said, 'I go to bed at around two and I get up at five.'

Walters looks at me across the round conference table in his office. "Spectacular human being," he says. "And that kid doesn't get into an Ivy League school today, and he probably doesn't get into a NESCAC school, either. Because under the current system, his academic credentials coming out of high school wouldn't be enough."

He stands and begins to pace. "One of the things that I worry about as this academic credentialing system becomes more and more 'precious' is that you lose the ability to pick and choose kids on the left part of the tail over here that are *stars*. So what happens is, we run the risk of becoming less and less relevant in the real world, as the tradeoff for becoming more academically pure."

As these elite undergraduate institutions begin to look more and more like graduate schools, filled with students who are more narrowly geared to pursuing Ph.D.s in academic areas, Walters fears fewer students will pursue leadership roles in society.

"I never talk about the narrow 'academic' mission of the university," he says, sitting back down. "Because I believe that part is subsumed under the broader 'educational' mission of the university. The academic mission is too narrow. We are about developing leaders." He lists a number of former Princeton athletes to illustrate his point.

"Richard Mueller, the captain of the lacrosse team, is the FBI director. Donald Rumsfeld was the captain of the wrestling team and lightweight football team. George Schultz played football. Bradley played basketball. Bob Ehrlich, the governor of Maryland, was captain of the football team. You look at the people that are in public service, and you see the number that participated in sports—and by the way, since the 1960s all of them have been recruited in some way, shape, or form. These people are really doing a significant job of contributing to Princeton and their nation's service, particularly those that were athletes."

Walters rises and begins to pace again. "The narrow specialization taking place in the academy, where you learn more and more about less and less, isn't relevant conceptually within the context of the real world as I see it. When you engage in this debate, the minute people want to put it on academic terms, it then becomes a zero-sum game between academics and athletics. You can't win that."

"But when you put it on the basis of broader educational goals and objectives, now you've got to make sure that athletics doesn't get out of whack. But you also have to make sure that you're not doing whacky things on the academic side, that aren't consistent with your educational mission."

He pauses for a moment, then continues. "All you have to do is look at the kinds of decisions that have been made in the name of pursuing narrow academic objectives that have compromised the institution's educational goals. You occasionally end up in positions where the professoriate itself has been professionalized pursuing research for commercial gain, conducting consulting activities on the side, and negotiating away teaching responsibilities, which is a perk of academic superstardom. The lines have become blurred: Is the professor a researcher, an entrepreneur, or a teacher? Does the faculty have a responsibility to the guild or to the university? Is the faculty fulfilling its social contract to contribute to the 'educational' life of the university? It's ironic, but I believe that those of us who are committed to the educational mission of our universities should be much more concerned about what I perceive to be the growing academic/educational divide than about the manufactured academic/athletic divide imagined by Bowen."

"I understand why they don't want athletics in the NESCAC and the Ivy League to get like it is in the rest of the world," says Kathy Delaney-Smith, the women's basketball coach at Harvard. "But these are people we should be proud of. Athletics is as important as their academics—and it should be. Because it does everything for them and for their future that the classroom does. So why isn't it equally valued? You ask any doctor, lawyer, teacher, 'Where did you learn more, in history class or on the basketball court?' They're going to tell you probably on the basketball court. I view my role here as an educator."

Sound like a cliché? Consider the words of Marvin Bressler, a retired professor of sociology at Princeton, who served as a faculty advisor to the Princeton basketball team for many years, beginning with the era when Bill Bradley and Gary Walters played for the Tigers.

"I learned a lot from athletes," writes Bressler. "I learned how rich the athletic culture is in academically relevant ways. The basketball team is, among other things, a debating society. They ask a lot of questions pertaining to organizational theory. Is it important for players to like each other? How much do character and work ethic compensate for limited athletic ability? What's greater as a motivating force, praise or blame? If you examine these questions, you will see that there are many great courses devoted to the same ideas."

"What also interested me was coaching," he continues. "Coaching is really quite a curious combination of liberal and conservative approaches to teaching. You have the benevolent coach, the belief in hard work, the sacrifice to the larger purposes of the group, the nineteenth-century conviction of the repetitive drill. Side by side with that you have the liberal conceptions of educational philosopher John Dewey and his belief in learning by doing, the whole person, the conviction that people should be judged by the same standard regardless of social position or background, some conception of cooperative learning, and you have the blending of talents."

Delaney-Smith has blended the talents of her players brilliantly, creating successful teams that have won eight Ivy titles and competed in five NCAA tournaments in the past fifteen years. Over her twenty-two years at Harvard, 75 percent of her basketball players have graduated cum laude or higher. Her program has produced more doctors than any other men's or women's basketball team in the country, Division I, II, or III. Over the past twelve years, half of her team has been pre-med. One hundred percent of her athletes, when high school seniors, have been offered basketball scholarships; yet they have chosen to attend Harvard for its unique combination of academic excellence and athletic challenge, often making a financial sacrifice to do so, in the form of student loans and work-study.

"One of the things about athletics," says Walters, "is that our coaches utilize not only the John Dewey teaching method of learning by doing, but they expand upon that philosophy to include learning by doing with all of your senses. We believe in values-based coaching at Princeton and that our playing fields should serve as an extension of, and a complement to, the learning that takes place in the classroom. A former Nobel prize winning economist at Princeton, Sir Arthur Lewis, said it best: 'Excellence is achieved not only by intellect; it derives even more from character . . . only the humble achieve excellence since only the humble can learn. . . . In the university we build character no less than brain, since brain without character achieves nothing.' Interestingly, Professor Lewis made those comments in the mid-1960s. I wonder how relevant those comments are now, forty years later, to the teaching that goes on today in the classrooms of our colleges and universities. I know it has great relevance to the coaching, teaching, and learning that goes on at Princeton's playing fields."

Unfortunately, athletes at Ivy League schools have been known to try to hide their athletic identity from professors, fearing discrimination and reprisals because of their participation in a varsity sport. Jake McKenna, an All-Ivy lacrosse goalie and captain at Harvard who graduated in June 2004 with a degree in art history, told me that he succeeded in hiding his lacrosse-playing identity from about half of his professors over his four years on campus. He felt they would not take him seriously as a student if they knew he played a varsity sport, even though he entered Harvard from Taft, an elite prep school, where he carried an A- average and scored 1430 on his SATs. McKenna said he loved Harvard and greatly appreciated the opportunity he had to attend the school, but the only professors he told about lacrosse were those he absolutely had to every spring term, when he needed to miss an occasional class to travel to an away game. Scott Turco, another Harvard graduate who played four years of varsity hockey for the Crimson, told me, "Being an athlete may be a help getting in, but once you're there, it can really work against you. Playing sports definitely hurt me." Antiathlete editorials in *The Crimson*, the Harvard student newspaper, and an antiathlete bias from some of his classmates and professors left Turco with mixed feelings about his Harvard experience. Like Jake McKenna, Turco came to Cambridge from an elite prep school, Phillips Andover, where he earned good grades and scored 1330 on his SATs. He chose to attend Harvard because he felt the school offered "the best merger of academics and athletics," and because he wanted to follow in the footsteps of his father, a physician who had starred for the Crimson hockey team thirty years before. While the younger Turco loved Harvard, he was a victim of an antiathlete bias held by some professors on campus. Athletes at other Ivy League schools, including Dartmouth, Brown, and Yale, shared similar stories of bias against them and of trying to hide their athletic identities from professors.

"I know individual faculty members who I see at every sporting event," says Fred Hargadon. "And I have heard faculty members who are just so anti-athletics it's not even funny. My hunch is the great majority are somewhere in between: 'Don't know, I could care less,' but aren't anti-athletics. You know, the one thing about academic institutions is that they're as vulnerable to stereotyping as any institution in the country. Everybody gets up in arms when the state police are accused of profiling—stopping drivers because they're black. But my hunch is there's profiling that goes on in academic institutions when they see a kid who is 250 pounds with a big neck and baseball hat on; I've got to imagine that people profile him."

"A life spent in Admissions has really helped immunize me against stereotyping," continues Hargadon, "but it's also made me very sensitive to how some of the smartest people in the world can be some of the worst stereotypers of all. Students do it. Everybody does it. It's not the kind of thing you would think would take place as much on college campuses, but it does. It's like thinking every Asian-American must play the violin. I think actually there are classes, campuses, where probably there are some faculty who have negative attitudes toward athletes. It upsets me when athletes, as a group, find themselves denigrated in public statements by a college's faculty or administration. I think this profiling of athletes is no less objectionable than the profiling of any other identifiable groups in society."

As a former Dartmouth skier told me, "I had never seen anyone who was really big and really smart before I came to Dartmouth." The idea of both qualities, brains and brawn, being combined in one individual who happened to play football (stereotype: dumb jock) was alien to him. Bowen and his coauthors have fed this stereotyping by dehumanizing athletes with their charts and tables, numbers, and statistics, and by employing a politically correct double standard.

In *Reclaiming the Game*, Bowen and Levin express their support for the academic exceptions made for some minority students, who have been recruited to attend elite undergraduate institutions despite lower academic credentials than their incoming classmates. The authors share their view that "the notable success achieved by so many minority graduates of these academically selective colleges and universities, not only professionally but in providing leadership in civic and community affairs, speaks for itself."

What, then, of the notable success achieved by so many of the recruited athletes (minority and nonminority alike) who have been admitted with lower academic credentials than their incoming classmates, who have graduated from these highly selective schools, and who have gone on to make significant contributions to society? Does not their professional success and leadership in civic and community affairs speak for itself as well?

Bill Bowen should talk to former Senator Bill Bradley about SATs and GPAs, the lessons gained from sports, the value of leadership, and the intangible, intrinsic qualities that Bowen values in students of color, but ignores in athletes of any color. It is extremely dangerous to generalize about individuals as gifted and driven as Ivy League athletes and their Division III brethren in NESCAC. The overarching educational mission of these schools includes their goal of fostering leadership and public service, rather than simply championing the narrow academic criteria of test scores and grades. The individual athlete is just that—an individual. Assessing the individual is exactly what the Ivy and the NESCAC admission process does in a highly disciplined, thorough, and selective fashion. I am a former college athlete who should know better than to stereotype and generalize, yet it took me several interviews before I realized that a 6-foot-9-inch basketball player from the ghetto in Philadelphia could not only be a force on the court, but an utterly determined student, bound against all childhood odds for medical school. Or that an immigrant from war-torn Bosnia who had won two consecutive Ivy League Player of the Year awards in women's basketball and turned down full scholarships to Top 10 schools could also be a brilliant student carrying a 4.0 average as a pre-med student at Harvard.

The vast majority of Ivy League athletes are extremely impressive young men and women, with talents, drive, and character that will surprise and impress you, both on and off the playing field. They are the finest blend of student and athlete of any students who are athletes in any league in the nation. But to fully appreciate their accomplishments, you must look at them as individuals. And to fully understand their mistakes, you must remember they are eighteen to twenty-two years old and still growing up.

I'll let a more experienced voice than mine have the final say on the subject of these athletes' academic performance.

"I don't think the issues raised by Bowen, et al, should be addressed, either by proponents or opponents of Bowen's thesis, by focusing on GPAs or 'underperformance,'" Fred Hargadon wrote me. "I think the more fundamental questions are: (a) what is a college for?; (b) how accurately does a student's GPA at graduation measure all that student has gained or learned from his or her college education?; (c) what 'mix' of students ought a college seek to enroll and educate, and for what reasons?; (d) what do we know about the differences in 'value added' student by student, between those who graduate at the top of their class and those who graduate in the bottom quarter?; and (e) how much of what a student gains from college derives from the mix of students he or she lives with, goes to class with, studies with, participates with in one or another extracurricular activity, socializes with, etc.? In sum, I think many of the questions raised by Bowen's books are really questions about differing 'visions' of what colleges are, or should be, about. And well-meaning people obviously differ here."

Chapter Eight

Show Me The Money

"I sure don't want us to get into a spot where we're competing for athletes based on how large a financial aid package is. That, it seems to me, is not consistent with the Ivy League principles. I think a lot of schools worry about this a lot."

James Wright
Dartmouth College President

The worry is well founded. Ivy League principles are indeed being tested, and even, in some instances, ignored or discarded. Money, the root of so much trouble in big-time college sports, has caused plenty of problems in Ivy League athletics as well. With apologies to James Wright, I believe Ivy schools are *already* in a spot where they are competing for athletes with the use of large financial aid packages, and no solution appears to be in sight.

One answer, uniform athletic scholarships for all, is not viable for a number of reasons, not the least of which is the cost of funding scholarships for thirty-plus teams. Even assuming the League could adopt an open policy of paying athletes to play (just pretend for a moment), from a strictly financial perspective the idea is ludicrous, since providing scholarships for players on thirty-plus teams would add up to over $250 million a year. Such annual spending would threaten even the largest Ivy League endowment—Harvard's $19 billion—because it would increase spending from the standard accepted rate of 5 percent of the endowment per year to 6.4 percent a year. Or consider another way to look at the idea: in order to finance athletic scholarships at $250 a million a year, every Ivy institution would have to increase their endowment by $5 billion.

The monetary issue has resulted in plenty of rough sailing in the Ivy League, including a financial aid scandal at Brown; a trend among coaches in the League to press kids for decisions by holding financial aid offers over their heads; and a feeling among League administrators and coaches that money is helping wealthier schools attract better players and win more Ivy championships.

It's hard to argue with this last concern, an understanding of which is vital to our consideration of the first two issues. Financial aid in the Ivy League is not equal across all schools, not for athletes or for any other students. Some schools are simply better endowed than others. And one school, Princeton, has eliminated student loans altogether, awarding grants-in-aid to every student who qualifies for financial aid, whether he or she is a cellist or a quarterback, a math genius or the editor of a high school newspaper. The Princeton Trustees made the change to address a concern that loan indebtedness at graduation was tilting the job preferences of graduates in undesirable ways—say, to Wall Street instead of to teaching or government service—not to benefit athletics. But in the process of eliminating student loans, the institution has attracted the best and the brightest applicants from every economic background, and, not surprisingly, it has also dominated Ivy sports through the past decade, winning more Ivy championships than any other. Princeton has emerged as the New York Yankees of Ivy League athletics in the hunt for titles every year, thanks in large measure to its wealth. The Tigers have the money to build and operate first-class facilities, including a stunning new pool and a $43 million football stadium. They are able to pay an excellent staff of coaches large enough salaries to keep most of them from moving on to other, higher-paying jobs. And they can offer athletes who qualify for financial aid something no other school in the League can match: generous financial aid packages that are free of any student loans. In an era when many Ivy athletes will go on to attend professional schools (and take out student loans in order to earn their legal, business, or medical degrees), graduating without any undergraduate student loans to pay off is, as the commercial says, priceless.

Princeton's advantage is not limited to money, of course. The school enjoys an unsurpassed academic reputation. *U.S. News & World Report* has ranked it as the top undergraduate institution in the country for several years in a row, its name synonymous with Ivy League excellence. And the school's dean of admission during its decade-long run of Ivy championships, Fred Hargadon, is widely credited around the League for his support of Tiger athletic programs. As a result, good athletes who are good students now flock to the school, attracted by a commitment to excellence in academics and in athletics that is unmatched in the League. Princeton is the only Ivy League school (and the only nonathletic scholarship school in the NCAA) to ever crack the annual Sears Cup rankings for the nation's top fifty Division I athletic programs, placing as high as twenty-fifth in 2000. Recruiting athletes to Princeton is arguably the easiest sell in the Ivy League. And the school's financial aid policy makes the whole Tiger package that much sweeter. It's hard to imagine a player saying, "No thanks, I'd rather take the $20,000 in student loans and go to Cornell."

As Brown Athletic Director Dave Roach put it, when asked how many prospects Brown coaches lose each year to Princeton: "It's not even so much who you're losing. It might even be who you're never in the game with."

How did Princeton ever gain such an advantage?

"The Ivy League used to have three types of rules," explains Roach. "Playing and athletic rules. Admission rules. And financial aid rules. The playing and athletic rules are still the same. The admission rules are still the same. But now everybody can do whatever they want in financial aid."

The reason schools can do whatever they want within the federal guidelines for financial aid (which include some significant gray areas) is that the Justice Department filed an anti-trust suit against the Ivy League and about twenty other institutions in the late 1980s, claiming that the schools' "overlap meetings" on financial aid were illegal on the grounds of price fixing and collusion.

"We were all institutions that gave only need-based aid," says Jeff Orleans. "And many, although not all of us, were need-blind in our admissions. 'Need-blind' meaning the admission office admitted without regard to whether the kid needed financial aid. 'Need-based' meaning you got financial aid based on need, not on merit."

Groups of those schools, including the eight Ivies, would meet every spring as admission letters were being prepared. Financial aid officers would compare the financial aid forms that applicants had filed, and come to a common definition of "family resources" for students who were about to be admitted to more than one Ivy League institution.

"The idea," says Orleans, "was that a student would pick a school, not based on the financial package, but on academic or other considerations. The finances would be the same."

"It was really a very noble intention," says Bob Ceplikas of Dartmouth, "to create a situation where students were choosing among Ivy League schools on criteria other than money. So they were making the choice based on what institution would really be the best match for them, rather than, 'Who will give me the most money?'"

But, says Orleans, "The anti-trust division's theory was, in terms of taking price out of the equation, it may or may not be a valid educational goal, but anti-trust laws don't allow it."

What the Ivy League was doing behind closed doors, argued the Justice Department, was tending to drive up the cost of attendance for individual students. Since schools were often agreeing to a higher level of contribution from a student than at least one of the overlapping institutions was planning to require (based on their interpretation of a family's financial need), students were required to pay more than they might have if the overlap meetings had never taken place.

In 1991 the League agreed to sign to a consent decree that said, in effect, "The eight Ivy schools may not talk about financial aid policies, or levels, or ways of looking at student assistance, except to discuss publicly announced policies that have already been adopted for coming years. And the eight schools may not have any kinds of discussions about historical, publicly announced policies from past years that would lead the Justice Department to think that they are trying to signal each other about what they are going to do, but haven't announced."

These latter discussions are known as "conscious parallelism," an anti-trust violation that grew out of GM and Chrysler's discussions when they dominated the car market. "They'd all sit there and say, 'Well, what are you thinking of doing next year?'" says Orleans. "And they wouldn't agree, but somehow the price increases seemed very similar."

The consent decree was for ten years, and expired in 2001, but when it ended, says Orleans, "The League's lawyers essentially said to the schools, 'You know, this has become pretty subtle anti-trust law, and some general advice is that we should continue to act as if the consent judgment was in effect.'" As a result, today the Ivy League may not talk about anything related to financial aid that is not already public; may not have any discussions that would lead people to think it is engaged in conscious parallelism; may not have any agreements about how schools are going to administer their aid programs; and may not share information on specific people—with one exception.

"You can continue to agree that aid for your athletes will be based only on need," says Orleans. "And you can use outside auditing to verify compliance with that." In the latter half of the 1990s the League did just that, hiring an independent auditor to review three hundred cases where coaches had questions about possible financial aid issues at other schools.

"He found one case where he wasn't a 100 percent certain," says Orleans of the four-year investigation. "And he wasn't 100 percent certain because it was a different enough case that the institution hadn't anticipated this particular issue, and there didn't happen to be any comparators. So he was only about 98 percent sure. His conclusion was, 'Yes, people are treating their athletes the way they are treating their nonathletes.'" Orleans pauses, then confirms what everyone in the League is concerned about. "Now that means Princeton's athletes are getting a better package than Dartmouth's athletes." Just as Tiger athletes are getting better packages than athletes at Cornell, Penn, Harvard, Brown, Yale, and Columbia.

"For the first few years after the consent decree was signed," Ceplikas says, "there were minor variations in packages around the League, but it was very, very rare for an individual applicant to get very different financial aid packages from different Ivies. But as time went on, and as the wealthier institutions wanted to devote more money to financial aid—not just for competitive reasons, but also to provide more access to more families to be able to afford their institution—the packages across the League became less and less consistent. And those who were the wealthiest, Harvard, Yale, and

Princeton—I mean, it's no secret, they've got the hugest endowments—were flexing their financial muscle, and the rest of us were getting outbid."

And the schools getting outbid had to find ways to combat the problem.

At Brown, the search for ways to compete with the wealthier schools for athletes led to the League's most public athletic controversy since the presidents approved a waiver for Columbia football and allowed the Lions to admit several players below the A.I. floor in the late 1980s. Brown wound up being penalized by the League in 2000 for the actions detailed below, but the irony is that no money ever changed hands and no players ever benefited from a misguided attempt to enrich the financial aid packages of a few athletes. Nevertheless, the actions were illegal. The League, facing its first financial aid scandal, was in many ways unprepared to deal with it. These events could have happened only in the Ivy League, where aid is based on need, where some schools are better endowed than others, and where competition for athletes and championships is fierce.

According to Jeff Orleans, the trouble started with the executive director of the Brown Sports Foundation, the late Dave Zucconi, a legendary figure at Brown whom Orleans describes as "legendarily ungovernable." But according to Brown coaches from that period, some of whom have moved on the other jobs, that characterization is inaccurate. "Dave Zucconi," one coach told me, "was absolutely governable. And he loved Brown. Whatever he did stemmed from wanting the best for Brown the most." Another former coach expressed his view that "it would not be accurate or fair" to place the blame solely on Zucconi's shoulders, for others at Brown, including financial aid officers, were also involved in the effort to improve the financial aid packages of recruited athletes.

When the problems at Brown occurred in 1999, Zucconi headed the Brown Sports Foundation, an arm of the Brown development office that oversees fundraising for the Brown athletic department. Fundraising is responsible for generating nearly a quarter of Brown's annual sports budget each year, with revenue from ticket sales contributing another 11 percent. In total, 35 percent of the Bruins annual athletic budget comes from raised funds, with the balance consisting of university operating funds and endowment funds.

"We raise 60 percent of our annual football budget," says Brown's Dave Roach. "Everybody in the League does it all a little bit differently, so you can't really say that every sport or every coach [at every school] has to raise x amount of their budget." But at Brown, coaches are expected to help raise a percentage of their annual budget through fundraising efforts, including direct appeals to alumni athletes, running golf tournaments, securing sponsorships, and using other accepted ways of raising money. As a result, Zucconi had plenty of direct contact with Bruin coaches.

"Zucconi had been at Brown since coming there as a student in the early '50s," says Peter Lasagna, who was the men's lacrosse coach at Brown when the scandal occurred, and who now coaches at Bates. "And he had been in Admissions, he was key to the founding of the Sports Foundation, and he was just a great person, a great friend to Brown University in all ways, and really did a lot for Brown athletics."

Zucconi was fully aware of the challenge that Brown coaches faced in the recruiting process, as athletes weighed financial aid packages from scholarship schools and from other Ivies, a number of which are better endowed and therefore able to structure more attractive awards for any student, athlete or not. Brown's financial aid officers were also aware of these monetary challenges and together with Zucconi they set up a meeting for all of Brown's varsity coaches to help them find ways to stay competitive with wealthier Ivy schools.

"It started as an information thing," says Lasagna, explaining how the violations originated, "in the context of the constantly escalating costs of the schools, and the limited ability of schools like Brown and Brown University's financial aid office to meet the need of many of the students that we were recruiting in our sports. . . . If you've been in the League for a long time, or at the institution for a long time, you knew that other things [ways of finding more aid] existed. [But] if you're new to the Ivy League, it's a very unique situation, and so here are some avenues that all students have—not just recruited athletes—their families can apply for these outside scholarships."

At the informational meeting, all of Brown's varsity coaches were encouraged by the school's financial aid office to have recruits apply for such outside aid. "It certainly didn't start with the athletic department," one Brown coach said of the directive.

According to Dave Roach, the trouble was that Dave Zucconi then encouraged coaches to have recruits apply to some specific foundations for scholarships.

"Just by virtue of being there for so long," says Lasagna, "he had more information than many of us, and he knew more people—both Brown graduates and people that graduated from other schools—that were doing well in life and had foundations. Dave would be a person, whether you were instructed to by your athletic director or not, that you would go talk to about these scholarships. And he would sometimes have suggestions that were really helpful, and he would sometimes have suggestions that didn't lead you anywhere. Because these scholarships were open to anybody, different coaches would encourage different prospects to apply for them or not."

The problem was that a couple of the outside scholarship offers to Brown recruits came from foundations controlled by Brown alums. And according to Dave Roach, in one case Zucconi had gone to a Brown alum and said, "'You have a foundation, why don't you create some outside scholarships?' And the guy said, 'Okay.'"

"These were people of impeccable reputation," says Jeff Orleans. "They had no idea that the sequence of events in which they were being involved would be wrong. I don't believe they were trying to do the wrong thing. I don't believe Dave Zucconi was trying to do the wrong thing."

The violations, says Orleans, occurred primarily in football. "Another Ivy institution was recruiting one or more of these kids, and the kid basically said, 'Well, I'm getting this scholarship from Brown, from this Brown Foundation,' or whatever. And the coach went to his athletic director and said, 'Is this okay?' And the athletic director rightly thought that if that were true, then it was not okay and he called us."

"They were only offers," says Roach. "They were never given. No one had ever played a game as an ineligible person and gotten something that they should not have gotten. The executive director assumed an outside scholarship was an 'add on.' It really wasn't an 'add on.' It took away loans and work-study. So in essence, it would have saved Brown some money. But it was still illegal."

Orleans cites an ongoing theoretical debate in criminal law over a "law of intent" and a "law of execution." "And certainly," he says, "if you're looking at a code that seeks deterrence and punishment as two of its goals, it shouldn't matter whether it [an infraction] actually happens or not."

"From our perspective," says Orleans of his office, which investigated the infractions, "this was money that would have made a recruiting difference, was intended by at least some people to make a recruiting difference, that would have gone to athletes that otherwise would not have gone to anybody else. And whether it was intended to be manipulative or not—it was wrong."

"The great irony of being involved in collegiate athletics with these institutions," says Lasagna, "is that none of the programs that got in trouble, none of these prospects ever received a penny. And I know that one of the coaches in particular, who was brand new to Brown, felt particularly unfairly singled out. . . . Here's a guy who was in his first year at an Ivy League institution, and he was literally following the same instructions that every other head coach had gotten—encouraging a family to apply to these foundations for these various loans—and he got pulled in with other people that the Ivy League decided had done something untoward."

It was the first time the League had ever had something that looked like a major financial aid violation, and they did not have a committee, beyond Jeff Orleans and his staff, to oversee an investigation. "We didn't have a structure for having institutional supervision of that process," says Orleans. "The big-time conferences have a faculty committee or whatever it is because violations happen more often." To cope with the Brown infractions, the League constructed an ad hoc process in which the presidents were deeply involved (too deeply, in Orleans' view), and Brown paid the price of being the first school that the League punished for a financial aid violation.

Out of the crisis came a process, in the form of a standing committee, which includes one person from each Ivy school balanced among the athletic, admission, and financial aid offices. "If we have something that looks like a major case," Orleans explains, "we now have a process for deciding, including involvement from the presidents, and we would need to involve this committee in working with our office. They are the committee that acts. Not the presidents, not the athletic directors. And everybody is now comfortable that if we have something that looks like it might be a major violation, there's a way of getting institutional input into what we do, and at the same time not have the kind of ad hoc politicized result that occurred. The Brown guys, unfortunately, were the test of birthing."

Even though Brown had already penalized people and put restrictions on recruiting in certain sports, the League piled on more punishment. "The presidents extended the penalties," says Orleans, "in terms of penalizing admissions in certain sports for a couple of years, and making Brown ineligible for the football championship. And there's a second level of resentment at Brown about that."

"It became pretty nasty," says Dave Roach. "In retrospect, if Brown had removed that person [Dave Zucconi] from that position, people would have been more willing to compromise. There was a lot of miscommunication on the whole thing."

And there was a lot of finger pointing at Brown, where the school's internal investigation was conducted by Vice President for Student Life Janina Montero (who had recently arrived from Princeton, only to be thrust into the storm), and Mike Bartini, the school's director of financial aid. The financial aid officers were not eager to point a finger at themselves for encouraging coaches to have their recruits apply for outside scholarships. Instead, Zucconi wound up bearing the brunt of the blame for his role in the controversy.

Other actions taken by Brown in the wake of the League punishments turned out to be equally harsh and politically motivated.

"I had a player who was one of the students who was involved in Brown's own investigation of it," says Lasagna. During the player's junior year, his father died suddenly of a heart attack, while skiing with the player's younger brother. The Brown lacrosse team was in Syracuse at the time, preparing for a game. The mother called with the news.

"It was an extremely traumatic situation," says Lasagna. "He had to get home right away, and I took him to the airport and sat with him until his plane came, while the Brown lacrosse team was practicing at the Carrier Dome. And he went home and did everything he had to do, and they buried his father a few weeks later."

Overnight, the player had gone from being a "no-need" student at Brown to being a "full-need" student at Brown, because the father had reinvested all his life insurance and other assets into his company. There was nothing left to pay his son's Ivy League tuition, room, and board. With one year left, his future at Brown was in peril.

"So the mom went online and did a ton of research and applied to as many foundations as she possibly could," recalls Lasagna. "And she got a few of them. But because one of them was a foundation—I don't remember which one—that had some affiliation to somebody who had at some point had something to do with Brown University, even though they had given scholarships to many, many other people at schools all over the country and the world, somebody went, 'Oop! Brown! Brown!' And this family had to go through a world of trouble.

"It all ended up being fine, but it was a terrible experience for them, and just an example of, 'Who's at fault?' I'm not sure who's at fault. It ended up having a happy ending, but boy did this family have to jump through a billion hoops.

"What was so frustrating about this case," says Lasagna, "is you could look and see, 'Well, here's the foundation that gives money to college students every year.' And it would be very fishy if you looked at their awards over the last ten years and it said *Brown* every time. Or a *Brown athlete* every time. But it didn't. It was MIT and Michigan and Stanford and Harvard, and all over the institutional map. But because this person was a student-athlete, it raised every flag. From an NCAA standpoint, or an Ivy League standpoint, should it? I don't know.

"You're not talking about someone getting their financial aid package boosted when they don't qualify," he says, summing up the issue. "You're talking about people that qualify getting scholarships."

There are other scholarships that coaches encounter while recruiting in the Ivy League. One of them specifically helps coaches at Yale, the other benefits coaches at Princeton. These awards have never been the subject of a league investigation, thanks to the language and timing surrounding their establishment. "You can get very specific in terms of awards for recruited athletes if you were smart enough to set it up ahead of time," explains Lasagna. The Yale scholarship serves needy students from Duxbury, Massachusetts, which now seems ironic, given the current high level of wealth in the community. Yet, at a cost of $40,000 a year, Yale continues to have applicants from Duxbury who qualify for aid. "I'm sure it's worded such that it could be awarded to any student from Duxbury, Massachusetts, that goes to Yale," says Lasagna, who knew of lacrosse players who qualified for the funds, "but it just so happens that these awards are often made to needy student-athletes."

At Princeton, coaches can benefit from the William Cane Scholarship, which was endowed fifty years ago and is awarded to needy public high school students from New Jersey who attend the school. Its special provision is that students are not asked to work, either during the school year or in the summer. Again, the wording of the Cane Scholarship is such that it can be awarded to any student who meets the criteria, not just a recruited athlete, but athletes are considered and they have received the Cane Award.

"It always seemed funny to me that if you were smart enough or old enough to have set this up years and years and years ago," says Lasagna, "you could specifically say, even word it, that this award is going to go to an athlete from this town, or in this sport, or whatever, and that's legal."

The folks at Brown could very well argue that a double standard is at work here, and they would have a point. But the benefactors who endowed the funds have every right to specify who will receive them, and the schools, grateful for the aid, work within the legal language to find qualified recipients. In the end, these targeted scholarships increase the overall aid pool, which is a good thing for all financial aid recipients.

Looking back, part of my need-based financial aid package at Middlebury came from such a scholarship. The scholarship was endowed by the parents of a former Middlebury two-sport athlete from New Hampshire, Bayard A. Russ, who had died in Vietnam. To honor his love of sports, his parents worded the endowment in such a way that the scholarship could be awarded only to a student who was also a varsity athlete. As a two-sport varsity athlete who was also from New Hampshire, and who played soccer (just like Bayard A. Russ), and who qualified for need-based financial aid, I was an ideal recipient for the award, in the view of Middlebury's financial aid director and Mr. and Mrs. Russ. The scholarship had nothing to do with my recruitment by the soccer coach or the hockey coach. It was never mentioned during any of our conversations. In fact, my need for financial aid was never raised with the Middlebury coaches. The scholarship was simply, and generously, a part of my financial package, which arrived along with my acceptance letter. I was very grateful to receive the grant, for it greatly reduced my need for student loans. Similar scholarships have been endowed throughout the Ivy League and NESCAC. And other scholarships have been endowed as well for students from specific places, from specific backgrounds, and with specific talents in the arts, the sciences, the humanities, and other disciplines. These grants are all welcomed by the institutions they serve and by the students who receive them. If they were to be deemed illegal for athletes, then they would have to be deemed illegal for any other student who is singled out for consideration by the benefactors. Their existence is ultimately positive, and hardly seems surprising to me.

What is surprising, given the financial aid fiasco at Brown, is that in the years immediately following the League's consent decree with the Justice Department, which eliminated the overlap meetings, Brown's financial aid office quickly established a reputation around the League for being the most responsive and thorough in providing early financial aid reads to recruited athletes. They were so good, in fact, that coaches around the League would encourage the prospects they were recruiting, who were also being recruited by Brown, to ask Brown for an early financial aid estimate, so that their school would also have an accurate gauge of the student's need.

"It was a big plus for us," explains Lasagna, "being able to give these families the information that they needed desperately to figure out, 'Does it even make sense for me to consider applying for Brown? Let me find out what the ballpark money looks like.' Then, because our financial aid office would get stuff turned around the most quickly, we started to be used and abused by every other Ivy League financial aid office." He laughs at the memory. "And if a kid was being recruited by more than one Ivy, the Yale office, the Harvard office, the Dartmouth office, the whatever office, would say, 'Look, why don't you get a read from Brown first and then show it to us.' And that's what started to happen. And it hurt us."

In response to this trend, the Brown financial aid officers became more and more conservative—first, because they didn't want to get burned and abused, and second, because some coaches didn't do a thorough job of identifying prospects. "The financial aid office just got slammed by doing these early requests, these early reads, for kids that would end up not applying to Brown," Lasagna explains. So the office stopped doing hundreds and hundreds of early reads for prospects, and streamlined their internal process to avoid being taken advantage of by other schools. "As a result, the other Ivies got more and more aggressive, and we fell behind. And then," he adds, sounding the death knell, "Princeton started waiving self-help, and that's what really changed the nature of Ivy League recruiting."

Lasagna pauses, thinking about some of the rule breaking that emerged in the wake of the consent decree and Princeton's waiving self-help. "If you have billions in your endowment, of course you can be truly need-blind, and if you don't, you can't. So it shouldn't be surprising to anybody that people have to find other avenues if they can."

The other avenues he told me about are murky, the result of a convergence of factors, not the least of which is the ever more aggressive recruiting undertaken by scholarship schools, with whom the Ivies compete for a majority of their athletes. With the recruiting timeline accelerating rapidly, as scholarship schools pressed kids for verbal commitments during their junior year at high school, Ivy coaches began to bend the rules in an effort to keep up.

"The financial aid read is where I think some of the most borderline unethical things were happening," says Lasagna. "It started in football first, and hockey, and then it just made its way through all the sports including lacrosse. An Ivy coach would say to a prospect or a prospect's family, 'I can get you a great early financial aid read, but I can only put it in writing if you commit to apply early to *fill-in-the-blank* school.' And they would sometimes put this pressure on student-athletes who had not done their official visit yet. It was happening earlier and earlier and earlier in the process."

Coaches were not only trying to keep pace with the scholarship schools, they were also trying to lock up kids before their Ivy competitors could match an offer.

Lasagna explains: "Scholarship schools say, 'We'll give you this amount for a scholarship, but we're not going to put it in writing,' because they wouldn't want it to get matched by another school. Or, 'We're not going to put it in writing until you commit to the school.' And this was happening maybe in the kid's junior year, but certainly in the summer between their junior and senior year, when they haven't done their official visits yet. And it worked its way down the food chain into the Ivy League. And it really hurt us at Brown because we went from having the most proactive financial aid office in the early days to having the most reactive. And so our best opportunity to get a competitive financial aid read would be by saying,

'Would you please fax me the award letter that you got from another Ivy?' And as time went on, it got harder and harder to do that because the [other Ivy] coaches just would not commit those things to writing.

"In men's lacrosse particularly, as the whole process got more and more accelerated, people were holding support over these kids' heads. And if scholarship schools are putting pressure on kids to commit in April of their junior year, you're gonna get left behind if you don't start to bring up early application. And so, as time went on, more and more and more of your list, the vast majority of it—seven or eight kids—would apply early. And whether it was Early Action or Early Decision, frankly, didn't matter that much—except the occasional time you would get burned by a player or the parents. And then maybe one kid or two kids would be there left at the end of the process that you might be supporting for regular decision. That's just the way it is now."

Playing the early application game involved more than holding financial aid over kids' heads. In an effort to get into the picture early enough to compete with the scholarship schools and promote Early Decision, Ivy coaches began to have more illegal contact with prospects and their parents and coaches at contests during the athletes' junior year, an action known as "bumping."

"You would hear about coaches bumping parents or bumping students at contests," says Lasagna. "All the different Ivy coaches and the illegal contacts that they were having with [high school] coaches and athletes. I heard much more of it in football and hockey, outlandish things in terms of coaches bumping parents or bumping students." But as Lasagna admits bumping also happens in other sports like soccer and lacrosse that have showcases and tournaments for top high school players. There is an unwritten rule, however, that lacrosse coaches will not turn each other in for these recruiting violations, and one wonders how much this "professional courtesy" extends into other sports.

"There are Division I scholarship lacrosse coaches that will tell you right now that people are calling underclassmen all year long," Lasagna says of a common rule violation. "But no one wants to turn anybody else in."

Why not?

"If they're not guilty now," he says, "they might be guilty someday, and they'd rather not turn the light onto the current rule breakers."

According to Lasagna, some of these coaches are Ivy coaches, but most, he says, are scholarship school coaches. And the reason for their illegal calls is simple: "Because they have money, they can force a decision much earlier."

In the era of Ivy overlap meetings, "forcing decisions" came much later in the recruiting process. And for athletes who were accepted at multiple schools, and who qualified for financial aid, there was always just one universal offer to consider.

"There was no negotiation," John Lyons of Dartmouth says of the days before the anti-trust suit settlement. "Now, it's better for families. But I feel like Monty Hall on 'Let's Make a Deal.' Listen, here's what happens. The kid sends his paperwork to us, Harvard, and Princeton. It comes back, and generally Princeton's got the best read, then Harvard, then us. I have a hard enough time trying to land a kid involved in Harvard and Princeton. What shot do I have when we come back as the third-best package of those three schools? What do I do then? Well, we'll match it."

Matching a financial aid package is legal under the consent decree, for all students, not just for athletes. Regardless of who is involved, the process is overseen by the financial aid office and based on the written offer from another school. But for athletes, the timing comes long before an acceptance letter has been mailed, during a recruiting process.

"You've gotta understand," Lyons continues, "that those two coaches are saying, 'Dartmouth doesn't want you, 'cause if they did, our initial offers would be the same.' So you're behind the eight ball. The stuff they use is unbelievable. We're not supposed to be negatively recruiting, but there's a lot of that that goes around. It's unfortunate. And I tell our guys not to do it. I don't think, in the long run, it does you any good. Because these people are smart and they're going to figure it out."

Figuring out if a family is willing to make the sacrifice required to attend an Ivy League school is one of the first things that coaches identify in the Ivy recruiting process. For high-income families, money is not a problem. For lower-income families, the League is a great option due to its need-based aid policy. But middle-income families, as one coach put it, "get screwed." Several Ivy coaches told me that they can tell within minutes of walking into a recruit's home whether or not the family values education enough to make the financial sacrifice necessary to attend an Ivy League school. (In the 2003–04 school year, the average cost of undergraduate tuition, fees, and room and board at an Ivy institution was nearly $38,000. Add another $3,000 for books, supplies, travel, and other expenses and the annual cost topped $40,000.)

"It's usually the middle-class families that are completely caught," says Cornell's Jenny Graap. "They're making a little bit too much money, and it's just a sad situation. They don't feel like they're making enough, and yet Uncle Sam is saying, 'You're not meeting our criteria for financial aid, so you're not getting anything.' The really wealthy people don't even bother to ask about it. And the people that are really needy, they're going to get decent packages. That's all part of the recruiting process. As the coach, you have to have that understanding of the family. 'Is this family, number one, going to be able to afford this Ivy League education?' Because if the answer is 'no,' then no matter how great you are as a recruiter, and no matter how awesome your university is, and no matter how much effort you're willing to put into this prospect, chances are you're not going to land them—if a family really doesn't feel that they can afford it, or if it's not worth it for them. If the value of taking out all these loans and doing all this paperwork, and the value of the education that their son or daughter is going to receive—if they don't perceive that as worth it, then you might as well just cut your losses and go for someone else. Because it's just a nightmare."

A dream scenario for Graap is finding a lacrosse player from New York who wants to attend one of Cornell's three state-supported schools, where tuition is at least $10,000 less than it is at Cornell's endowed colleges, each of which has a comparable price tag to the seven other Ivies.

"If you happen to reside in New York State and you happen to apply to one of our state-supported colleges, then you're allowed to pay the in-state rate," Graap explains. "It does sometimes help." In 2003, she had one national All-American and two regional All-Americans from New York who were enrolled in Cornell's state-supported colleges. They paid considerably less than they would have paid to attend any other Ivy League school.

That same year, Graap had another regional All-American from New York who was enrolled in Cornell's College of Arts & Science, an endowed college, not a state-supported one. "She wanted the liberal arts," says Graap. "So it doesn't always happen that the reason why a player from New York is looking at Cornell is because they want some type of financial benefit." But for families who face a financial sacrifice, the benefit of in-state tuition can indeed help Graap's recruiting.

"Obviously, we want to get focused on people who are willing to make the sacrifice," says Bob Ceplikas of Dartmouth. "Because I don't care how much the [federal] formula allows us to provide someone in terms of financial aid—whether the family ultimately qualifies for a very large aid package or a very modest one, for every one of those families it's a sacrifice. So you've got to get a sense for that, early on."

Mike Noonan, the men's soccer coach at Brown, says, "I'm not selling four years at Brown. I'm selling the value of a Brown education over forty years, over an entire lifetime. If people don't see that value, that's fine. Not everyone wants to make the sacrifice."

Noonan uses an interesting analogy to compare his job to those of his counterparts at highly regarded academic schools that also offer soccer scholarships, schools like Stanford, Duke, Notre Dame, Virginia, and SMU. "I'm selling a Mercedes. Those coaches are selling a Rolls Royce. It's hard to win that battle for a kid, where he goes to a great school, with a great soccer program, *and* gets a scholarship. I can be in the top five choices for that kid, but I'm not going to get him very often." Especially if he comes from a middle-income household.

"The Ivies are in a tough situation because, first of all, a lot of kids that they'd like to have as athletes wouldn't ever survive academically," says Bruce Bailey, the director of college counseling at the Lakeside School in Seattle. "And then when they get kids who are good students and get offered an athletic scholarship, that's a huge decision for those kids."

Making the sacrifice required to pay for an Ivy League education is a huge decision for all middle-class families today, regardless of whether an athlete is involved. According to Bailey, an increasing number of attractive options are becoming available for top students from middle-class households. "Public universities are developing these 'schools within a school' for the best and the brightest—with the best teachers and small classes— and going after kids like we have here," he says. "The University of Washington, for example, has seven kids out of our class going to their honors program next year [2003–04]. It's a very high-powered group of students, and I can't say for sure in every case, but I think finances have been a huge part of that decision. Along with the fact that the honors programs are getting pretty good, they're also so much cheaper that kids can come out of college without debt, and perhaps have money to go to graduate school, which most of them are going to do anyway. So that financial deal is getting bigger and bigger now as those college tuitions are so way up in the stratosphere."

Bailey compares the financial and educational value of these public university honors programs with the financial and educational value of an Ivy League or a NESCAC education. "Say I have a family that really wants me to prove to them that the $40,000 a year investment at Middlebury or Yale is going to be that much better than the $10,000 a year investment at the University of Washington Honors Program," he says. "My argument is that at these elite schools, it's the kids you're bringing together and how they learn so much from each other that may be the difference. But now these honors programs are doing exactly that. They're bringing the best and the brightest into one group. So that argument doesn't quite hold the way it might if you said, 'best public university, flat out.'"

Other colleges and universities are trying to lure strong students to their campuses by offering them money to attend. Says Bailey, "One of the other great, interesting phenomena that's taken place, and that's quite controversial, is the huge amount of what you might call 'merit-aid,' which just kind of drops out of the acceptance letter from schools, particularly schools just below the Ivy League who are really trying to go after good kids. And so they'll accept a kid, and then all of a sudden, 'And by the way, we're offering you $75,000 over four years to come here.' Now again, in this day and age of high tuitions, that's pretty heady stuff and for families who are a little squeezed that becomes, 'Whoa!' I just totaled up the [2003–04] merit scholarship number for our kids—and I still haven't even heard from all of them—but we had well over half a million dollars given to twenty kids, unsolicited, in the admission letters."

"Schools are making internal decisions at the board level," Bailey explains. "They're saying, 'We want to up our profile,' or, 'We want to attract the best we can, and the way to do it is to give merit aid.' Then they're going out and raising that kind of money. But it's still in their aid pool, so it's x minus this amount that's going to financial aid based on need. Now that'll never happen in the Ivy League. They're strictly financial aid based on need. They don't have to resort to merit aid because of the kind of demand they have. But if you're trying to compete and to raise your school's profile, this is a very effective way to do it, I think."

While the demand for an Ivy League education may be great, so is the cost of attendance. And the high price tag has altered the composition of team rosters.

"I think it's really become more of an elitist, or rich kid's, league," says John Lyons of the high cost of attending an Ivy school. In his view, and in the view of nearly every coach and administrator I interviewed, the number one issue facing the League is the increased cost of attending the schools. Stratospheric tuition bills are driving many players from middle-class backgrounds to accept athletic scholarship offers. As a result, Ivy rosters are now laden with high-income kids who require no aid, and low-income kids who qualify for good packages—with some "willing-to-make-the-sacrifice" middle-income kids sprinkled here and there. But, as Lyons points out, many of the lower-income kids face a challenge getting in, thanks to the heavy reliance on test scores in computing an Academic Index that just continues to rise. "I think there are a lot of kids that deserve an opportunity, particularly some kids from tougher back-grounds that aren't getting a shot anymore. The lower-class kids will get good packages now, but what they need to get accepted has really jumped up because of the Index."

Today the middle-income kids compete for football scholarships at such state schools as UNH, UConn, UMass, and the University of Rhode Island, all of which compete in Division IAA football, just like the Ivy League. "As scholarships came in and the Ivy [academic] quest kept going up, the whole thing changed," explains Lyons. "Dartmouth went through some really tough times trying to compete with UNH, and for a while had to drop 'em because we weren't competitive. The finances are a big factor. And what it takes to get into these schools now, it's so different. Kids I either went to school with [at Penn], or kids that I coached earlier [at Dartmouth], these guys don't get into these schools anymore with the credentials that we all had. And a lot of these guys have gone on to become very, very successful in a lot of different fields."

Some schools in the League have had more success than others recruiting kids from lower-income households, where the financial aid comparison between an athletic scholarship and a need-based award is more apples to apples.

"We've done a great job of recruiting kids that have a high need," says Dave Roach, the Brown athletic director. "And that kid, as a league, I think we're in the running for."

Indeed, the Brown men's basketball program has undergone a resurgence under the guidance of Coach Glen Miller, who has developed a winning program by competing for talent directly with scholarship schools. One of the first three questions Miller and his staff ask when placing calls to learn more about a kid who has landed on their radar screen is, "Does he require a lot of financial aid?" If he does, and if he stacks up academically and as a player, then they move forward. If he doesn't require a lot of aid, they drop him.

"There are 320 schools that play Division I basketball," says Roach, "and all but ten of them have scholarships. Eight of the ten are in the Ivy League. So the kid who gets offered a scholarship at a lower-level Division I school, we're gonna steal from people. We're gonna attract kids who have high need that could go to certain state schools on a basketball scholarship, but they want a great education."

To help attract these high-need players, Andy Partee, one of Miller's assistants, has installed a toll-free phone number at his home, and pays the bill out of his own pocket. "The scholarship schools have toll-free numbers so kids can call them," he explains, describing one way that basketball coaches skirt the rule that prevents them from calling players prior to March of their junior year. (Basketball recruiting is the most accelerated and, arguably, the most aggressive, of any college sport, allowing the earliest legal call from coach to player.) In any sport, though, it is perfectly legal for players to call coaches as underclassmen, and this is something that all coaches, at all schools—scholarship *and* Ivy—encourage top prospects to do through letters and emails to kids. "The toll-free number puts us on an equal footing with the scholarship schools," Partee says. Intrigued and excited by his idea, the Brown athletic department looked into the cost of installing toll-free numbers for all their programs, before balking at the price tag. For now, Partee continues to pay for his toll-free number at home. "If it helps us win," he says, "it's the least I can do."

Today 50 to 65 percent of all Ivy athletes enroll through an Early Decision or Early Action program. As a result, the comparison shopping for financial aid offers from around the League starts early.

"Top prospects don't lose financial leverage by going Early Decision," says Bob Ceplikas of Dartmouth. "And you can see how crucial those early readings are, because there would be plenty of families out there who would say, 'Well, I can't afford to just go with the one offer, I've got to wait until I have a chance to shop.'"

Ivy schools have to pick their spots providing these reads because, as we saw in Brown's case, neither the admission office nor the financial aid office can possibly spend the time it would take to provide hundreds and hundreds of families with early financial aid estimates. At most schools, there are now other mechanisms in place to deal with the large number of prospects who get screened through the wide net of Ivy recruiting, including both a hard-copy version and an online version of a financial aid estimating worksheet.

Oddly enough, both Yale's football coach, Jack Siedlecki, and Cornell's Jenny Graap will direct recruits to the Princeton website to get an early financial aid read.

"It's kind of ludicrous," Graap admits, "but sometimes I will tell my recruits to go on the Princeton website and fill out the Princeton estimator, because it's right there online. I feel ridiculous doing that, to be honest, because I don't really want them looking at Princeton. But we all follow the same [federal] formulas [that govern all schools, not just the Ivies], and our tuition is very comparable in the endowed colleges, so I'll just direct them that way if they want a quick and easy answer."

If a recruit's financial situation is atypical, due to divorce, trusts, or a complicated situation beyond salary and money in the bank, then the simple online calculators do not work well, and a full financial aid application must be processed.

Within a few years of the consent decree, a competitive shift in the balance of financial aid awards within the League began to emerge. Schools with the financial resources to do so began to beef up their financial budgets and push the envelope in the gray areas of the federal formulas in order to be more generous.

"They were all still within the proper federal formulas for need-based financial aid," explains Bob Ceplikas, addressing how the richer schools began to attract richer pools of talent in the mid-1990s, "but we went through a period of several years where we were hammered by Harvard, Yale, and Princeton, in particular."

One gray area exploited by these schools has to do with family situations involving divorce and separation. "They are very murky," says Ceplikas. "Whether you should be counting the income from both parents, or just the one that the student is living with. . . . The federal formula allows you to count just the custodial parent, but for many years because schools didn't have the financial aid budgets to allow for it, generally most schools were counting both parents. If you had enough financial resources, though, and if you wanted to be more generous, you could decide to only count the income of the one parent. It's all legal. It's all within the federal formulas."

But it favors the schools with more money to award.

Another gray area lies in a key factor for calculating financial aid—determining how many kids are in college at the same time.

"That obviously has a huge impact on what a family would have available," says Ceplikas. "Well, the federal formula will allow you, if you wish, to count children who are in graduate school as well. But traditionally, they haven't been counted by most colleges because we haven't been able to afford it." Again, this is another example of how schools with enough money could, and did, increase a prospect's financial aid award by counting siblings in graduate school.

As time went on, and as the wealthier institutions with the largest endowments chose to devote more money to financial aid—not just for competitive reasons, but also to provide more access to more families to be able to afford their institution—the packages across the League became less and less consistent. Harvard, Princeton, and Yale began to outbid the other schools in the League.

At Dartmouth, this trend hit football recruiting harder than any other sport.

"It was devastating," says Ceplikas. "When I say that we were sitting there in '96 and knew we were in trouble, it's because that's when we were just beginning to get outbid on our top-tier recruits. So we knew that we were down to John's second- and third-tier recruits before we were getting kids to commit to Dartmouth.

"If, all of sudden, your potential pool has shrunk so that it's only the same small pool that Harvard, Yale, and Princeton get to fish in [due to the sharp increase in Dartmouth's mean A.I. that occurred in 1996], *and* they have more money, *and*, let's face it, they're more a household word in East Overshoe, Texas, that's a triple whammy."

When James Wright replaced James Freedman as the Dartmouth president in 1998, he wasted little time in addressing the school's shortfalls in financial aid. Within a month of taking office, Wright and the Dartmouth Trustees announced a $6 million infusion into the financial aid budget. A few years later, they made a second infusion.

"Of course, the public spin was not, 'We're doing this to get competitive with Harvard, Yale, and Princeton again,'" says Ceplikas. "It was just the platitudes about access for more families and these wonderful things—and it's all true. But in the world of athletic recruiting it was, 'Whew, we're back in the ball game with Harvard, Yale, and Princeton.'"

"The second time was not a planned follow-up to the first," Wright told me. "We looked at it again, and decided to do something. And that was not driven by athletics or athletic recruiting, it was driven by really two things: trying to provide competitive financial aid packages at Dartmouth so that those students that we wanted to recruit, no matter who they were [artists, mathematicians, scientists, musicians, students of color, athletes, or others], would look at us just as they were looking at other places. But I think even more important than that was to provide financial aid packages that would enable students to come to Dartmouth. I value immensely the opportunity that we have here, and even the obligation that we have here, to make a Dartmouth education available to a wide group of different students—that one's capacity to pay should not be a factor in whether or not a student comes to Dartmouth."

One's capacity to pay is even less of factor in whether or not a student goes to Princeton. Imagine, no loans for four years. Little wonder the applicant pool at Princeton is so rich in talent of every variety. When the consent decree was signed in 1991, there were significant concerns that Princeton or Harvard would dominate Ivy athletics by having the most attractive financial aid packages. To make matters worse, under the decree members of the League would not even be able to discuss the issue, or to agree what steps to take to alleviate it. Athletic dominance by the richer schools loomed as a real fear.

"When Princeton really did change its financial aid policies," says Jeff Orleans, "and Harvard followed suit somewhat, as did Yale, there was even more concern that that athletic dominance would be the case. And, when Princeton won double-digit Ivy championships every year of the '90s, it was a significant issue."

Says Mike Goldberger, the director of admission at Brown, "There are some pretty big disparities out there, and I know it's going to get worse. It leaves other schools to try to come up with creative ways to balance that or counteract it. What in the world do you do when Princeton has no loans, and you're trying to recruit a kid, and at Cornell she's going to have $20,000 in loans, and you're sort of in between? Nobody is blind to the fact that there are competitive problems."

Thanks to the anti-trust settlement, the schools, as we have seen, cannot address these issues together as a league. "Absent a consent judgment," says Jeff Orleans, "if we were free to make agreements about athletics without having to go back to the Department of Justice, I think there might be some interest in trying to find some way of looking at the athletic part of financial aid." Orleans admits that this could stir up concerns among some "nonathletics people" that schools would be treating athletes more favorably than nonathletes by having a financial aid agreement for athletes. "What the Justice Department relationship means is that even though the consent judgment is done, if we wanted to refine this financial aid agreement on athletics we would need, I think, to go back to the Justice Department, and there's a real reluctance, obviously, to do that.

"I think the athletics piece of the original consent judgment could have been negotiated better," he adds. "I think the people who were negotiating really didn't understand athletics very much. A lot of the lawyers did not spend as much time thinking about that as they could have, but, you know, that's history."

A few case histories of financial aid awards for Princeton athletes following the consent decree are enlightening. Rob Chisholm, the index booster from Nova Scotia and the Middlesex School, who wound up making the Tiger hockey team after all in the fall of 1998 and playing regular shift, told me how his financial aid worked at the school prior to the enactment of Princeton's no-loan policy.

"Princeton said, 'Here's your need. Here's what we'll give you.' They gave me most of it. I paid very little my first year, maybe $1,500. Then they said I had to work for $2,000 at a job on campus. But I could walk into the financial aid office on day one and say, 'I'm not going to be able to work. I'm too busy because I have to play hockey four or five hours a day, so what can we do?' And they'd say, 'Well, how much money do you have?' And I'd say, 'Well, you told me I had to work for $2,000. I can't work for any of it. I need it all.' And they would say, 'Okay, we'll give you $1,000, and we'll loan you $1,000.' The fact is, all I had to do was walk in and say, 'I need more money,' and they'd give me $1,000—plus an interest-free loan. It was basically free money.

"My second year, it was a little less: I had to work off a little less, and I paid a little less. And by my third year, I was getting paid by the University. They were actually going to credit my account $2,200 to pay for books and all the little expenses that aren't covered with tuition. They were actually going to try to cover some of those for me."

Chisholm never received the money. He decided to leave Princeton three weeks into his junior year, frustrated by his lack of motivation in the classroom, where he had always excelled. He eventually transferred to Middlebury where he was able to pursue his passion, environmental studies, and play varsity hockey. Elected captain of the team as a senior, he graduated summa cum laude, won the Environmental Studies department award, and earned a prestigious post-graduate Watson Fellowship, which allowed him to travel the world for a year, studying indigenous fishing communities. The switch of schools proved very successful, albeit more costly.

"Princeton just gave me more financial aid," says Chisholm. "They calculated my need as higher. Middlebury sort of assumes that they're giving you a minimum loan no matter what. They don't care how much money you make; they just assume you'll be able to pay it off at some point."

Nor were the Middlebury loans interest free, as Princeton's had been. "They're just at a very low rate, 5.7 percent," Chisholm says. "And repayment doesn't start until nine months after you graduate."

Another Princeton athlete, swimmer Maura Bolger, who graduated in 2003 with plans to attend Pepperdine Law School, told me her financial aid award was "surprising," more generous than she or her parents had expected. The New Jersey native was an all-state swimmer and all-state cross-country runner at Manasquan High School, where she carried a 4.0 average and scored 1340 on her college boards as a sophomore. During four years of high school, she competed in eight Junior National swimming championships, which caught the attention of coaches at Princeton, Harvard, Duke, UNC, Penn State, Boston College, Illinois (which offered her a half scholarship to swim), and several other schools. She eventually narrowed down her list to five schools, and applied to all of them under regular decision.

"I just wasn't ready to make a decision," she told me. She eliminated Harvard after making an official visit, and was on her way to make an official visit to Duke, driving through Virginia with her parents in mid-April, when she learned she had gotten into Princeton.

"My grandma was checking our mail and the acceptance package came from Princeton," she says. "It was the best school I had applied to, and if I was going to get in, I was going to go. So I called the coach at Duke and I said, 'I'm not coming for the visit because I am going to Princeton.'"

She pauses, then adds with a laugh, "So the next week I got a rejection from Duke." It was the standard reply in the recruiting game, especially at an elite academic school, including those in the Ivy League: once a coach knows a player is headed elsewhere, the precious admission slot is used for another recruit.

"I was number two in my high school class," Bolger says, "and the girl who was number one was wait listed Early Decision by Princeton, and then eventually accepted maybe a week before graduation. But that was tough, considering she was number one and I was number two, and then I got accepted. She ended up going to Brown. She wasn't a recruited tennis player for Princeton, but she played tennis, was on the student council, National Honor Society president, you know, the typical Ivy League things, and so that was a weird situation."

Bolger's decision to attend Princeton had nothing do with money, but when she looked at her financial aid award, she was taken aback. "It was surprising," she says. "At Princeton, I guess they have a reputation of being pretty generous, giving all students some kind of aid. I was just surprised that we had any aid because I had heard prior stories of friends who had both parents working, and the school gave them $1,000 or something. And I was just surprised that this is Princeton, and they were giving so much."

Bolger's mom, who had stopped teaching full-time when Maura was in seventh grade, worked as a substitute teacher, and her father, a lawyer in private practice in Ocean County, was a partner in a law firm, specializing in medical malpractice, earning what his daughter described as "a good living."

"He defends the doctors," she says, "so I say he's on the 'good side.'"

"I'm an only child," she adds, talking about her aid. "That was another thing. I think they were surprised, too, with how much I got."

Bolger received $10,000 a year to attend Princeton. "And as tuition increased, the aid also increased to $12,000 this past year [her senior year]," she says. The money was all grant-in-aid. No loans.

"I was impressed with anybody who'd try to do swimming and have a job," she says of her teammates who tried to balance their time commitment to swimming with their studies and an on-campus job. "Because we did the NCAA rules to the max with the number of hours they limit you to practice. And we went over with optional hours that you're supposed to go to. That wouldn't count on the sheet because they're 'optional.'"

Such intensive training is not limited to Princeton women's swimming. I found cases of it at other schools around the Ivy League. One Ivy rower told me she and other varsity athletes routinely exceeded the twenty hours allowed under NCAA rules, usually training for twenty-five hours or more each week. On this matter, I agree with Bill Bowen: Many Ivy athletes today spend too much time training for their sports, which in turn affects the amount of time they have to pursue other activities, to interact with students other than their teammates, and to meet the demands of their schoolwork and on-campus jobs. In some cases, the intense training also places their health in jeopardy.

Bolger says she has "no doubt" that the level of training required by the Princeton women's swimming coach led her to develop a severe case of mononucleosis during her sophomore year. She describes a demanding weekly practice schedule that ran for the first two months of the team's six-month-long season: four days a week (Monday, Tuesday, Thursday, and Friday) she attended two-hour morning practices from 6:30 to 8:30 am; five afternoons a week (Monday through Friday) she swam for another two hours from 4:30 to 6:30 pm; then on Saturday morning she went to a three-and-a-half-hour practice, starting with an 'optional' half hour swim at 7:30 am with the other long-distance swimmers, followed by two more hours of swimming with the entire team, followed, finally, by one last hour of dry-land training (a circuit with weights, medicine balls, sit-ups, stadiums, and jump rope that would change each week). Sunday was a day off.

"Sophomore year I was swimming pretty well in the fall after summer training on my own," she says. "But then I started just getting really tired by Friday morning practice, Friday afternoon practice. Then I would feel really strong on Monday after the day off. And by Tuesday afternoon, I'd feel dead. Finally, I swam [in] a meet and was terrible. I was tested for mono, and I had mono. So I lost my sophomore season. . . . I'm still a little bit angry that I didn't get tested until December 5, when over Thanksgiving weekend I lost four pounds—over Thanksgiving, eating the Thanksgiving meal. I clearly had it, and you know I could have seriously hurt myself diving into the pool with my spleen and stuff like that. It was a little frustrating. . . . I think that was a product of having such a big team that the coaches weren't really noticing that I was struggling in practice."

Having a big team allowed the coaches to foster an intense competition for the limited number of spots on the Tiger team that would swim in the Ivy championship meet. But one wonders how the coaches could have missed the signs that Bolger was struggling when she would emerge from the pool at practice on the verge of tears.

"I would get out of the pool, practically crying, and say to the coaches, 'I'm hurting and I don't know what's wrong.' And they would be like, 'Oh, okay. Well, take the day off,' or 'Come back tomorrow and try. . . .' They would ask, 'Are you getting enough sleep? Are you eating right?' It was more things geared toward the sport, not necessarily your academics. That's a big thing: a lot of the kids, with schoolwork won't sleep. And so that was what they would ask. That would bring in the academics. 'Are you getting enough sleep,' which means, 'Are you spending all your time late at night doing your homework?'"

Doing homework until one o'clock in the morning is exactly what Dartmouth running back Mike Giles was doing during the winter and spring terms of his freshman year. The government major with a 3.8 GPA would then rise at 5:00 am, grab a bite to eat, and report promptly at 6:00 for a two-hour team running and agility session. From 9:00 until 2:00 in the afternoon, he attended class. Then he reported to the football weight room at 3:00, where he worked out for two more hours. "So now I've been going nonstop since 5:00 am," he recalls. "I go to dinner, get back to my room by 7:00, and then I have all that homework to do until 1:00 in the morning— but I still have to get up at 5:00 the next morning." After several weeks of pushing his body to the limit in this fashion, Giles developed such a severe case of mono that he wound up connected to an intravenous drip in the Dartmouth infirmary. He remained there for five weeks.

"The way many students handle the academic workload," says former Dartmouth Freshman Dean Steven Cornish, who is now a dean at Brown, "is to go without sleep. And it catches up with some of them." Not just athletes contract mono, but the rigors of training year round to play a Division I sport, on top of meeting the intense academic demands of an Ivy education make athletes vulnerable to illness.

For some athletes the challenge is not just to stay healthy, it is to stay motivated. By the time they are seniors, nearly half of all recruited Ivy athletes will have quit, only some because of injury. (In football the percentage of those who stop playing by their senior year is closer to two-thirds.) This attrition is built into the Ivy recruiting system, and it's easy to see why: some high school stars, accustomed to the spotlight and plenty of playing time, "walk off" a team frustrated after sitting on the bench for a year or two; other athletes stop playing to delve more deeply into academic majors or other co-curricular interests; and nearly all who quit want relief from the intense time commitment required for training.

Former Harvard hockey player Scott Turco described his in-season training regimen as follows: early morning stationary bike riding for an hour three mornings a week; afternoon practice for two to three hours, five days a week; weight lifting after practice; back-to-back games on Friday and Saturday nights. "It's insane now," he says. "And some of the

Canadian guys were so unprepared academically, they were struggling just to keep their heads above water academically. Then throw on top of that their work-study jobs, and then on top of that the hockey, which is like a full-time job, and I always heard them complaining about how they were just getting run into the ground."

When I asked him if he saw a solution to the demands placed on him and his teammates, his answer surprised me: "I think there should be some [financial] compensation. . . . You should definitely be able to get some of your education paid for."

Pay for play is hardly an Ivy principle, but Turco's point is valid and his honesty refreshing. "As other schools are improving their academics and giving out scholarships," he points out, "it's going to be harder and harder [for the Ivy League] to compete athletically." In an effort to keep up, Ivy athletes invest just as much time and effort into their sports (through official practices and by investing their own time and energy) as their scholarship school counterparts. And the demands of working at their sport all year round, "doing a job," are intense.

"I think most high school kids, at least ours, have no idea of the commitment that's necessary in any college program, even Division III," says Bruce Bailey of the Lakeside School. "They just don't have any idea. They've done it all in high school, they figure they can do it all in college. It ain't gonna happen. And so some of them burn out. At least at the Ivy League they don't own you, and you can go on and do other things."

Bailey advises parents and athletic recruits: "You've got to really be proactive, try to get a handle on the coach and the players that play for the coach. Talk to those players when you visit. Do they have a life? That's always my question. Are they able to do other things and take advantage of the resources of an Ivy League school? I think it would be a travesty not to be able to do other things."

Mike Goldberger believes this issue lies at the heart of the debate over Ivy athletics, but he points out that major time commitments are also required of Ivy League students who participate in other co-curricular activities.

"I think in terms of learning the work ethic and learning what it takes to get things done, I learned a lot of that in athletics," says Goldberger, who played two sports at Middlebury and was a football coach at Brown before becoming an admission officer. "I think other people learn that in the orchestra, other people learn that in working on assigned projects together, and others learn it from community service. But I think it is an incredibly valuable opportunity that's important to make available to people. The question at issue now is, 'How much time should be devoted to it?' I think people see a disconnect of saying, 'Why is it okay to limit athletics, but not to limit music?' And I'm struggling with that a little bit. I like the notion of kids participating in lots of different activities, and not just being a student and an athlete, but being able to be in the theater, being able to be in the school paper. And I think that is what the Ivy presidents are doing, when they are saying they would like to try limiting the amount of [practice] time in the off-season.

"I remember having this conversation with somebody whose daughter was going to be the editor of the Brown student paper," Goldberger continues. "He was so fearful that that was all she would do that year—and in fact, that *is* all she did that year. There is no way that you can aspire to get to that level; you don't get to be the editor of the paper without making that commitment. You can't say, 'I want to do the paper, but I also want to be in a play, and I also want to do that.' You know, on the one hand, I don't like that. On the other hand, I think it's great. So it's something that I am struggling with right now in terms of what's right, what's the right balance."

By her senior year, Maura Bolger was eager to find a better balance. Burned out by all the 'optional' hours and the intensive training, she left the Princeton swim team and walked on to the cross country team, where a close friend was enjoying her experience. When a leg injury stopped her from competing, she delved into other interests, including student government, winning a spot on the Alumni Council for her graduating class. Her social circle expanded. Her grades improved. And although she had quit her "job" with the swim team, her financial aid did not change. In fact, her aid was higher her senior year than any other, reflecting the increase in Princeton's rising tuition.

Around the League, Princeton's financial aid policy is a formidable obstacle in the athletic recruiting game. Even with the "matching offer" policy of all the schools, the reality of the recruiting process makes it virtually impossible for athletes to get competing offers based on a

Princeton package. Jenny Graap of Cornell explains why: "I believe that Cornell will try to match offers, not only for recruited athletes, but for any student. But in my world, it doesn't really happen all that often because in order for the recruit to actually get a financial aid offer from Princeton, we're not talking about matching the estimator that's online. We're talking about matching the actual package. They have to really be one of the coach's top prospects. They would basically have to go through the whole process telling that coach at Princeton, 'Yeah, I want to come here.' And then get all of the benefits of that, which is number one, in their admission process, and then get this financial aid package. Then they'd have to give it to Cornell to match. In my experience, it sounds great that you could say to all of your prospects, 'Oh my gosh, please go and try to be recruited by Princeton, so that you can benefit from this wonderful financial aid that Princeton offers.' But I think that Princeton is pretty savvy about all that, and they know who they want. They pick who they want, and then these other kids who are just below their list or are just below their cut, they're not going to bother with them. So they just say, 'We're not interested in you. We've already filled our recruiting class.' And then this poor kid, who would certainly benefit from this wonderful Ivy League matching of financial aid, gets left out because there's nothing to match. The kid then says, 'I wasn't on their list, they weren't interested in me after all, and so I don't have the package.' Philosophically, it sounds great that we can all match Princeton's packages. But the truth is they get the first cut of the kids. It's also not fair that the kid you want to benefit from this wonderful, new aid package that Princeton offers, they can't even get to that level. Princeton's just going to cut them loose and say, 'Sorry, we're not interested.'"

In recent years, Princeton administrators have argued that their high A.I. is a disadvantage that balances, or even outweighs, any competitive edge they may gain in the recruiting game, thanks to their financial aid policies. But, says Brown Director of Admission, Mike Goldberger, "Every coach at Brown would say, 'I would give anything to have that disadvantage if I had the facilities and if I had the financial aid packages of Princeton.'"

Goldberger goes on to point out that in football, "If you look at the League over the last seven or eight years, things are pretty balanced.

Except for Columbia, who has struggled. I think everybody else has won at least part of the title. And they have had good years and bad years. Brown's had a title, Harvard's had a title, and Dartmouth. I think every one of the Ivies, except for Columbia, has had part of the title or the outright title."

In terms of overall Ivy titles in the past decade, however, Princeton stands alone at the top with double-digit Ivy championships for ten straight years. And the reasons are clear to everyone in the League. "I think people who have really thought it through," says Jeff Orleans, "their conclusion is that certainly financial aid makes a positive difference, but so do facilities, and so does coaching, and so does recruiting, and so does Admissions. And they give the financial aid at Princeton some credit, but they also give Fred Hargadon credit for who he admitted, and they give [Athletic Director] Gary Walters and his predecessor Bob Myslik credit for hiring the Princeton coaches, and they give the endowment managers at Princeton credit for building Denunzio Pool and Princeton Stadium."

Orleans chooses to use "credit" where others might prefer the word "blame." If you are recruiting against Princeton, it can feel as if the odds are stacked against you. And, in many ways, in many sports, they are.

"The thing about Princeton, it really recruits itself," says Maura Bolger. "I don't think the coaches have to work too hard."

Chapter Nine

Studs, Lies & Videotape

"The game gets played in the Ivy League because there is no Letter of Intent . . . so parents and kids can tell you anything that they assume you want to hear with no recriminations attached to it. Absolutely nothing."

Pat O'Leary
Dartmouth College
Assistant Football Coach

Pat O'Leary knows a thing or two about recriminations. For ten years, he was a New York City cop. Prior to that, he served a one-year tour in Vietnam with the 101st Airborne Division. In both jobs, recriminations came with an unforgiving, sometimes lethal, precision. Then he joined the Ivy League, and for the past twenty years has watched people get away with murder.

"I'm telling you," he says of the League's reliance on a verbal, rather than a written commitment from recruits, "it's a disaster."

Many agree. Deans of admission have suggested reform, coaches have lobbied for a change in the system, and athletic directors have cried foul. But the Ivy League presidents, aware of the public relations challenge they face regarding recruited athletes, have chosen not to alter the Likely Letter system that provides a recruit with a written commitment from a school without asking the recruit for a written commitment in return.

Unfortunately, the Likely Letter policy has fostered a recruiting environment that is no better, in some ways, than that of the big-time schools the Ivy League likes to keep a stiff arm's length away, on the basis of its claim to moral superiority.

"I think the [NCAA] Letter of Intent is more of an Ivy principle than the [Ivy League] Likely Letter, even if you are going to talk about integrity and honesty and morality," says the League's executive director, Jeff Orleans. "Because it's inviting problems the way it's set up now."

Indeed, the NCAA Letter of Intent is clean and transparent compared to the Ivy League Likely Letter. Under the Letter of Intent system, which is honored by all scholarship schools competing in Division I, a recruit must sign a letter by the first Wednesday in February of his or her senior year, stating his or her commitment to attend and play for one school. In this way, each recruit's plans for college are made open and public. In contrast, the Ivy League does not require a recruit to sign a thing, only to make a private verbal commitment to a coach to attend a given school. In return, the coach arranges for the school's admission dean to send the recruit a letter stating that he or she is very likely to be admitted to that Ivy institution when their official acceptances are mailed in April. Unlike the Letter of Intent, there is nothing open, public, or binding for the recruit under the Ivy Likely Letter system.

Not surprisingly, problems ensue. These include players and parents who lie to coaches, coaches who pressure players to make commitments, coaches who ignore the commitments players make to other schools, and an environment that is rife with mistrust, denunciation, and denial. It's hardly a one-way street of deceit. The ugliness cuts two ways. Some players, parents, and high school coaches simply lie to Ivy coaches. And some coaches twist the truth to suit the needs and goals of their programs. No coaches admit to any conscious wrongdoing. It's always the other coach at the other school who is at fault. Or it is the Ivy system that is to blame. But in the age of Enron, Tyco, and Bill Clinton and George W. Bush III (a couple of Ivy Leaguers with degrees from Yale), it is no surprise that someone's word, or a verbal commitment, means nothing. ("I did not have sex with that woman." "We have evidence of a nuclear weapons program in Iraq.") What is disappointing in the case of Ivy League athletic recruiting is that there is a simple solution to the problem, one that would end much of the ugliness overnight. But the presidents of the Ivy League seem to act as if the problem did not exist, perhaps because they do not want to come fully clean on athletic admissions.

"We need to acknowledge that athletic admissions are different," says Jeff Orleans. "And that the way to be faithful to Ivy principles is not to insist that we treat athletes like nonathletes, but to find the right way to treat athletes. Because the ingrained principle is that you don't treat athletes differently. But we already are. And it's just hard to get the presidents to focus on."

Within the past ten years, the presidents have focused on at least one proposal that would have alleviated much of the trouble, when Fred Hargadon of Princeton offered the League a solution based on his experience at Stanford, where recruits sign an NCAA Letter of Intent when they accept an offer to attend the school.

"Somewhere in the middle of my fifteen years here," he says, "I went out on a limb and said I thought there ought to be a Letter of Intent in the Ivy League as well. But people in their minds connect Letter of Intent with athletic scholarship so closely that they just weren't able to disassociate it. They thought, 'Oh my god, if everybody finds out the Ivies have Letters of Intent it will be a disaster.' I think a Letter of Intent would make a lot of sense. The kid can collect offers, but on a given date, make up his or her mind in time for the coach to be able to recruit somebody else. It never flew."

Instead, what has flown is some bad behavior on both sides of the ball.

"When everybody started catching on to this game in the mid-'90s, coaches were getting burned by probably a dozen kids a year," says Pat O'Leary of the Likely Letter abuses, which have always been most prevalent in Ivy League football recruiting, where players make their official visits to schools on consecutive weekends during the month of January.

"Say I'm the head coach, and you're the recruit," O'Leary says, explaining how the problems emerge. "I'm going to say to you: 'How'd you like your visit?'

Oh, I had a great time, coach.

"Okay, what have you got going?"

Well, coming up next weekend, I've got a visit at Yale, and the next weekend I've got a visit at Princeton.

"Okay," says the coach. "You're a tight end. We're taking two tight ends this year. One is already committed to us. We have one slot left. The next two weekends, while you're at Yale and Princeton, we're bringing in other tight ends. If you want to wait those two weekends, that's fine. But if we get a tight end next weekend that commits to us, we're taking him. Just so you know, up front."

So the kid says, *Okay, fine.*

Then, O'Leary explains, the kid goes home and during that week, he calls the head coach and reports: *I've thought about what you said, and it has sunk in. I'm bagging my Yale and Princeton visits. I'm going to commit to you.*

"Great," says the head coach, who then contacts Admissions, where they pull the player's folder and say, "He's a good kid, great student, we like his essay, everything's fine. We'll take him." The admission office immediately mails the recruit a Likely Letter, which says the player is highly likely to be admitted in April, when the Ivy institution's official acceptances are mailed, provided he maintains his current good standing in the school and the community.

In the meantime, however, in some cases, "the kid is just telling us a big fat lie," says O'Leary. "Unless we assign a private detective to him, how do we know he's not going to visit either Yale or Princeton?" The kid makes his other visits, and in the process collects one or two more Likely Letters.

"Any [Ivy football] coach who is honest with you will tell you that it happens one or two times every year," says Yale head football coach Jack Siedlecki. Admittedly, that's better than a dozen times a year, as was the case ten years ago. But multiply those one or two players by eight schools, and you're looking at over a dozen cases annually of outright lying.

"Now the kid's got two Likely Letters," O'Leary says, "and there's nothing you can do about it. Once he's got a Likely Letter in his hand, you've told Admissions that he's a kid you want, and they're saying we're taking him. The whole premise of the Likely Letter is that we will hold you a spot."

That premise originally grew out of the fact that so many Ivy athletes are offered athletic scholarships to attend other schools. Thirty years ago, as I weighed a full soccer scholarship offer from UNH, the Dartmouth soccer coach had no way of providing me with an early read from his admission office. I had to make a "blind" decision, and in the process I wound up without the scholarship or the Ivy acceptance. Today, that would not happen. A recruit who is weighing a scholarship offer now has the right to ask for an early "read" from both the admission and the financial aid office at one Ivy institution of his or her choice. In return, he or she will receive a Likely Letter (or an Unlikely Letter, as I would have) from Admissions, along with a financial aid package estimate, so he or she can make an informed decision about whether or not to accept the athletic scholarship offer. To prevent recruits from cheating this system, their high school guidance counselor must fax or mail a written confirmation of the scholarship offer to the Ivy school's admission office, to confirm that the offer is indeed legitimate. This whole scenario is known within the League as a "squeeze play."

"A squeeze play is when a scholarship school is squeezing a kid for a decision," says Yale associate head football coach, Keith Clark, "not when we are squeezing a kid for a decision."

What happens when Ivy football coaches squeeze kids for decisions is that the Likely Letter can backfire, as the following story from Dartmouth football coach John Lyons illustrates.

"We had a kid from Pennsylvania this year who came in early in January [2003] and said, 'Coach, I really like it here,'" Lyons explains. "I said, 'Okay, now what do you want to do? We're only taking a couple guys at your position, and in your band we don't have many spots left, but if you want to take another visit, go ahead.' He said, 'Well, I'm going to cancel my visit to Brown.' I said, 'Are you sure you want to do this?' His father was sitting right there, and the kid says, 'Yep, this is it for me. I really like it here. I want to get this over with.' Boom—we send him a Likely Letter. He's committed. And then, for the next three weeks, we can't get a hold of the kid. He's dodging our phone calls. Well, it turns out he did go to Brown. He got in there. And he's going there. And he wouldn't even tell us that he'd made that decision. And it really just pisses me off that a parent can sit there with a kid and allow that to happen. There's just no integrity at all. I don't know what it is. But I wasn't playing a game. I told the kid, 'I didn't create this system. I think the system stinks. But this is what we've got to live with.' Now, I never tell a kid, 'Don't take your visits.' I tell them, 'If you take one or two more, I don't know where we're going be with spots. If guys are all relative in ability, I'm taking guys that tell me when they want to come here. And if we fill up, we fill up. Some years we're taking two guys at your spot; some years it's five. This year, here's how many we took early, here's how many spots we have left at the position and in the band. Now, you want in, you tell me. But if you don't, I'm not making any promises. You're in now. I don't know how long it's gonna be there for. But I'll call you up before we fill it up.'"

Lyons says the kid who wound up at Brown felt pressured to make a decision. "I said, 'Look, I didn't pressure you. I said you can go make your visits, but I don't know what's gonna happen if you do.'" Lyons pauses, thinking about the dilemma he and other Ivy coaches face under the current system. "I guess that's pressure, but that was the truth. The thing that bothered me is that the father sat right there, and they didn't even have the courtesy, or the guts, or whatever it is, to call and say, 'Coach, something happened.' If they had told us after he was here, maybe we could have filled that spot up with another kid at his position." As it turned out, Lyons had to scramble to find another player late in the official visit process, one that played a different position and was rated much lower in ability than the original recruit.

"It seems to me they've created a system that really puts a lot of pressure on kids," he laments, "and there's no integrity now in terms of the process."

Tim Murphy, the head football coach at Harvard, says it's very rare that a recruit will commit to his program, only to turn around and enroll at another Ivy. "That's because of the type of character of the kids we are recruiting. The level of character that we're dealing with—whether they're rich or poor, black or white, Mormon, Catholic, Hispanic—is very high, and I think I've had two who committed to us verbally turn us down," over the course of ten years.

That may be the case, but according to John Lyons, when it comes to pursuing football players of high character, "Harvard basically does whatever the hell they want. That's the bottom line."

Lyons has had recruits commit to him by applying Early Decision, only to see Harvard catch wind of it. "They haven't recruited you, but they've found out that you're coming to Dartmouth," he explains. "They find out you're a good player. They say, 'You got in Early Decision? Well, I'll tell you what. We really want you here, and all you've got to do is withdraw that early decision thing, and we'll take you here at Harvard.' Now what kind of bullshit is that?

"I said to our admission people, 'Is this legal?'" Lyons shakes his head. "It's not what it's meant to be about, but they can do that. Now, what is that? I mean, what are you teaching these kids?"

Murphy says, "It's not easy. We have a lot of kids who [opposing] coaches will say, 'Well, they committed to us.' And I'll say, 'Listen, the only way I recruit is I listen to what a kid tells me. If he tells me Harvard is his first choice, I'm not gonna give up recruiting him'—no matter what the coach said. Because in the end, this is still about the student-athlete. If Harvard's his first choice, then I'm not gonna give up on him just because some coach tells me, 'He's committed to going to our place.' I want to hear it from the kid. If the kid says it, then I'll stop recruiting him."

In January 2004, Murphy offered Ryan Darnell, a wide receiver from El Paso, Texas, a spot in the next Harvard football recruiting class after Darnell had made his official visit to Cambridge. The offer came over Darnell's family cell phone as he and his parents were sitting in the airport, preparing to fly home from Boston. Murphy had just looked at the player's videotape and was blown away by what he had seen: a 6-foot-3-inch speedster, the top sprinter in El Paso, with great hands and a solid build. The coach raved to the family about what he had seen and told Darnell, whose academics placed him in the high A.I. band, that he had a spot at Harvard.

"They weren't even recruiting him until we offered him a visit," says Pat O'Leary of Dartmouth, who learned all the details of the Harvard exchange from Darnell's mother. "They were looking at him in the fall and tried to get him to go Early Action, but the kid is such a good player he was waiting for an offer from UT [University of Texas] or A&M [Texas A&M]. I had been in touch with him since last May. Then I visited his home in December, and when we offered him a visit, Harvard came in late and offered him a visit when they heard we were interested."

O'Leary knew Harvard would pressure Darnell when he made his official visit and he had warned the family what to expect. "The family assured me, 'We'll handle the pressure. We'll deal with it,'" he recalls. "They said, 'You've been the school showing the most interest and we definitely plan to make the visit to Dartmouth after Harvard.' But then they got the phone call from the head coach saying he had just looked at the film *after* the kid had visited. I mean, that's backwards. Our head coach looks at the film two or three weeks *before* a kid comes to campus. That tells me how late they were coming in. Murphy must have spotted the kid walking around during his visit and noticed him. I mean, he's a great looking kid, really put together."

O'Leary shakes his head. "They were hot and cold with him. I'd seen the kid's tape from his junior year, which was even better."

Unaware that any offer had been made, but well aware that Harvard could put the squeeze on a recruit they really wanted, O'Leary called the Darnell home on Monday night at nine to confirm Ryan's flight and travel itinerary for his upcoming visit to Dartmouth. Ryan's mother said he was unavailable to come to the phone. "At nine on a Monday night?" O'Leary recalls thinking. "You're kiddin' me. Now I'm thinking the mother wants him to go to Harvard. But she says, 'He's going to make his visit to Dartmouth.' So I call the next night, Tuesday, to confirm the e-ticket schedule and everything, and again Ryan's not available. Now I know there's a problem. And then his mother tells me that Harvard called that day and told them, 'If he visits Dartmouth, we're pulling the spot.' And I said, 'Wait a minute. He's going to make the biggest decision of his life based on one official visit? After all we've been through? After you all said he wants to come up and we bought the ticket and made all the arrangements?'"

The next night, O'Leary called again, certain Ryan would be around. This time the player came to the phone and confirmed he was going to Harvard. And then his mother told O'Leary that two Harvard coaches were coming to their house the next day for breakfast.

"The kid had an 8:30 morning flight to come up here," O'Leary says, "and the Harvard coaches flew down to make sure he didn't get on it." And then they turned around and flew home to Cambridge in time to host another weekend of official visits.

So much for the "level of character" that Harvard's Tim Murphy likes to trumpet. Yet his is not the only Harvard program that manipulates the Ivy system.

In March 2003, the Dartmouth men's basketball program lost a player to Harvard after the player had committed to Dartmouth. The recruit shared his decision with the Harvard coach over the phone, and thanked him for his interest. But the next day, the player received a phone call at his high school. It was the head of Harvard Admissions, calling to inform the player that he had been accepted to Harvard and that everyone wanted to see him in Cambridge. The player's parents, explaining their son's decision to switch schools, told Dave Faucher, the Dartmouth coach, "We just have to do what's best for our son." So much for Dartmouth's early interest and for their son's verbal commitment to attend school in Hanover. So much for the parents' failure to encourage their son to honor his side of the bargain. As John Lyons says, "What are you teaching these kids?"

"It gets ugly," admits Dartmouth President James Wright, who is currently serving a two-year term as the chair of the Ivy Group Presidents. "But then you end up making them stick to it, and that gets potentially ugly, too."

Perhaps that would be true under a Letter of Intent policy, but one wonders how much worse it can get, and why the presidents haven't addressed the Ivy recruiting process in a more meaningful way. Part of the problem is that the Council of Ivy Group Presidents has a revolving door in its membership. After just five years as the president of Dartmouth, Wright became the third most senior member on a Council of eight; and when Penn's president, Judith Rodin, stepped down in 2004, he rose to second in seniority after just six years. With such a high turnover rate, the Council is almost always in flux, and it can be difficult to build a consensus based on shared knowledge and experience. Not all members will recall or understand the issues that drove a key decision or led to the establishment of an important policy. What's more, each president views athletics differently.

"It's a hard group to speak on behalf of," Wright says of his role as chair. "There are a lot of people there who have their own views on any of a number of issues."

The pressure stems from the precious nature of admission slots at schools that reject 90 percent of their applicants. "Coaches do have to be very careful," says Wright. "I think they've learned that they have to use their slots with real care." Over the last twenty-five years, he points out, there has been a huge increase in the number of athletic teams at Ivy schools, thanks to the growth of women's athletics, while at the same time there has been an increase in recruiting, even aggressive recruiting, in sports beyond what might be considered the traditional sports for recruiting in the Ivy League, such as football, basketball, hockey, soccer, and lacrosse.

"Twenty-five years ago, you may have had students playing lacrosse at Dartmouth who hadn't picked up a lacrosse stick until they came here," says Wright. "I can't imagine that being the case today any place within the Ivy League."

Indeed, walk-ons are almost unheard-of in the Ivy League today. On the contrary, virtually every golfer, swimmer, cross country runner, water polo player, volleyball player, wrestler, tennis player, sailor, baseball player, field hockey player, and other varsity athlete on the thirty-plus teams most Ivy schools field has been recruited and allotted a spot in the admission process.

"Since I got here fifteen years ago," Fred Hargadon told me in June 2003, "we've actually reduced pretty significantly the number of athletes we actually admit, but have done very well with the ones that come. There were a couple of differences before I got here. One, there weren't as many varsity sports. Two, we used to admit a huge number for football: a) expecting that not all of them would come, obviously; and b) that when they'd get here, they'd sort them out—who would really stick out, who was good. And that was so alien to me, having come from Stanford, where the athletic quality of the player was determined far *before* I'd see them. I just said, 'We cannot afford to keep admitting lots of kids and then sort them out when they're here. It would be better to find out if they're any good before.' And so the coaches have really done a lot of work ahead of time now. That really enabled us to not have to use so many places in the class for prospective athletes."

Hargadon's method of cutting the number of spots used by athletes has spread throughout the League. And with Ivy coaches under intense pressure from their admission offices to fill a specific number of allotted slots each year, seventeen- and eighteen-year-old kids wind up in a vice, being squeezed for a commitment. Mike Giles, a Dartmouth football player, told me about one Ivy head coach (he would not share the coach's name or school) who made him promise during one recruiting phone call that he would not apply to Dartmouth. Feeling cornered, Giles agreed, "knowing it didn't mean anything." He just wanted to calm the coach down.

"You're at home trying to do homework at night during the season," Giles told me, "but the schools are just calling all the time. Call waiting would keep coming up. At first it was real fun, then it started getting old. They were pressuring me too much, because a lot of coaches are really aggressive. Some of them would ask me for double commitments right there: 'Please promise me that you won't go to Dartmouth, or go to another school.' And I was like, 'Yeah, yeah, I guess.' But deep inside I knew I wasn't sure yet what I was gonna do."

Other coaches will ask players to withdraw their applications to rival schools, and wait until they receive a faxed letter of that withdrawal, before they will ask Admissions to mail the player a Likely Letter. Such a request is against league rules. It is also against league rules for a coach to promise a player a place in the next freshman class, even after the coach has received a promising read on the player from the admission office. Coaches walk a fine line on this matter, and must choose their words with care: "Things look very good," or "Everything looks very promising," or "Admissions likes what they see" are all perfectly legal statements. Abandoning these favorite Ivy euphemisms, however, and announcing that the player will be accepted is not.

"One of the worst cases," says Bruce Bailey of the Lakeside School, "was the time a coach promised a kid admission to an Ivy League school as a rower and then the kid didn't get in. I called the admission office and said, 'Hey, on this day, this student was promised admission by your coach.' And in this case the school ended up taking the kid. I'm sure the coach wasn't around very much longer, but it's the 'promises, promises' thing that I think Ivy League administrators and admission officers have to spend a lot of time with their coaches on—coaches who come in from different environments, where they don't have to be quite as careful, or they can make those kind of promises. Ivy League coaches do not sit on admission committees, and Ivy League admission committees are very fierce about that. In recent years, Ivy coaches have been much better."

"I think honesty and integrity go a long way in this process," says Jenny Graap, the Cornell women's lacrosse coach, "because there are so many situations where families are nervous, especially with the admission process. I'm sure they would love to hear a guarantee that their son or daughter is going to be admitted to a certain university. . . . I've been in a family's house having dinner with a prospect, and the father said to me, 'Listen, coach, we want our daughter to apply to a school where she's going to get admitted. We don't want her to put all her eggs in one Early Decision basket and then be denied. Why should we apply Early Decision at Cornell, when you're telling us you don't know if she's going to get in, when we have heard definitively from other Ivies that if she applies early there, she will be admitted?' And that's really awkward. It's a situation that I had to deal with, and the reality of that situation is that other Ivy League coaches, although they may have this high level of predictability, and they may actually have on fairly good authority that this prospect will be admitted early at their institution, it's against Ivy League rules for them to tell the family that. And that's written in the Ivy manual. A coach is not permitted to give an admission decision. So basically what I'm hearing from this family is that other coaches are in violation of our own code of ethics and our own rule book—where it clearly states the coach is not to convey an admission decision."

In the case described above, Graap told the parents exactly that. "That's how I won their trust, and ultimately their daughter came to Cornell. I said, 'Listen, I'm not here to say my counterparts are cheating, but I can just tell you what the rule book says, and I'm gonna tell you that's what I'm going to abide by. You can listen to what these others say, but what happens if the coach says she's gonna get in, and then she doesn't get in? How's that going to make you feel? The reality of the situation is, they're not allowed to tell you that. So, you choose what you want to believe.'"

"If I could wave a magic wand," says Pat O'Leary, "coaches wouldn't even be involved in the recruiting process. Because we're too much salesmen and in a lot of cases, coaches will make things up, too, to tell kids."

And the kids, finding themselves the objects of intense desire, courted by professional coaches who earn their living by convincing talented players to attend their schools, will sometimes tell coaches what they think the coaches want to hear (as Mike Giles did), or they will have a change of heart—a symptom that is hardly unique to the Ivy League.

Julie Shackford, the women's soccer coach at Princeton, has experienced some parents and players who play the recruiting game by saying one thing and doing another. "A lot of kids don't realize that most coaches talk and if they're trying to play one [coach] against the other, oftentimes we find out about that," she says. "But it bites you on the butt sometimes. It's disappointing to find out that you've recruited this kid and she applied early [decision] somewhere else. And then I feel badly for the coach because had I known that, I wouldn't have even been recruiting the kid.

"I actually think that sometimes kids do make a mistake and realize they've made a mistake," she continues, "and I think in the end, some of them don't play a game but really were just put under too much pressure. . . . It comes down to being honest and having some integrity. The Yale [women's soccer] coach [Rudy Meredith] is somebody that I admire so much as a coach and a person. I can remember a kid who wanted to go to his school—who had applied early [to Yale] and then decided that she wanted to be at Princeton. And he called me up and said, 'Julie, I want her to be where she's happy.' And I thought, 'Wow.' So I think honesty and doing what's best for the kids is probably really important, too."

"I saw a list in a magazine not too long ago where a dozen to fifteen big-time football players switched commitments the day before signing [Letters of Intent]," says O'Leary. These high-profile players had verbally committed to one scholarship school, only to sign with another at the last minute. "You know, the verbal commitment means nothing. It's not binding at all." Kids can walk away without recriminations. But a school that backs away from a verbal commitment to a player is vulnerable to a lawsuit.

"The thing is," says Dartmouth men's lightweight rowing coach, Dick Grossman, "I feel as coaches we have to be honest. We are never going to lie to a kid. We are never going to say to a kid, 'We will list you,' if we don't list him. If we say, 'We will submit your name to Admissions,' we will submit their name. If we say, 'We will submit you as part of our target group,' then we will submit them as part of our target group. If we say, 'You're our number one,' then they are number one, and they're not going to move from number one unless something devastating happens and they do something wrong. Even if we find someone who's better, if we committed to a kid and said, 'You're our number one,' then he stays our number one. We feel we have to maintain our integrity."

But, Grossman points out, the kid and his parents can get away with murder, as this horror story illustrates. "I had a number one kid, who would be a junior now, and not only did he call me every week, but it was a constant thing between Dartmouth and another institution. He would call me every week and say, 'This coach told me this, and what are you gonna do, and where do I stand?' It finally got to the point where we ended up getting an early read from Admissions. We told him right up front he'd be our number one candidate, and we got Admissions to contact him in February and give him a Likely Letter. It even got to the point where the associate director of admission called him to tell him that he was likely to get in as they sent the letter out. And then his father was on the phone with me once a week. And then he got in and they didn't like the financial aid award, and the father was on the phone every day, and there was this constant thing going back and forth where we're going to get him more money. And then he showed up the first day of school and said, 'Well, there are other things I want to do and I'm going to play rugby.'" Grossman shrugs, holding his hands out. "What can you do? This isn't Big 10 football. You can't get him blackballed and take away his scholarship. He's here, he's gotten the money, he wins."

When you are coaching a sport, as Grossman does, that gets anywhere from three to six recruits a year (unlike football, which gets thirty), losing one player a year in this fashion can be devastating. Grossman is not alone. Coaches throughout the League experience such immediate losses, much as they work to avoid them. Kathy Delaney-Smith, the highly successful women's basketball coach at Harvard, told me about one huge catch that gave off a wretched stink.

"A 7-foot player from India and her 7-foot-4-inch-inch dad came over. Stanford, Ohio, North Carolina, Virginia, and Harvard all got in a recruiting war. This kid played in India, not at a great level, but she was 7 feet tall. She was the tallest woman in the world. So we fought and fought and fought, and I won the recruiting battle." Delaney-Smith shakes her head. "And she never played one minute. She used me to get in. She would not have gotten in without me."

A percentage of other Ivy athletes who would not have gotten in without the coach will eventually quit the team for various reasons at some point during their college career. This attrition is reflected in Ivy football rosters, which rarely have more than ten or twelve seniors still playing, from an initial class of thirty-five (now thirty) recruits. In my view, the option to pursue other interests, free of financial aid consequences, is one of the healthy, positive aspects of the Ivy athletic structure. But it does present a challenge to coaches.

During the Ivy recruiting process, it is the lack of a common final signing date to keep kids honest that generates most of the problems. "I was in one house with the high school coach, the mom, the dad, the brother, the sister," recalls O'Leary, "when the kid says, 'I'm coming to Dartmouth.' I tell the head coach, 'This kid committed to me in front of his coach and his parents.' So we turn around and send him a Likely Letter. A week later, a Princeton coach comes in and says, 'By the way, we got you in.' And the kid says, 'See ya, Dartmouth.'"

It seems ironic that Likely Letter abuses in football recruiting have been exacerbated by Princeton, since it was Fred Hargadon who recommended the League adopt a Letter of Intent. But, as John Lyons explains, "Princeton has always been late, because their admission guy, for whatever reason, his final thing of control is, 'I'll tell them when I want to tell them.' So, the [Princeton] coaches would find out on some kids early, and then not know about a group of kids—but that group of kids was getting recruited by other people. And those kids would say, 'Yeah, we'll commit to you' because somebody's squeezing them. But then they go back and take Princeton at the end of January when they find out they're in."

This reflects the Ivy League pecking order, based on national prestige and name recognition. "And Princeton is right up there," says Lyons. "Obviously, Harvard is the toughest. We can hold our own against Yale."

But no school can hold its own against kids and families who manipulate the system by lying.

"Just tell me you don't want to come here," says Lyons. "Because when you give me your word, and we go out on a limb and give you a spot, you're screwing not only us but you're screwing all these other kids behind you."

"If the kid is going to commit to you," says Keith Clark of Yale, "I'd like to get his parents and his coach and his priest and his principal, have them say it out loud in front of everybody. Videotape them, and send it over the Internet to every school. That would be the ideal world. But it's part of the recruiting process. I'd say once a year you get something like that where it's really just a blatant, flat-out lie—from the kid and his parents.

"I always remember who they are," Clark adds, when these players show up across the line of scrimmage, on another Ivy team.

"I think the commitment game has gone about as far, and maybe farther, than it should go," says Karl Furstenberg, Dartmouth's dean of admission and financial aid. Yet, he feels the pressure on recruited athletes is only fair, given the favorable treatment they receive in the admission process. "The other side of this is they also get an advantage. They get an advantage in a highly selective process at one of the best institutions in the world. And if you live by the sword, you die by the sword. I don't think it's unreasonable, if they're going to jump ahead of twenty other people in line due to their athletic talent, that that comes with some strings. I have no problem with that."

Furstenberg says he understands there is a "pragmatic reason" for a Letter of Intent, but for a number of reasons, he is opposed to adopting one in the Ivy League. "I think it is exactly the wrong message for the Ivy League to send to all the high schools in America: that Larry Linebacker can hear from Dartmouth in a formal way that he's in before Valerie Valedictorian can. I see a real mismatch there in terms of the fundamental mission. And it's just one step further away from the scholar-athlete."

But Larry Linebacker, I point out, is *already* hearing in a formal way that he's in before Valerie Valedictorian, thanks to the Likely Letter.

"Maybe," he replies. "But shouldn't this group of schools be the one to maintain the higher standards and not be drawn in the other direction?"

Furstenberg's counterpart at Brown, Mike Goldberger, identifies the crux of the problem. "What the Ivy League is struggling with is what they say they do and what they do. The problem is that the Ivy League principles say that athletes should be treated like everyone else, but they are not. And that is what they are struggling with: 'This is what the principles say, here is what the practice is, and how to do we get them to match?'"

A Likely Letter is indeed a part of overall Ivy policy and sent to students other than recruited athletes who are prized by a certain department or by the school. "We could send it to hundreds of kids," Goldberger says. "You know, they will send it to top students, and students of color, and things like that." But the Likely Letter's primary use is for athletes, and other students only began to receive them once they were developed for athletic recruiting. This enables league officials to say that they don't have a separate policy just for athletes, which would be a big no-no.

In Goldberger's view, "A Letter of Intent could actually give athletes a little more power and say so. In other words, if you would offer it to kids and then by a certain date the kid had to say, 'This is the school that I want to go to.' As opposed to, 'If you commit to come, then I will support you and try to get you a Likely Letter.' That is the ugly part of it."

Goldberger believes Likely Letters can still work, but even he admits that the scenario he describes breaks down under the real pressures of Ivy recruiting, where coaches are pursuing many of the same kids and pressing them for a commitment, sometimes within days of each other.

"What I tell our coaches," Goldberger says, "is that we don't need that commitment from the kid. What we need is a commitment from the kid that within a couple of weeks if they are not going to take it, that they withdraw. So a Likely would go to a kid who is ready to make a decision, but it doesn't have to be a quid pro quo—a Likely if you are willing to commit. It is a Likely if you are willing to make a decision in a couple of weeks. I don't mind the kid having three choices. And he says, 'You know what? I really think Dartmouth is the right place for me.' If the kid would withdraw and say, 'I'm going to Dartmouth, I'm happy,' that opens up a spot for somebody else."

In the real world of Ivy recruiting, however, a football coach (or hockey, basketball, soccer, lacrosse, swimming, or any other kind of coach) cannot always afford to wait three weeks to hear from a player, and in the meantime drop from landing a top recruit to seeking one who is rated much lower as a player. As Lyons told the prospect from Pennsylvania, "I have the spot now. I don't know long it will be there."

"The coach wants to get the best team he can," Goldberger says, summing up the challenge. "And the kids want to make sure they get into a school and they are nervous about it." The coach pressures the kid for a commitment, and the kid gives his word, which he may not keep.

"Most of the students that we're dealing with," says Karl Furstenberg, "if they make a commitment, they'll honor it."

"The kids are not bad kids," says Jeff Orleans. "And the coaches are not bad people."

It must be the process, then, that is rotten and in need of reform.

"I guess it is time to revisit it again," Mike Goldberger says, echoing a sentiment expressed by Jeff Orleans, Fred Hargadon, and others around the League who endorse the idea of adopting a Letter of Intent.

"One of the things that I think people understand is that you can decouple the idea of a letter from the idea of receiving money to play," says Orleans. "What you can't decouple it from is some sense of what your aid will be [at our need-based schools]." The League has already addressed this need for a financial aid "pre-read" for Likely Letter recipients, thanks in large part to school websites that enable applicants and their families to get their own financial aid preliminary readings by filling out forms online. "The schools are now much more able to make some legitimate early financial aid estimates," says Orleans. "They've moved that part of the process up to the point where it can work with the letter system."

Shifting that early financial aid read from a Likely Letter to a Letter of Intent would be simple. The difficulty lies elsewhere: in the presidents' inability to focus on the process, which seems surprising, given the behavior the current system engenders; in the public relations challenge of going public with a Letter of Intent, in contrast to keeping the Likely Letter policy a quiet compact between coaches, admission officers, recruits, and their families; in the current antiathlete environment fostered by the books of William Bowen and his coauthors, James Shulman and Sarah Levin; and, last but not least, in the Early Action admission policies of Harvard and Yale.

"There's all this moralizing in the League these days around Early Decision and Early Action," explains Karl Furstenberg, addressing this final issue. "And what you hear from the Early Action schools—Harvard and Yale, primarily—is this holier than thou, 'We don't think any student should be forced to make a commitment prematurely. Everybody should have until May 1.' Baloney. It's total baloney in my view, because they march up and down the East Coast and across the country doing precisely the opposite of that. So how would Harvard and Yale square a Letter of

Intent with their Early Action philosophy, that no one should be committed to come and make that decision until May 1st? They get to have it both
ways. I think there's a fundamental inconsistency with the way they operate one part of their admission process with the way they operate another
part, and they think everybody else should fall in line. They use Early
Action in a huge way for athletic recruiting. And let's face it, Harvard has
the highest yield in the country. Early Action for them is tantamount to
Early Decision. So they can afford to cloak themselves in sanctity, knowing
that there are no implications for them competitively."

The question now is how much longer the League can afford to cloak
itself in sanctity, claiming to treat athletes just like everyone else when in
fact they do not. Perhaps it is time for the League to live up to its noble
principles, as Jeff Orleans suggests, and establish a system that fosters
integrity and promotes honesty among athletes, their families, coaches,
and admission officers. Instead of cultivating hypocrisy on the issue, and
operating a system that encourages ugly behavior, why not embrace transparency and have a policy that supports and enhances all that is right and
good about athletics in the Ivy League?

This may be easier said than done. There will always be some lying in
athletic recruiting, from both coaches and families. But the issue is not
going to vanish, not in our sports-crazed culture, where kids specialize
early and develop more impressive athletic skills and abilities every year.
The Ivy League is a Division I sports conference, with a commitment to
excellence, and the level of play across all sports in the League continues to
rise, often at astonishing rates. These are gifted kids. Other schools offer
them money to play. The Ivy League does not have to mirror scholarship
schools with a Letter of Intent. It can do better than that. It can, and should,
as Karl Furstenberg suggests, "Be the one to maintain the higher standards
and not be drawn in the other direction."

How? As a fan of the League who would like to see improvement on
this issue, I propose the presidents authorize use of a *Letter of Ivy Intent*. As
the name suggests, a Letter of Ivy Intent would reinforce all of the positives of Ivy League athletics and eliminate many of the negatives associated with Likely Letters. A Letter of Ivy Intent would put an end to the athletic scholarship overtones associated with a standard Letter of Intent,
since financial aid in the Ivy League is strictly need-based. By placing the

emphasis exactly where it should be—on the word *Ivy*—the inherent message of a Letter of Ivy Intent would be clear and forceful: athletes who signed it would be intent on pursuing an excellent education at one of the finest academic institutions in the world, while also playing their sport for passion, not for pay. What's more, the athletes who signed a Letter of Ivy Intent would be making a public, written commitment to attend one Ivy League school by a final deadline. This would allow players to make all their official visits before making a final decision, reduce the pressure on athletes to make verbal commitments to coaches in order to secure a spot in the next class, alleviate the amount of lying from players, parents, and coaches, and put an end to the tampering that occurs when some Ivy coaches do not honor or respect a player's verbal commitment to attend another school. In this way, the presidents could enhance their league's image and greatly reduce the damage arising from the current policy.

That would be a victory for everyone.

Chapter Ten

Under Fire

"The interesting thing to me about the Ivy League is if you're a good coach and you have a successful program, the people on the outside won't give you credit for being a good coach. They'll say, 'Oh, Admissions have given him every-thing.' Or, 'Financial Aid is helping him.' You're never given credit for being a decent coach. It's always, 'Everybody did this for you.'"

Dave Roach
Brown University
Director of Athletics

"I think we all try to fancy ourselves as great basketball minds. The fact is, the better the player the more knowledge-able the coach is."

Fran Dunphy
University of Pennsylvania
Head Men's Basketball Coach

Fran Dunphy is the most successful active men's basketball coach in the Ivy League. On the all-time Ivy career wins list, he ranks second, behind only the legendary Pete Carril of Princeton, who retired from the Tiger program in 1996 after thirty years with 514 victories. In fifteen years as the Penn head coach, ending with the 2003–04 season, Dunphy has led the Quakers to eight Ivy titles (including four of the last six league championships), to four perfect Ivy seasons (14-0), to seven NCAA tournament appearances (including four trips in the last six seasons), and to regular-season victories over such non-league foes as Temple, Villanova, Penn State, USC, Saint Joseph's, La Salle, Holy Cross, and other prominent basketball scholarship schools.

Yet to many outsiders, Dunphy is the beneficiary of coaching at a school with a proud history of having a winning basketball program, where Admissions gives him everything and financial aid makes it easy for recruits to say they'll come. Is this true? Is it fair? Is he a great coach, or is he simply in a great place?

The true and fair answer is that Dunphy is a great coach *and* he is in a great place. After fifteen years of success, people forget that his predecessor, Tom Schneider, didn't get it done in the very same spot. Penn was 51-54 over four years under Schneider, who recruited under the same admission policies and the same need-based financial aid parameters. Within three years of taking over the Penn program, Dunphy led the Quakers to a share of the Ivy title, and then his teams went on a three-year tear, playing forty-two consecutive Ivy League games without a loss. Dunphy can coach.

Perhaps more importantly, he can recruit.

These days, the two go hand-in-hand, as he is the first to admit.

"Penn's success over the years has had a lot to do with its history, its tradition, its location, its competition, and its facility," he says. "We're in not only the Ivy League, we're in one of the most unique settings in all of college basketball, where we have six Division I programs in the city [of Philadelphia], and we play every one of them."

The five other Division I basketball programs in Philadelphia that he is referring to are at Villanova, Temple, Saint Joseph's, La Salle, and Drexel. The first four, combined with Penn, make up what is known as the Philadelphia Big 5, which offers an annual regular season competition complete with standings, all-star selections, and a Big 5 Hall of Fame. Drexel, the other Philadelphia school on the Penn schedule, is located so close by that the Drexel players walked to their game with the Quakers in November 2003.

The game was played in Penn's home facility, the Palestra, which is yet another big factor in Penn's success. The stadium holds seven thousand fans, more than any basketball stadium in the Ivy League, and it is set in the middle of a major market with a storied NBA franchise. For a high school star with an Ivy academic profile and aspirations of playing at the next level, competing for four years in the Palestra is the ultimate Ivy basketball experience. Even though Drexel is not a Big 5 game (all of which sell out), the November contest with Penn still drew five thousand fans. Penn's other early season home game in 2003, against the University of Wisconsin, packed the stadium.

"Of our first six games, we play three Top 15 programs," Dunphy told me, reviewing his 2003–04 schedule. "And two of the other three are local teams here in Philly, Drexel and Villanova, and later on this year we're playing two other city games with Temple and La Salle. We're also going to Madison Square Garden to play against St. John's and Holy Cross in Manhattan. So I would hope that if indeed being challenged is what you want [as a recruit], both in the classroom and on the basketball court, we can provide that for you."

"Penn is very difficult to overcome," says Glen Miller, the head coach at Brown, who led the Bears to a 12-2 Ivy League record in 2002–03, his fourth year at the school. The second-place finish was Brown's best since 1968 and added an exclamation point to Miller's turnaround of what had been the League's weakest program. In 2003–04, Miller's team again finished second in the League and posted the program's first-ever, fourth consecutive winning season. "We're not getting the highly rated player yet. There's different ways you can rate kids. One scouting service rates a kid from a two to a five. You'll find a whole slew of kids rated a three. That's considered a low-major player. A four is a mid-to-high major player. The UConns of the world, they're all bringing in fives. I think every kid in Penn's recruiting process is either a 3-plus or a 4-minus. Their tradition, their success, they can get involved with that kid. So can Princeton. We'll have a tough time."

"You have to understand," says Armond Hill, the last Ivy League player to be selected as an NBA first-round draft choice (by the Atlanta Hawks in 1976 after leading Princeton to a 14-0 Ivy record), who was the head men's basketball coach at Columbia through the 2002–03 season, "if I'm a high school student I want to play at the dance—in the NCAA tournament. And my chance of going there is a lot greater playing at Penn or Princeton because they've been winning for the last forty years . . . so if I can go to the dance two out of my four years, well, that's a pretty high percentage. I think that is as much of a draw as the school and the academics and everything else. If I'm a basketball player, that's what I want to do."

At Penn, Dunphy prepares his team for a chance to attend the NCAA dance by playing a very challenging schedule. "I think notoriously, or historically, Princeton has done that as well," he says. "I think Yale is starting to do it. I think some others are doing it on a selective basis. For us, it's almost built in with the other five teams here in the city, the challenging part of that. So we're a little different than most."

"A little different" is putting it mildly when you compare all of the selling points at Penn with what Dartmouth has to offer a basketball prospect. It's hard to imagine a more dramatic contrast than the difference between the basketball passion of Philadelphia and the basketball boonies of Hanover, New Hampshire. It is a study in almost complete opposites. For Dunphy, being a great coach in a great spot has led to almost complete job security after fifteen years. For his counterpart at Dartmouth, Dave Faucher, recruiting against Penn, Princeton, Yale, Brown, and other Ivy schools (not to mention schools that offer basketball scholarships) led to almost complete job insecurity after twelve years. Despite winning more games than any Dartmouth hoop mentor in thirty-four years, Faucher was under fire after a string of four straight losing seasons. In June 2003, he nearly lost his job.

By mid-February 2004, facing the prospect of winning just one Ivy League game and finishing the year with eighteen straight losses, Faucher resigned before Dartmouth could fire him. He planned to finish his thirteenth season as the Big Green head coach, and his twentieth year with the program, and then step down.

The lack of equity in Ivy League men's basketball recruiting is illustrative of a league-wide issue that affects every sport at every school. Tradition, location, support from the school's administration, facilities, financial aid packages, the institution's mean A.I., the size of the student body, the curriculum—these factors all affect every program at every Ivy institution to one degree or another. Not every sport is created equal or treated equally on every campus. Finding a way to balance a weakness (the lack of a winning tradition, for instance) with a strength (an open curriculum or a lower mean A.I.) is crucial to a program's, and a coach's, success. In some cases, the school and coach understand they will never compete for an Ivy title. Brown and Dartmouth will probably never take an Ivy squash title from Harvard, Princeton, or Yale, who have winning traditions and lure the best of a limited pool of players who qualify on the court and in the classroom. The same is true of other sports around the League.

But in the "money" sports that generate revenue through ticket sales— football and men's and women's basketball and ice hockey—and in sports that have a higher priority at a given school (what one coach calls a "tiered system"), there is greater pressure to win despite the obstacles, and coaches lose their jobs for failing to overcome them. Some Ivy coaches are in far tougher situations than others, and they must find ways to win despite the odds against them.

At Dartmouth, the men's basketball program has not had a coach with a career winning record in more than fifty years. Gary Walters, now the Princeton athletic director and a former Tiger teammate of Bill Bradley, coached in Hanover for four years in the mid-to-late 1970s. He posted a 44-60 record with just one winning season. He was followed by Tim Cohane (30-74), Paul Cormier (87-95), and Faucher (136-208). Cormier succeeded in posting four straight winning seasons, then moved on to Fairfield University. A few years later, Faucher put together his own string of four consecutive winning seasons, including second-place Ivy finishes in 1994–95 and 1996–97. This pair of four-year winning streaks had been unequaled since the 1950s. Unlike Penn, which was ranked as high as third in the nation under coach Chuck Daly (yes, the same Chuck Daly who later coached the Detroit Pistons to back-to-back NBA titles) in the early '70s, Dartmouth's last sniff of national basketball glory on the men's side dates to 1942 and 1944, when the Big Green played in the NCAA championship game. Dartmouth's last NCAA tournament appearance came in 1958, their last Ivy hoop title in 1959. In contrast, since 1959 Penn has captured twenty-two men's Ivy basketball titles and made twenty NCAA tournament appearances.

Today, Dartmouth plays its home games in Leede Arena, which resembles a glorified high school gym. The cramped locker rooms feature metal lockers, not the wooden stalls found elsewhere in the League. There is no space for viewing game tape, a crucial aspect of an Ivy team's preparation for their next opponent—not in the locker room or anywhere else in the basketball facility. The wooden playing floor lies directly on top of a concrete slab, rather than on top of the wooden subflooring found in college facilities across the League and around the nation, that provides a cushion and protects players from injury. (In 2003–04, Faucher's team was devastated by ankle, knee, and hip injuries, which proved lethal for their record and his chance of survival.) A capacity crowd is three thousand, a number hit most recently when the Harlem Globetrotters came to town in 2001 and played against the Washington Generals. Usually, attendance for a Dartmouth men's basketball game hovers between 750 and 1500, depending on the opponent. Standing-room crowds filled Leede Arena for games against Penn and Princeton back in 1997, when Dartmouth was in the Ivy title hunt. Since then, big-time schools North Carolina and Virginia have come to Hanover for easy wins, drawing large crowds in the process. But there is no Hanover Big 5 (unless it's a fraternal order of pizza lovers), and Leede Arena is a far cry from the Palestra. Even the Penn cheerleaders, the male and female acrobats who perform breathtaking stunts are a far cry from Dartmouth's halftime female dance troupe. When they appear in Leede Arena each winter, flying through the air to the upbeat tempos of the Penn pep band, the Quaker cheerleaders leave local jaws ajar. It's hard to say which is more impressive: the slam dunks of Penn's two-time Ivy Player of the Year, Ugonna Onyekwe, or the death-defying summersaults of the Penn female cheerleaders as they twist and turn fifteen feet above the court, only to be caught by their beefy male partners within a foot of the hardwood floor. Both acts say, "Welcome to the big time, folks."

For Fran Dunphy, recruiting players to Penn is a breeze compared to the job faced by Faucher.

"The two obvious places that would be difficult to recruit to are Dartmouth and Cornell," Dunphy says, addressing the challenge of luring male basketball players to isolated, frigid Ivy campuses far from major urban centers. "Just because of their proximity. But that's just the way it is.

There's not much you can say about that. Ours might be one of the easier ones because of our proximity, our history and tradition, the Palestra, and the Big 5. You know, we have a lot of things in order, in place. . . ."

Cornell and Dartmouth also have proud traditions in men's ice hockey, reinforcing Fred Hargadon's theory, shared with a laugh, that success in hockey is relative to a school's proximity to Canada. In the case of Penn, this view holds true: the Quakers dropped their men's hockey program in the late '70s, after struggling to compete with their Ivy foes and growing weary of long bus trips north, where all their competition was based. Today, the Penn athletic director is a former basketball star, Steve Bilsky, the point guard for the 1970 and 1971 Quaker teams that went 53-3, lost just one regular season game, were ranked third in the nation, and made it to the Eastern Regional finals of the NCAA tournament. Success in basketball matters to Bilsky, just as it matters to Gary Walters at Princeton, where as a Tiger player his team was also ranked as high as third in the nation, and made a trip to the NCAA Final Four.

At Dartmouth, the school's skiing program is the emperor, ranked among the nation's best teams each year, with a proud history of producing Olympians and national champions, including the last three straight NCAA men's slalom champions. The Big Green skiing program maintains a relationship with the athletic department for NCAA compliance purposes, but its premier status on campus is reflected in its separate offices, budget, and fundraising activities, all of which function outside the athletic department, under the aegis of the Dartmouth Outdoor Programs office, which in turn is overseen by the Office of Student Life. Perhaps most significantly, the program's admission liaison is Dean of Admission Karl Furstenberg, an avid Nordic skier. Just beneath the emperor is the king, the Big Green men's hockey team, and the queen, the women's hockey program, which is ranked among the nation's very best teams each year. (Furstenberg played club hockey at Wesleyan before the school had a varsity program.) The winter princess is women's basketball, a program that has enjoyed great success over the years.

If you're a hotshot female basketball player who is interested in playing in the Ivy League, you look first at Dartmouth and Harvard, just as the top male basketball players look first at Penn and Princeton. Those are the two schools with a winning women's basketball tradition and a commitment to their programs (although in recent years Penn and Princeton have also bolstered their women's basketball programs, with Penn capturing the Ivy title in 2003–04). At Harvard, the coaches promote their tradition and the Harvard name. At Dartmouth, the school's rural location (which works against the men) works in favor of the women: here is a top school in a safe place where parents can send their daughters with peace of mind. Within a few years of launching its women's basketball program in the late 1970s, Dartmouth enjoyed success under head coach Chris Wielgus, who has subsequently built an impressive 245-177 career record over eighteen seasons and two tenures at the school. As many coaches in the League told me, such success breeds success.

. "The success of our women's basketball program over the years means we can attract a nationally ranked, high-profile player," says Karl Furstenberg. "Our men's team is not going to attract the same caliber of player." One of these highly rated women was recently admitted with a few Cs on her transcript, a break that a men's basketball recruit would never enjoy. In 1999, Craig Austin, a Big Green basketball recruit with good grades and an A.I. well above the League floor was turned down by Dartmouth Admissions in the Early Decision process, only to wind up at Columbia where he became the Ivy League Player of the Year. Had Austin been admitted to Dartmouth, other Ivy coaches acknowledge that Faucher's record over four years would have been much improved. The Big Green coach might never have felt forced to resign.

This disparity in the academic credentials of recruits who are admitted to play different sports is not unique to Dartmouth or to basketball. Admission exceptions for different sports are a fact of athletic life around the League, in various programs at various schools. Some sports are simply a higher priority than others, favored by school tradition, the admission dean, or the athletic director. For coaches, such academic exceptions beg the question: what comes first, the players or the success? The wins or the commitment to winning? When jobs are on the line, these are more than simply rhetorical questions. They cut to the core of people's livelihoods.

"Both of those places are great schools," said Fran Dunphy of Dartmouth and Cornell, "and they have two hard-working, good guys that are at the helm of the basketball programs. But it's not easy. Those guys, they work hard at it. And there's given years where Coach Faucher's had a terrific basketball program. And how much of that is a commitment by the university, I don't know. But I do know that's a quality guy, a talented guy, who works real hard at what he does."

Indeed, Faucher succeeded in convincing a number of talented individuals to come play basketball at Dartmouth. Over thirteen seasons, ten of his recruits scored one thousand points or more, the latest being forward Charles Harris ('03), who is now playing professionally in Germany. Forward Ian McGinnis ('01), who led the nation in rebounding as a sophomore, became the first Ivy player since Bill Bradley to reach one thousand rebounds in his career. And Flinder Boyd ('02), a devastatingly quick point guard, became only the fourth Ivy League player, and the first Big Green player, to amass one thousand assists and 150 steals in a career. In the mid-to-late '90s, Faucher's teams finished as high as second in the League twice, and third on three occasions. In one of those seasons, they held the nation's longest winning streak at ten games. Even Penn got stung by Dartmouth during this period, when the Big Green ended another Quaker unbeaten Ivy streak at thirty-four games.

But entering the new millennium, things began to slide in Hanover. Ivy victories became harder and harder to come by for Faucher's teams, as schools other than Penn and Princeton made a commitment to their men's basketball programs. Yale, rarely a threat, emerged as a contender after firing their coach in 1999 and hiring James Jones to take over an ailing Bulldog program. Jones had served as a Yale assistant for two years under Dick Kuchen, and then spent two years as an assistant at Ohio University before returning to New Haven as the new head coach.

"I had an idea of what needed to happen for this program to be successful," Jones says. "And you know the main thing you gotta do is change the mindset. You gotta make people *believe* that you can win. Obviously, you gotta believe to achieve. And you know we were very aggressive recruiting-wise and we have been since. You can coach 'til you're blue in the face, but you've gotta have some kids with some talent that can obviously play a little bit for you to be successful. And we were able to come in and do that here our first year."

By his third year, Jones had led Yale to a share of the Ivy League title with Penn and Princeton. By his fifth year, his team led eventual national champion UConn at halftime before losing by ten points. Soon after, the

Elis beat Clemson and Penn State. Jones credits Yale Athletic Director Tom Beckett with playing a crucial role in helping to turn the program around.

"Tom's been here now for almost ten years, I think," says Jones, "and he was the catalyst for getting financial aid and Admissions on the same page with athletics and trying to help bridge the gap, anyway, to try to help the athletic programs. He's unbelievable. And that's the one thing that you look at when you go to work for somebody: who that person is. And you know, when I got the job the first thing I asked him was, 'How long are you gonna stick around?'

Jones says Beckett assured him that he would be around for quite some time. Feeling well supported, the new coach began his mission. "When I was an assistant here, we never got anybody that Penn and Princeton were recruiting," he says. "We never got any of the top guys. They always looked at the school because of what Yale has academically, but because of where the basketball program was, we never got any of those kids. We feel that we're getting some of those kids now. We've certainly gotten kids that both of those programs have looked at. Penn and Princeton both recruited Casey Hughes [a Yale player] last year. They recruited Sam Kaplan [another Yale player] last year as well. And we've lost our share. We were recruiting the Schafer boy [Max Schafer, who started at guard for Princeton as a freshman in 2003–04]. I mean, that was all done. He was ready to commit to us and then some other people started negatively recruiting against us, telling the kid that I was going to be leaving, that I wouldn't be around."

Jones says a coach outside the League at a scholarship school told Schafer that Jones would be leaving to take another, higher-profile job. "But sometimes that stuff goes on inside the League as well," he adds. "Most of the kids that you recruit are intelligent enough to see through that stuff. I talk to kids when I go out recruiting. I say, 'Listen, you're gonna hear a lot things about Coach Jones.' When I first got here, it was, 'Well, you don't want to go to Yale because he's a young guy and he doesn't know what he's gonna do over there.' Then the second year, it was, 'Well, they're rebuilding, you don't really want to go there.' Then after the third year we won a championship, and it was, 'Well, you don't want to go to Yale because Coach Jones is leaving.' There's always gonna be something. So you tell kids that you recruit, 'Listen, you have to listen for yourself and do what you think is right. You gotta listen to what comes out of the horse's mouth and do you believe me or don't you believe me?'"

"We don't deal with any of the paying guys off or the financial stuff like that," says Jones of the sort of recruiting games played by some scholarship schools. "I think the [Ivy League] recruiting for the most part is clean other than verbal abuses that may occur."

At Brown, where the coach was also fired in 1999, Glen Miller breathed new life into what had historically been one of the League's worst basketball programs, and in just his fourth year, he led the Bears to a 12-2 Ivy record and a post-season appearance in the NIT. Miller's success sheds some fascinating light on the recruiting and admission disparities within the Ivy League, and magnifies the challenge faced by a coach like Dave Faucher, who had no hope of luring a player from Penn, and, as we shall see shortly, could not touch some of the players admitted by Brown.

Glen Miller arrived in Providence after six years as the head coach at Connecticut College in the NESCAC, where he took over a program that was 4-22. Within six years he led the team to an undefeated regular season, the Division III Final Four, and a final record of 28-1. The stunning turnaround caught the attention of Brown Athletic Director Dave Roach, who was also impressed by Miller's previous experience: seven years as a UConn assistant, serving as Jim Calhoun's primary Xs and Os guy during the establishment of the Huskies as a national power; and a successful playing career under Calhoun at Northeastern, where one of his teammates was Reggie Lewis.

"He had head coaching experience," says Roach. "He knew Xs and Os. And he'd built a program." He also had a plan, a blueprint to employ, based on his experience at Connecticut College. "I saw Brown as the same type of opportunity as Connecticut College," Miller says, "with a lot of similarities within the League. Within NESCAC, Connecticut College was a terrific school, but not rated as highly as Williams, Amherst, Wesleyan. It was kind of a poor sister of the League in some ways, and I saw a lot of parallels here, and thought that I could use the same recruiting strategies here as I did there to improve the program. Saying that, no one ever explained the Academic Index to me before I took the job. I had no idea. I got in here and a couple weeks into the job, they said, 'Oh, we have this Academic Index.' From that standpoint, I didn't know what I was getting into."

"They probably don't mention a whole lot of the negatives," he says with a laugh. "The Academic Index is just hush-hush, it's something that's not talked about a lot, we're not supposed to talk about it for whatever reason, and it's something that a whole lot of people don't know about."

The A.I. may have come as surprise to Miller, but it didn't alter his ultimate strategy. "Maybe they could find a coach that could get the 220s [A.I.s] and 230s who are great basketball players—go head-to-head with Princeton, and beat out Princeton for that 220 or 230. I'm not that coach. And this program hasn't won here in ninety-something years. I think all too many years, they were probably just trying to get that kid. What happens is they'd end up getting Princeton's third and fourth choice at that position, so we'd finish at the bottom of the League every year. So I did the same thing as I did at Connecticut College. We didn't have an Academic Index there, but if I was to go head-to-head with Williams College for ten players, 99.9 percent of the time I'm losing nine out of ten, so we're not going to beat 'em. I didn't fathom we could *ever* become as good as Williams College without their players. But we found a way, and that was with low-income kids. And these low-income kids weren't horrible students, but some of them got in, and then they did well academically. If they flunked out, well, there goes your strategy right out the window. Because ultimately if the admission office is going to take a chance on a kid, that kid has to come through and perform and make you look good and be a good citizen at that college or university, and then maybe you get the next kid. So you get the low-income kid. At the same time, you go head-to-head with Williams, but you don't for the higher-income kids, the high SAT kids. If you lose that kid, you have the other kid who would be just as good, if not better, as a basketball player."

"I have to be able to get in some of these kids to be able to compete," he explains, summarizing his situation at Brown. "I don't know why they haven't won here because our diversity is terrific, the city of Providence has improved dramatically in the last ten years, and our curriculum is a strong point. People like the Yales and the Harvards and Princetons will use that against us because it's so different. But the fact is that you can come in and there's no core requirements outside your major or your concentration. You can get into your area of interest right away. If you're taking courses where you have a high interest, you're going to be motivated, and your chances of success are so much better, I think. The grading system where you can take most any course for a letter grade or on a pass/fail basis—there's a lot of strong points that probably allow a kid who may not have the best preparation to survive initially, and then to go beyond surviving and start to flourish. I think it's a great place for that. We need to recruit toward those strengths, which we're doing."

For Dave Faucher, the difference in the Brown curriculum is the difference between kids who can succeed at Brown and kids who might fail at Dartmouth. "When Brown comes to play us, a lot of the players that are playing significant minutes couldn't get in at other Ivy League schools," he told me the summer before he resigned, confirming the effectiveness of Miller's strategy. "My gut feel is, if I had the players that they have as students at Dartmouth there would be a chance for a significant percentage of them not making it at Dartmouth—because we have a difficult core curriculum. We have requirements in our liberal arts. They're a liberal arts school without a core. You're allowed to selectively choose your courses as you go through, not having to fulfill a distributive requirement. And that is a *huge* difference. Because it's one thing about giving kids an opportunity, but you don't want to put kids in a position where they can't do it. . . . It's a little more difficult with a core curriculum."

Miller agrees that he is in the right place, but he also makes a point that he is not alone in taking kids on the low end of the A.I. "I think that if Yale or Princeton say they don't take kids near the bottom of the Academic Index they're absolutely full of it, because they do. Cornell has a lot of different areas where they can hide those kids, protect those kids in different colleges. We're not going to get a kid in as easily as the Patriot League, I can tell you that. We're not going to get a kid with 900 SATs. I'd say the lowest SAT that you can have, and have a chance to meet the minimum on the Academic Index, is probably 1020, and that's really stretching it."

Says Faucher of his staff's initial screening, "We wouldn't look at anybody under a 1000 SAT score." And between such a junior year score and the player's final application, that total would have to rise by at least seventy points.

"Penn will take more kids toward the minimum," says Miller. Harry Sheehy, the athletic director at Williams, who was a top Division III basketball coach for many years and knows Penn's reputation in the recruiting world, agrees. "Penn's going to do some things in basketball that I'd guess they're not doing in soccer. If I had a few bucks in my wallet, I'd bet on that.

Says Miller, "Princeton took a kid we were looking at. He had a 154 A.I. going into his senior year. He must have really boosted his test scores to have reached the 169 he needed to get in.

"Harvard bends the least or gives the least," he adds. "Yale is making a big-time commitment in football and basketball. Are the Yale coaches working hard? Absolutely. But at the same time Yale is saying, 'We'll take some kids down at the bottom.' They're good kids, with good recommendations and all that."

The truth is, no Ivy school is holier than thou. Harvard and Princeton both had men's basketball players who were academically ineligible during the 2002–03 season. A few years earlier, Dartmouth lost a key player for a season because of academic problems. (He later returned to school, re-joined the team, and earned his degree.)

"It doesn't matter what type of a kid I get in here, a 238 or a 171, they've got to be successful," says Miller. "Otherwise, that goes on my track record, and it's going to hurt me down the road if they fail. We're held accountable for successes and failures."

His formula for success is not without its challenges. "A lot of low-income kids, the people surrounding them, all they can think about is big-time basketball and scholarships," he explains. "You have to not only find the low-income kid who's motivated in the classroom and has done well in the classroom, but you have to find that kid who is surrounded by people that understand this is an unbelievable opportunity—to get out of this environment and change his life."

Alai Nuualiitia (pronounced Ah-LAH-hee) had a high school coach who understood the opportunity. Greg Downer of Lower Merion High School in Philadelphia opened up a whole new perspective for his star player.

"I was looking at basketball as a way to get to college," says Alai, who graduated from Brown in 2003 after a brilliant career as a 6-foot-7-inch, 230-pound power forward. "But my grades were pretty good, so my high school coach said, 'You can go to an Ivy school, and you could probably take care of your family forever.' I hadn't thought about it that way. I said, 'Okay,' and that became my goal."

The seventeen-year-old senior was already taking care of his family, although few people other than Downer were aware of his plight. Late that fall, on Halloween night, Alai had returned home from his girlfriend's house, where he had been helping her hand out candy, and found his father was gone.

"He took almost everything," he says, "All his stuff, a lot of our stuff. Took off. He abandoned everybody."

Everybody included his second wife and their two young children, plus Alai and his younger brother, Aleni, who was sixteen at the time. An older brother, Amante, didn't live with the others, but came and went as he pleased. "She didn't work," Alai says of his father's wife, who sought refuge with other family members. "He was the one who worked and provided everything, so I'm thinking, 'What am I going to do now?'"

The family had been living above a Methodist church in an unoccupied parsonage. When they told the church that Alai's father had left and they were all by themselves, with no idea what to do, the church's reply was that they had to be out by the end of the week.

Stunned, Alai couldn't believe what the church proposed next. "They talked about taking my younger brother from me, sending him to an orphanage." He shakes his head. "I'm like, 'All right, we'll just leave now.'"

With nowhere else to go, they moved back to their mother's house, where their father's first wife lived in an impoverished neighborhood. "But she's not really there," he says, "so there's nothing really there. We were pretty much going from being left with nothing to going back to nothing."

His mother was incapable of caring for herself, let alone her children. In and out of mental hospitals for years, she suffers from bi-polar disorder. "The doctor's treatment is just to sedate her," says Alai. "I don't know if I'd rather see my mother talking to herself, or doing nothing, just drooling, because the drugs are so strong. I don't think people understand what it's like when you have to sit there and watch it, and you can't do anything about it."

His mother had first become ill years earlier, when Alai's father had left her and their three boys, and vanished for the first time. Alai was eight when his father abandoned them for four years, and he watched as his mother, who was an orphan, broke down under the stress of being the lone parent.

"She was sick all the time," he says of this bleak period. Alai attended a middle school in his poor neighborhood, where he was the only white kid.

When his father reappeared, he moved the boys out of their mother's home, and placed them in school in Lower Merion, a better school district that began just over the county line near her home.

"It was a Jewish-dominated high school," Alai says of Lower Merion. "One extreme to the next, I guess."

He absorbed the culture shock by getting involved in organized sports for the first time in his life, figuring it was a great way to make new friends in a new school. He played football and basketball, and made the varsity hoop team as a sophomore, where he spent most of his time on the bench watching a senior named Kobe Bryant lead Lower Merion to a state title.

"I watched him and learned a lot from him," says Alai, "but I didn't play much."

The next year, as a junior, he was the sixth man, getting more time, more points, and more rebounds. His father told him that the only way he was ever going to college was if he got a basketball scholarship. That was his ticket. His father had never been to college. He rode Alai, telling him he needed to play and work and improve.

And then his father's mother died back home in Samoa, and his father began talking about moving the family back to his native land. "He wanted to go back," says Alai. "I said I wanted to stay in school here. We got into a big fight. There was a lot of tension. We began fighting all the time."

When his father pulled the cruelest trick of all the following Halloween, "All of a sudden, I didn't know what to do," Alai says. "It took me a little while to figure out things. But then I thought, 'I can sit around and mope, or I can try to do something.'"

The first thing he needed to do was line up work. He and his brother got jobs at a friend's shop in a food marketplace in Philadelphia. The shop sold fresh and roasted chicken and other foods. Alai went to work after practice and on weekends. His brother, who was not as gifted or as driven an athlete, went to work directly after school. "Thank god we worked at a food place," Alai says. "They would help us out now and then and give us food. We made money there, too. It's not like I hadn't worked before. I've been working forever. But to support yourself, it's a little bit different."

After buying food and paying for utilities, the brothers didn't have a lot left over for clothes and other staples. "My brother and I used to share clothes all the time. Everything was shared. There was nothing that was yours, which was fine. It's like basketball 'cause you're a big family."

Basketball became his focus, his means to an end more than ever before. He committed himself to doing as well as he could in school, and to being the best possible player on the court. Somehow he found the strength, in the midst of what he calls "the worst year of my life," to overcome the adversity in his personal life and average twenty points and ten rebounds a game as a senior.

"I think basketball helped me a lot," he says. "Always trying to be the best. I just put it into my head that I was going to college, and not just any college, an Ivy League college, and I was going to play basketball."

"My coach told me how great the Ivy League was, and then I talked to my guidance counselor about it and she told me, 'You'll never go to an Ivy school.' My grades weren't as good as the other students they had who were thinking about Ivy schools."

But that didn't deter Alai, who was now in the sights of Fran Dunphy at Penn, whose history of recruiting talent in his backyard is well known in Philadelphia. The Quaker coach had heard about the season Alai was having from his good friend Greg Downer, and he loved all of Alai's numbers—with the exception of his SAT scores. He recommended that Alai attend prep school for a postgraduate year, boost his board scores, and then apply to Penn.

But the prep school Downer found, Northfield Mount Hermon, in rural Northfield, Massachusetts, felt like it was in the middle of nowhere to Alai when the city boy went for a visit. His immediate reaction was that he didn't want to go there. He didn't want to leave Aleni or Amante, who had moved in with his brothers, or his mother behind.

"It's probably one of the hardest decisions I've had to make, to leave my family behind. But what was I going to do? Stay home and be stuck in a trap? Or do something and get out?"

His first week at Northfield Mount Hermon, he didn't want to leave his room. He had never been alone away from home before and stayed in his bed the whole time. His roommate, another postgrad, was from an entirely different world. Alai had shown up with two duffel bags, on a full scholarship through the Transitional Year Program for disadvantaged urban kids. Cassidy Freidman had arrived fully equipped with a computer, a stereo, plenty of stuff, and plenty of clothes.

"It was one of the best things that ever happened to me," says Alai. "He was a surfer from California who played soccer, and I was a basketball player from Philadelphia who listened to rap and punk. He opened up my eyes to a lot of different things. He opened up this whole other world."

The roommates became good friends. Cassidy showed him how to use the computer and shared his worldly possessions. Alai slowly emerged from his shell, and by the time basketball season arrived, he had made other friends as well. Even so, he never fully adapted to the constraints of prep school life, which felt unnaturally restrictive after he had been responsible for everything back home in Philadelphia. "I can't say I really liked it there," he says, "but I think it really taught me a lot."

Beyond teaching him good study skills through mandatory evening study hours, and preparing him for an Ivy education with rigorous courses, the school also taught him the value of having a backup plan. In his meetings with the director of the Transitional Year Program, Ms. Shoemaker, Alai repeated one refrain: "I want to go to Penn. Penn. Penn. Penn. Penn. Because that's all I wanted to do. I just wanted to go back home, go to a good school, and play basketball."

Shoemaker said, "No, we have to throw out a big net and see what we get."

It was good advice. Because when Alai hadn't heard from Dunphy in months, he called the Quaker coach to check in—and got bad news. Dunphy had found two other players at Alai's position, and he rated them more highly. "He was nice about it," says Alai of the bad news. "And he offered to make some calls to other coaches for me. I said I'd appreciate it. But I was really disappointed."

He wasn't going home to play at Penn after all. And, for a while, it didn't appear he was going to play anywhere in the Ivy League. The whole idea seemed cursed. He applied to Yale, where the coach wanted him, but after another losing season, the coach was fired. He applied to Columbia, where he was eventually accepted without any support from

Armond Hill, who was trying to balance his team's A.I. and could not fit Alai onto his list as a result. Alai recalls being told by Hill that he could walk on. Hill says he was impressed with Alai's ability, wanted to recruit him, and felt frustrated that his team's A.I. average had no room for the promising forward. Either way, Alai says, "I thought he was making a big mistake." Indeed, Hill wound up with the League's worst record during Alai's college career and was fired in the spring of 2003. Alai also applied to Dartmouth, where he was not recruited, and to Brown, which did not recruit him, either. The Bears' lack of interest was surprising, given the fact that Alai's coach at Northfield was a former Brown football player who encouraged him to apply to Brown. But the basketball coaches did not pursue him. Marquette did, but then that coach was fired as well. When he promptly landed another job down at LaMar in Texas, he called and tried to interest Alai in coming south on a full scholarship.

"I was real big into academics at that time," says Alai, who thanked the coach for his interest and then declined his offer. "I felt I had to go to a really good school to help out my family. So I wanted to go to an Ivy League school."

The trouble was, no Ivy League school wanted him to come play basketball. A few NESCAC schools expressed an interest. More than one coach had told him during the previous year, "I don't see you as a Division I player, but you can probably play Division III."

"But I wouldn't take it," he says. "I said, 'No thanks.' I didn't pick up the game that early, and I thought I could get better."

Bucknell, a D-I school in the Patriot League, was interested. He went down to the Pennsylvania school on an official visit. "It was an awful trip," he says. "I hated it there. But it was my only choice. I was going to call up the coach and say, 'I guess I'll come to your school.' I had no other choice.'"

But first he went home for spring break, postponing a call he didn't want to make. When he returned to Northfield Mount Hermon in the middle of April, he found a voicemail on his phone. It was from Glen Miller, the new Brown basketball coach, who had just been hired to take over the League's worst program. He wondered if Alai was still available, and if he wanted to make an official visit to Brown. Colgate was also interested in having him make a visit, following his strong showing in the prep league tournament just prior to the spring break. He called both coaches and arranged back-to-back official visits—the first weekend at Brown, the next weekend at Colgate.

The odd thing was, he had already been turned down by Brown.

"When I came on my visit," he recalls, "I sat with the A.D. and the assistant coach and I said, 'What happened before?' And they said, 'You didn't get any help from the coaches, so you didn't get in here. So we just had to get you some help from the coach.' And he got me in.'"

"I remember when we read Alai's file, we thought he was terrific," says Mike Goldberger, the Brown director of admission. "I mean, a great kid, and the type of kid that we would really want to have here. But we were looking at him as a regular applicant and then as a basketball player. We could look at it and say, 'He's a great kid and it would be nice to have him here.' But that is true with probably about 75 percent of the kids that apply. To move him into, saying, 'The basketball coach would like to see him as one of his recruits,' and to add that to the, 'Wow, he's a great kid and we would love to have him here,' it became pretty easy."

The year at prep school had finally paid off with an Ivy League admittance *and* a coach who wanted him on the team. His boards had risen from 1030 to 1150, and so had his stock as a basketball player.

Says Miller, "We were recruiting kids from Northfield Mount Hermon for Connecticut College, and I knew Alai was a level above the NESCAC. I had a chance to see him play a few times that year and knew he was a good player. He visited here, and we revived his application, and he got accepted. I was delighted. He was my first recruit."

Miller's evaluation of Alai's potential as a college player contradicted the view of many of his Ivy coaching peers. But spotting promise where others see limitations is a key to success when you're lower in the League pecking order.

For a good basketball player, says Miller, "If I'm going to the Ivy League, I'm going to Penn or Princeton. I'm going to go to the NCAA tournament every year. I'm not going to consider anybody else. It's either Penn or Princeton—or I'm taking the scholarship. Brown, Yale, we've moved up. We're competing. Are we there yet? We still have a ways to go, but we're knocking on the door. Hopefully, in time, that perception will change. We'll start to build a tradition, where if a kid starts to think about the Ivy League over a scholarship, and he's that good a player and a student, he'll start looking at us in the same way as he's looking at Penn and Princeton. In the meantime, we get back to having to make great evaluations on kids that aren't rated that high."

Alai was not rated as high as other players on Fran Dunphy's list. And neither was Earl Hunt, the other player who turned out to play a huge role in Brown's turnaround under Miller.

"Earl Hunt was not rated high at all," says the Brown coach. "Matter of fact, Penn recruited him a little bit. I want to say he was their second or third choice at his position. Earl decided, 'Well, at Brown I can start right away and maybe be part of the building process—be an impact player.' I didn't recruit Earl. All I had to do was get on the phone and convince him that things were still going to be good for him with me here, because another coach recruited him and then got let go. So it was just a matter of me convincing him to stay with his commitment."

As seniors, both Hunt and Alai were named first team All-Ivy, recognized for their role in taking Brown from Ivy pretender to Ivy contender. Hunt finished his career as Brown's all-time leading scorer, with 2,041 points, while Alai wound up as the third-leading scorer in Bruins history, with 1,344.

"We have to make those evaluations," says Miller. "Those kids have to come in and we have to develop them and they have to be motivated and they have to turn out to be *better than their rating right now* for us to be able to win the League. And hopefully through some of the success that we've had in the past few years, they start to look at us in a different light."

In many ways, Miller's very first recruit at Brown turned out to be his best. "He's as low income as you can get. He probably came here, his first year I want to say he had a $1,000 loan, that was it. No parental contribution, no student contribution, no expectation for summer job. Well, there was expectation for a summer job, but Alai's a kid that has supported his family and their bills at home through his income. So the people at Northfield Mount Hermon wrote a letter stating what he did with his income and Brown waived his summer earning contribution."

Remarkably, neither Goldberger nor Miller knew all the details of Alai's story until the player's senior year at Brown. Nor did the majority of his teammates, and none of his classmates. They knew Alai held jobs on campus, in addition to majoring in biology, completing a pre-med program, and starring on the basketball team. They knew his parents never came to any games, but they didn't know why. They knew he was one of two key players behind the resurgence of the Brown basketball program, but they didn't fathom the depth of the opportunity that competing and studying at Brown meant to him. They didn't know he sent money home from campus each month to help support his family. He didn't want them to know.

"For the longest time, I didn't want anybody to know what happened," he says. "Because then I'd be different. I didn't want to be different. I just wanted to be like everyone else. I put on this front—everything was fine. I was embarrassed."

His girlfriend at Brown finally convinced him that somebody reading his story might find it helpful, and in the winter of his senior year he went public in an article written by a local sportswriter, Bill Reynolds, who had played basketball at Brown and wrote for *The Providence Journal*. The story seemed to break open a dam.

"So many people at Brown had no idea. The only reason I did it is maybe it will help somebody else. I'm going to the school next week," he says of the local elementary school where Brown athletes volunteer in the classroom, "to talk to some troubled kids. Hopefully, that will help them out."

Looking back, he says getting into Brown was everything he wanted. "It was great, everything I set out to do. But at the same time, I was coming to a school where basketball meant close to nothing. I came in and they were 4-22. The guys were like, 'Whatever.' I came in here with a goal to try to change things, and that goal happened.

"I came in here, I didn't know I was going to be pre-med. But when I said I was going to do it, some people said, 'You're not going to be able to do it with basketball.' And I did it anyway. I really didn't need people telling me that I can't do stuff."

He finished with a 3.0 GPA as a pre-med biology major. He mailed the checks home to his brothers. He started 110 consecutive games, playing through knee and leg and other injuries, to set a new career record at Brown. He received the coach's award, given to the player who, through total dedication and loyalty, has given the most of himself to the team. He served for three years on the Student Athletic Advisory Board. He volunteered at the local school.

"I sometimes think that athletes get a bad rap at some of these schools," he says. "People think they don't know anything, or that they're dumb—

that they just got in because of their sports. But if I had as much time as they did to study for these classes, I'd do just as well."

In the weeks prior to Alai's graduation in June 2003, he was trying to hook up with a professional team in Europe. He still wanted to play for a few more years. "I've talked to some people who said that three, four years out, it's all over," he told me, "so I want to take advantage of it while I can. Play for a few years and hopefully make a little bit of money and put it toward med school."

Glen Miller didn't have any contacts in Europe. UConn sends players to the NBA, and Connecticut College sends players to rec leagues. A few other coaches in the League had those contacts, but they weren't close friends of Miller's, and he didn't call them to ask for help.

"It's very difficult to be friends with people that you're competing with," Dave Faucher said at the time. "Because you know what's at stake, too, when you play. It's not just, 'Oh, okay they won, see ya.' It's important in their livelihoods. I think people are guarded about getting too close."

In the midst of a highly publicized job review, with rumors flying that he was about to get fired, Faucher knew what he was talking about. When he heard from a mutual friend that Alai was looking for a pro team in Europe, he offered to help. During the week when his job hung in the balance, he picked up the phone and made a few calls. Soon, he had found Alai an agent, who placed him with a team in Spain.

Faucher downplayed the effort afterward, preferring to focus instead on what lay ahead for his team. He had managed to save his job, negotiating another year at Dartmouth. He did not believe it would be his last. He felt good about his team's prospects for the coming season.

"I talk to recruits about here's a chance to be a part of something special. I believe that. My team believes it—*right now.* I think we have a good team. I think we have good young players. And there's no senior influence, everybody's coming back, so to me, I think we're going to stick our nose in this year, and I think the year after, we're gong to be one of the favorites.

"You have to believe that there's a way and it will happen," he continued. "You know: we've been close before and we'll be close again. What if we're close and we catch a break? Then we could do something that people say we can't do. That's a pretty rewarding experience. And that's almost worth working a little bit longer, dealing with a little more frustration, dealing with a lot more adversity. Achieving that once or twice in a career, to me, may be more rewarding than for some of the others that achieve it all the time."

He paused, then reflected on the difference between his program and Brown's. "I've been at Dartmouth nineteen years and our record is much better than Brown's over that period of time. Now, granted, they hit it with two kids that Dartmouth wasn't going to get in [because of the difference in mean A.I. and admissions], but no other schools were going to let them in either. Two kids that give them a different impression of their place. And we'll see what happens now that they've graduated. But that to me is all it is. It's not a coach, it's not a school, it's two kids."

Earl and Alai. Two impact players who turned a program around.

Faucher needed a few impact players of his own, players who could turn his program around and make the difference between his getting fired and getting a new three-year contract. Freshman guard Leon Pattman, a gifted player from Memphis, had the potential to be one of them. But who would make an impact for the Big Green down low, playing inside? In March 2003, Faucher had lost a talented recruit, 6-foot-7-inch forward/center Brian Darcy of Shrewsbury, Massachusetts, to Harvard when the Crimson coach and admission director made a classic Ivy League recruiting play for a player who had already made a verbal commitment to another school. It was just another sad example of how the lauded Ivy principles are ignored in the pursuit of athletic superiority.

"Harvard didn't accept the kid's verbal commitment," Faucher says matter-of-factly. Faucher was finalizing his priority list for Admissions when he called the recruit in March to check in. "I like to get a commitment from a kid before I put his name on that list. I told him, 'I gotta know, my final admission list is due. I don't get another kid at this position. I gotta make sure. I have someone else who has an interest in coming; I'd rather have you, so evaluate things and let me know.' And he says, 'Coach, I want to come to Dartmouth. It's what I really want to do.' I said, 'Okay, welcome to the family.'

"That night, I tell my assistants, 'He committed, it's over.' Harvard calls the kid and he says, 'I've committed to Dartmouth.' He tells them, 'I appreciate the recruiting.' Next day, their admission director calls him at school, and says, 'I just went over your file, you just got accepted at Harvard. Congratulations.' They chose to accept him, even though he had committed to Dartmouth. And then they say, 'Hey, come on over. You got nothing to lose, just take a visit.' So now he goes over, he likes it, he has friends that are going there. It's really hard on a Massachusetts kid, the Harvard community, and he decides to go to Harvard."

Faucher shakes his head. "I said to the father, 'It just looks like Harvard picked up their interest after we were interested, and even after he was accepted [at Dartmouth]. And he said, 'Well, it looks it, but I really think he's not making a basketball decision, he's making a school decision.'

"It's a good family," the coach continues. "They're good people. The father's a doctor. But this process can easily get confusing. It's not like Harvard's a bad choice. No matter what happens in basketball, in the end he's made a choice that he thought was best for him. But it was a gut-wrenching experience, because he said he wanted to go to Dartmouth."

Armond Hill sums up the recruiting challenge in Ivy men's basketball this way: "You lose players to Penn and Princeton. You lose parents to Harvard and Yale."

Losing Brian Darcy to Harvard was especially painful for Faucher because Darcy had the potential to become the force inside that the Dartmouth coach needed to keep his job. "They've got to find a way to make commitment a two-way street," he said at the time. "They really do."

The irony is that the new Dartmouth coach is likely to enjoy a greater commitment from the athletic department and from the admission office than Faucher ever received. The new coach is also likely to be better paid. Faucher earned $80,000 a year in his final seasons with the Big Green, by far the lowest salary among Ivy men's basketball coaches. In 2003–04, a Columbia assistant coach earned $80,000. Every other head coach in the League earns a six-figure salary, and the dean of Ivy men's hoop coaches, Fran Dunphy at Penn, makes three times what Faucher was paid.

Traditionally, when an Ivy athletic program has been in trouble and a new coach is brought in, schools make a commitment to work with the newly hired coach. In the past, such increased support at Dartmouth has led to a reversal of fortunes in both the men's hockey and the men's football programs. Bobby Gaudet, the current men's hockey coach, has enjoyed more support from Admissions than his predecessor Roger Demment ever received. Several years ago, according to Dartmouth football coach John Lyons, "They [Admissions] did things for Buddy Teevens that they never did for Joe Yukica." Eventually that honeymoon ended. Teevens grew frustrated with the Dartmouth admission office and left Hanover to pursue other opportunities. Today, under President James Wright there are "new marching orders," according to one Big Green coach, and Admissions has been asked to work more closely with Dartmouth coaches.

"I had some good recruiting classes the past few years," Faucher admitted in his final season. Indeed, his top recruit in 2003, Leon Pattman from Memphis, was named the Ivy League Rookie of the Year three days after Faucher cleared out his office.

The coach was proud of Pattman and excited to report that Dartmouth Admissions had decided to accept another player Faucher had recruited from Memphis. "They're going to take Jonathan Bell," he said. "He's the kid from Leon's high school. He's just an amazing kid and a great player. He took his boards again and got them up over the [A.I.] minimum, so they're gonna take him."

"The program's in a lot better shape than it looks," he added, ever the optimist.

Even on his way out, Faucher was still pulling for recruits to get in.

Chapter Eleven

Better Than Harvard, Princeton & Yale

"We just did a better job of recruiting. The relationships, the Trinity family, the welcome he received on campus. It was just a really good process for him. Players were helpful. Faculty members met with him while he was here. He met with the president, which doesn't happen at other places. President Dobell sat with him and said, 'You know, Marcus, we don't really want to lose to Harvard anymore. You could be a big part of that.' So it was really kind of a nice recruiting process."

Paul Assaiante
Trinity College
Head Men's Squash Coach

Paul Assaiante had been the Trinity squash coach for two years when he was called into President Evan Dobell's office in the spring of 1994. He had previously coached squash at Williams College, and, prior to that, at West Point, where he spent twelve years guiding the Cadet squash and tennis teams. He had come to Trinity after a stint as a squash club pro, and was eager to coach in college again.

"When I came to Trinity ten years ago," he says, "I fully expected to be coaching the sort of white toast, Main Line, Greenwich, Brookline, prep school–type kids who grew up learning the game and came here. Trinity had always had a pretty competitive squash team, and one year in the '80s they even were ranked as high as number two. But they were always competitive in the six, seven, eight range, where Williams and Amherst always used to jump around. I was excited about the opportunity to do that and teach lifetime lessons through sport. There's a plaque on the wall at West Point, and the plaque says: *On the friendly fields of strife are sown the seeds that on later fields will bear the fruit of victory.* That's been the driving motivator in my life as a coach. Teaching kids how to deal in life through the experiences they learn in sport—because you don't learn this stuff in a chemistry lab. You don't deal with the immediate flight or fight impulse at the moment. You don't deal with immediate failure or immediate success. Your character is not challenged. How do you deal with that close call? These are life issues that we get hit with every day. So that's what brought me here."

What brought him into the Trinity president's office, however, was quite another matter. Evan Dobell had perceived a unique opportunity, thanks to the unique status of men's college squash, which is governed outside the jurisdiction of the NCAA, under the aegis of the United States Squash Federation. Under their rules, there are no distinctions between Division I and the Ivy League and Division III and the New England Small College Athletic Conference (NESCAC), in which Trinity competes. Any one of the thirty-five colleges and universities that field a men's squash team can compete for and capture the national Intercollegiate Championship.

Assaiante recalls the meeting. "Evan called me into his office and he said, 'Coach, here's the deal. I noticed that the squash team plays the highest caliber of institutions in competition. You play Dartmouth and Penn and Yale, whereas your tennis team plays Williams and Middlebury and Bowdoin—and that's all great. But I need to be able to walk into boardrooms and raise money and get people excited, because I'm trying to give this school a facelift and a morale boost. And the fact that you're competing with those schools is very important to me. And my question to you is: how do we take it to the next level in that pond? Because if the tennis team wins the Division III national championship, that's great, and we can promote it. But if the squash team wins the national championship against a Princeton or a Harvard or a Yale, that's *very* compelling.'"

Assaiante was in a unique position to answer the question, thanks to his additional role as the national coach for the United States Squash Team.

"'Well,' I said, 'since you asked, I am the USA coach, and the one thing I can tell you in my world travels is that the best squash is not being played in this country. I coached the US Team in Cairo. We had our best finish in over a decade: we finished seventeenth. So, you've gotta let us begin looking in different ponds. And these are not ponds that other schools have not already looked in. But the NESCAC world has never looked in them.'

"And he said, 'Fine, Coach. Here's the deal. We will not compromise the school's standards one bit. These kids have to be academically competitive. And number two, we will not give scholarships because we're a Division III school. We give financial aid based on need, and that's all we'll do.'

"I said, 'Thank you very much, President Dobell.' And as I stood to leave the room, he said, 'Now Coach Assaiante, don't screw this up.'

"Yes, President Dobell."

The meeting took all of three minutes.

"This is the way Evan Dobell's mind works," Assaiante says. "Evan is the most out-of-the-box thinker I've ever been around. And it was a magical carpet ride with Evan Dobell—for the college and for sport in general, or at least for the game of squash in America."

In 2001, Dobell left Trinity after five years to accept a position as the president of the University of Hawaii school systems, but not before leaving behind a legacy in Hartford, Connecticut.

"Evan is a very tall, very imposing looking person," says Wendy Bartlett, the women's squash coach at Trinity. "Very much of a businessman, very slicked-back hair. He made it clear he was not an academician. He came in as a visionary and a businessman and a politician, and did a tremendous amount for Trinity. People might not have liked the way he went about it, but he got an awful lot done.

"He was super at fundraising," she continues. "He would go to an event and somebody would say, 'I'll give $10,000,' and he would say, 'How about if you give $50,000?' And they would do it. He spent a lot of money. He did spend a heck of a lot of money. The learning corridor. The admission building. On all kinds of things. So when Dick Hersch [who succeeded Dobell as Trinity President] came, he was sort of cleaning up after all the money Evan spent."

But Dobell's biggest legacy is arguably the school's dominant squash program. At the time of writing, Trinity had won six straight national men's squash championships. Over those six seasons, the men had not lost a single match, compiling a 108-0 record. By 2002 and 2003, the Trinity women had followed their lead, completing two undefeated seasons, and capturing back-to-back national titles. Paul Assaiante had not screwed it up. On the contrary, he and Bartlett had searched the world for better players and made Trinity squash a winner. Evan Dobell had been able to walk into boardrooms and proclaim that Trinity was better than Harvard, Princeton, and Yale. And in the process of building a dynasty, he and Assaiante and Bartlett turned the world of American squash upside down.

"He loved winning," says Bartlett. "He loved winning."

Ever since the first squash match in America was played at St. Paul's School in Concord, New Hampshire, in the late 1880s, the game has been an upper-middle-class sport in this country, played mainly by members of the well-to-do East Coast establishment. And for more than one hundred years, the squash played in America was a different game from the squash played in 132 countries around the rest of the world.

"For whatever reason, when the game came over from England, whether it was a court space issue or access to the proper ball, a different game got started in the United States," says John Power, a Canadian who coaches the Dartmouth men's and women's squash teams, and whose son, Jonathon, has been ranked number one in the world. The different American game was played on a smaller court with a hard ball, while the international game was played on a larger court with a soft ball.

There are conflicting views about the origins of squash. Some say it was started in the prisons of England. Others claim it began in the very upper English classes. But regardless of how it originated, the game was spread throughout the world primarily by the British military, whose members brought the game to every corner of the British Empire. This is why the top players in the world have historically come from such Commonwealth countries as Australia, Pakistan, and India. More recently, European players have made advances, with Peter Nichol of Scotland holding the current world's number one ranking for men, after dislodging Jonathon Power.

"There's been no American man to ever break the top fifty in the history of the sport," says Dartmouth's Power. A few American women, however, have joined the game's elite. In 2004, American sisters Latasha and Shabana Khan of Seattle were ranked twenty-first and thirty-third in the world respectively, and a number of years ago Demer Holleran and Alicia McConnell both achieved solid world rankings. Natalie Grainger, currently ranked third in the world, lists the United States as her country (she is married to an American and now lives here), but she mastered the game in her native South Africa, a squash hotbed. In Power's view, American men have not been as successful partly because "the Americans went on the whole different stream of the hardball game. And it was a very successful game, albeit played mostly on the East Coast of the United States, a little bit in Mexico, and in Canada, in the older private clubs."

In the 1980s things began to shift in North America, as Canada moved away from hardball squash, adopted the international softball game, and joined the rest of the world. By 1992, the American collegiate game was following suit, reflecting a wider trend in the United States. The days of hardball squash were nearing an end. Private clubs, exclusive prep schools, and elite East Coast colleges, the traditional strongholds of the hardball game, were all adopting the international game. For three years between 1992 and 1994, American collegiate teams alternated between hardball and softball matches, as schools went through a transition in facilities from the old hardball courts to new, larger softball courts. By 1995 the change was complete, and college squash had become exclusively softball, the international game.

This is why, when Evan Dobell asked Paul Assaiante to make Trinity the best squash team in the country, Assaiante immediately started fishing in international waters. American juniors simply weren't the best players. And it is also why, when Assaiante's team started winning title after title, the wealthy old guard squash establishment in the United States began bad-mouthing what he'd done—partly because he recruited many of his international stars while traveling to international tournaments on the US Squash Federation's dime, in his role as the US national team coach. He was, at best, a turncoat.

"The knee-jerk reaction in the little world of American squash has been negative," says Assaiante of his team's ascension to the pinnacle of America college squash. "We have been bashed in the cocktail parties around America because of jealousy and prejudice. But it's been the best thing for the college, and it's been the best thing for the game because if you truly want to stand on the podium and say you're the best, then you better be the best. This isn't a private country club. You don't get to exclude people. And if you're going to be calling yourself the national intercollegiate champion, and there are people academically qualified out there that could come to that school, then they should be at that school and you should be competing with them."

As Assaiante pointed out to Evan Dobell at their meeting, schools outside the NESCAC, in the Ivy League, had been casting in international ponds for squash players long before Trinity joined the fishing derby. But the affluent parents of many top American juniors didn't appreciate it when the NESCAC school started hauling out the best, and eventually, the biggest, catch.

"I'm shocked at the prejudice in our country," says Assaiante. "These kids, our best American juniors, come up through the white toast, Main Line affluent world, and yet there's a sense of, 'Well, then we should be able to control our children's college journey. And we may tolerate Harvard's having an international group, thus my son might not play number one at Harvard. But it's not tolerable at a school like Trinity or Williams or Amherst.' And over and over again, I have people come to me and say, 'So, how many English-speaking people do have on your team this year?' And I've reached the point where I feel like somebody walking up to a successful college basketball coach and saying, 'How many whites do you have on your team this year?' It feels the same way from this side. And you see the thing that I find problematic about that is, I didn't enter this game with this goal in mind."

That may be true, but once he entered it, Assaiante played the recruiting game masterfully. The story of how he found so many gifted players, created a national powerhouse, and helped Evan Dobell fill the Trinity coffers is astonishing.

"We began throwing our hook out there," Assaiante says of his first international recruiting efforts, "casting around, seeing if anybody would bite— just by making it clear in the world of junior squash that Trinity College was going to try to become a player in the game. I knew all the national coaches from the other countries. And I would call the English national coach who's a friend of mine and say, 'Listen, E.P., are there any kids out there in your world of junior squash that are academically inclined, and looking to go to university?' And so little by little, we started to have interest."

"Now interestingly enough," he continues, "in that world out there—Hong Kong, Malaysia, Singapore, Australia—everyone's heard of Harvard University. None of them had ever heard of Trinity College. And in those cultures, the name *college* means something quite different than university anyway. Those are high schools."

Assaiante had to educate the squash community, through the coaches, that Trinity College was the same thing as a university, only smaller—a small institution in the city of Hartford, with a fine facility and a commitment to look after players who would be in school far from home.

"What I have to do in the recruitment process," he explains, "is I have to educate the family as to, 'Why Trinity?' If you're going to a university, why *not* Harvard University? Why here? Well, in many cases squash in other countries is not a high demographic sport. It's a much more public sport. So for these kids, they're not coming from the economic backgrounds that some of our kids are coming from. The point of that is, these are kind of old-fashioned, small-town families. And the youngster from Bloomington, South Africa, that mother and father are sending Jacques to me, knowing that they may *never* see the college. I've had kids come through the program, whose parents never saw the college, didn't even come to graduation. They couldn't afford it. So the differential in some ways becomes the relationship that the coach can develop with the family, because they're sending Sparky to *you* and entrusting him to *you* for four years. So that's been the challenge in getting the word out: you know what, we really do care, we love your boys. We will protect him. We will be there for him through the peaks and valleys that are four years of college. We will call you when he ends up in Hartford Hospital because he drank too much. Or we will help him when he needs some academic guidance. We're small, and can do that here."

The other thing Trinity did from the very beginning was commit to providing need-based financial aid to its international squash players. Unlike some of its wealthier NESCAC cousins—Williams, Amherst, and Middlebury—Trinity is not need-blind. Hence, the school admits each student knowing exactly how he or she will impact the school's overall financial aid pool. With Evan Dobell's support, squash players were a high priority to receive need-based aid. And for years they have all qualified for awards, thanks to their backgrounds, to brutal exchange rates against the dollar, and to a lack of college savings by their parents, who live in countries where going to a university is inexpensive or covered by the government. These international players are the equivalent of the low-income Ivy League recruits, whom coaches love because their large financial aid packages compare favorably to a full ride at a scholarship school.

Last but not least, Assaiante was offering these kids the chance to come to America, which for many was a dream come true.

"All of a sudden, this started to catch fire," he says. "The next thing you know, three years later, we're in the finals of the Intercollegiate Championships." Their opponent was Harvard, the defending national champion and the country's most storied program with the greatest winning tradition in college squash.

Ironically, Assaiante's top player that year was a young man named Marcus Cowie, a former world junior runner-up from England, who had been rejected by Harvard under Early Decision. When Assaiante heard from the Harvard coach at the time, Bill Doyle, a Trinity graduate and close friend, that Marcus was not going to get in there, he asked Doyle's permission to contact the player.

"He said, 'By all means, feel free,'" says Assaiante. "I called that morning, and the time differential is always tricky on these calls, it's five hours ahead there, Singapore's thirteen hours. . . . I started calling and the line was busy, and I didn't reach him until 11 pm their time—and I was the sixth coach to reach him that day. All the fishing lines were in the water."

Assaiante began the process of trying to reel in his biggest catch yet, competing for Marcus with a number of Ivy League schools.

"We had alums in England that were very successful businessmen," he says. "They were happy to drop him a line, say they'd had a positive experience at Trinity, and hope he'd consider it. Just like any other business deal you're closing, you need to look at the Rubik's Cube from all angles."

Under NCAA Division I rules, the Ivy League coaches could not employ their alums as recruiting allies. Trinity, bound by much looser Division III regulations, faced no such restriction.

Soon, Marcus had narrowed down his list to a few schools. Then, unlike the vast majority of Trinity's international squash recruits, who never make a campus visit before they enroll because of the cost of airfare and distance barriers, Marcus decided to come see Trinity. This is when President Dobell sat with him and said, "You know Marcus, we don't really want to lose to Harvard anymore. You could be a big part of that."

For a player who had been rejected by Harvard, this was the perfect sales pitch. Marcus chose Trinity. Assaiante had made his first huge catch.

"It turned out that Marcus was bigger than life," the coach says. "Marcus was just everywhere. He came here really to get an education, so in his four years here, and I laugh about this, and I say this often, but I have probably turned around more squash players and watched them deteriorate under my watch than probably any other coach in America. Because they come in world-class juniors and by the time they leave, they're American college–educated kids and they've gotten into the social world and everything else. So Marcus was brilliant when he came, he was pretty damn good in the middle, and by the time he left, he was just a very talented guy, and that was it."

That first, brilliant year, Marcus helped Trinity beat Harvard for the first time in school history, 6-3, during a regular season in which the team's only loss came to Princeton.

"So now we go into the Intercollegiate Championships," says Assaiante, "and we have Princeton in our semifinal, and Harvard is in the other half. Evan Dobell is in San Francisco, and his secretary calls me and she says, 'When are the finals?'

"I said, 'What do mean, when are the finals?'

'Well,' she said, 'Evan's flying back from San Francisco for the finals.'

"This was the only time I felt pressure in my entire coaching career," recalls Assaiante. "I said, 'Well, we just lost to Princeton [at the end of the regular season]. We're playing Princeton here, at Princeton, and he's flying back for the finals? I can't guarantee you we're *in* the finals.'"

The coach laughs. "Talk about crapping yourself. So, anyway, his secretary says, 'Well, he wants to know when the finals are.' Classic Dobell. So I told her." He smiles and continues. "Well, we beat Princeton 7-2 to make it to the finals. So now we're in the finals, first time in college history, and Dobell flies back from San Francisco, and we lose a barnburner, 5-4, to

Harvard. It was just amazing. But you know the old saying, 'You have to be in the dance before you know how to win the dance.'"

Marcus had been to big dances before, including the World Junior finals, and he knew how to boogie. He took the sting out of the team's loss to Harvard by capturing the individual intercollegiate singles title. But for Assaiante, the singles final was a bittersweet experience, a dramatic introduction to coaching a player from squash's highest level.

"Marcus was just a flamboyant, artistic player, who could be quite contentious in the heat of play. And he was always right. He was a wonderful kid, truly a special human being with a great soul. But when he got on the stage, you never knew what you were gonna get."

Marcus played Daniel Ezra of Harvard. "They were there in each other faces," recalls Assaiante. "About calls, positioning, gamesmanship. Now in theory, this game, the sport of kings, is supposed to be a self-refereed, collegial, congenial experience. Well, in many cases it's much more dramatic than that, and we were not expecting that, we didn't know that. It was like icy water being thrown on you.

"So here I am, coaching a player, my first player's national singles championship—and it was such a contentious match that I wanted to be anywhere other than there," says Assaiante. "Here I'd coached my whole life to be coaching a national champion, and we're on the cusp of that experience, and as life always tells us, 'This isn't what I really had in mind.'" He laughs.

"Daniel was a little smoother about it. He was always like the lamb with the lion, but they were both getting their stuff in there. Marcus was very MacEnroesque. He was brilliant, but he was at times a handful."

The freshman from England ended up winning the match, his first of two consecutive national intercollegiate singles titles. But the team remained a step away from the top.

Nevertheless, Evan Dobell was very pleased. Assaiante remembers, "He said to the team, 'This is great, and I'm proud of you guys. Keep up the good work.'"

To Assaiante, the president said, "We can do this. We can break through. We're so close. Let's keep this thing going."

"I'll never forget," Assaiante says, "he said to me, 'Coach, wouldn't it be great if we could win one national championship?'

"Yeah, Evan, it would be awesome."

The first national title came the next year, and the way in which Assaiante and Trinity engineered it sent shock waves through the Ivy League. Through his international coaching contacts, Assaiante found a hot prospect in South Africa, a player named Loua Coetzee.

"Now, again, we've never been in the South African marketplace, and we don't know what to expect," says Assaiante. "Well, much to our surprise, the kids' educational background in South Africa is terrific. So this kid came in a rocket scientist. He was pretty heavily recruited by the Ivies, and it was pretty clear that he was going to get into those Ivy League schools."

But instead of choosing to attend one of the Ivies who were pursuing him, Loua opted to enroll in Trinity—in January, midway through the squash season.

"This is another thing that we are able to do here that other schools are not," explains Assaiante. "Loua finished his schooling in December. That's when they finish their high school. We have a January admission, so what we were able to help the family understand was simple: 'Surely, you can wait until September and go to other schools, or you can come here. If you're comfortable with us, why don't you just start in January?' We're able to get a real jump on the competition through the use of the January admission. And so we've gotten four boys in through the January admission process that have all turned out to be All-American squash players."

Loua was the first. And just to make it worse for the Ivy League, he proved to be the difference in Trinity's quest for their first national title.

"Is that cheating?" says Assaiante. "No. It's working within the framework of what we do as an institution. The fact that it's not done at Cornell is not my problem," he adds with a laugh. "We've made great use of that. We've had kids come who were admissible to Ivy League schools, but they wanted to get started and the parents were very comfortable with the relationship that I had worked with them. And when Loua's father said, 'You know what, I see the difference in the institutions, but it's not—you know, little me, a pharmacy worker in Port Alfred, South Africa—it doesn't mean enough to me to wait. I want my son to get his education right away. So we're gonna go ahead and pass on this and go ahead with Trinity.' That caused a real knee jerk through the Ivy community, because it was like, 'How does this happen? Why would a kid go to Trinity, as opposed to waiting, and we're going to admit him here anyway?' And that was really shocking to everybody."

The shift in the balance of power, from the traditional Ivy elite to the upstart Trinity, grated on the old guard.

"Trinity?" says Assaiante, echoing the reaction of his competition. "How the hell can it be Trinity? How dare you! When we play Harvard it's such a treat, because you walk in there and they sit there with their arms folded and they look at you and they just basically say, 'How dare you!'

"I love it," he says. "We always pull back into this little place in Hartford, Connecticut, and it's really fun. But you know, it starts spinning around: 'You guys must have compromised your academic standards. You've got to be cheating out there.' There's not enough time, and there's not enough effort, and there's not enough need to run around to every cocktail party that's happening this weekend in America to dispel those myths."

The surprising truth is that the international kids Assaiante began recruiting were, by and large, academically much stronger than the homegrown kids Trinity was already bringing in.

"Traditionally, Trinity has been, not a second choice school, but not always a primary choice school," he says. "Certainly not in relation to the Harvards and the Yales of the world. To a Middlebury and a Bowdoin and a Williams, we were always sort of in the middle of that NESCAC pack. Now we started bringing in kids that were academically off the charts from our standards. Some are very focused, and they're very disciplined, and they're into it."

Even so, the adjustment of being so far from home and of being a college student can be difficult for the international players, and Assaiante, who serves as a surrogate parent as well as a coach, has set up a support system to make sure they are well cared for.

"We have an academic advisor for each sport. It's more like a team mom or a team dad. But because it's a small school—and it is what we promote, 1,800 students—the fact is, you have to try not to be able to get through. If you're communicating with your professors from day one: 'I'm sorry Mr. Bosenberry, I didn't understand the lecture,' they will go out of their way to help you. The classes are only twelve to one, so they are very good about helping kids help themselves. The team really helps each other. It's very cute to watch the upperclassmen hover over the younger kids. And then lastly, we try to have no person in a class that a teammate isn't in. Because by doing that, they can never lie to me. So if I say, 'How's it going, Johnny?' And he says, 'It's going fine,' I can ask Bill, and Bill will say, 'He's not been going to class, Coach.' And then I'm all over Johnny—because, again, these parents have entrusted this kid to me."

For Assaiante that trust is established almost exclusively through email during the recruiting process. "If I sense from the tone of the email that it might be going in the wrong direction," he says, "I get on the phone, because you have to hear the voice to know the tone. I probably email these kids just little blurbs three or four times a week, once I've established contact. In this business it's all relationship building and communicating."

In recent years, Assaiante says most of the contact has been initiated by recruits, who have heard about Trinity out on the junior circuit from a national teammate or from a competitor who has come to the school. The simple truth is one great player has led to another, and the men's and women's teams have cross-fertilized each other with recruited talent, a tribute to the job Assaiante and Bartlett have done with the players on their rosters.

"It really is so much word of mouth," says Bartlett. "Marcus, our first international player, really set things rolling. The day he got here, I said, 'Do you know any girls in England?' And he said, 'Yes, I know Gail Davie.' And I called her in September, and she was all set to go to Manchester University there. And she totally switched gears and started in January at Trinity. So that just started the whole process going. She was so excited to be able to do both academics and squash. That was our first international player."

In turn, Gail Davie suggested Clare Austin, another English player. A year later, Gail's mother told Bartlett about Amina Helal, yet another English player, who was the 2002 and 2003 women's intercollegiate national champion at Trinity. Her father, a world-class squash player for Egypt, is now a pro in England.

"Amina is the best player to ever come to the United States, in my opinion," says Assaiante. She is also a top student, a German major with a 3.9 GPA.

"As a player, it was sort of known in England that if you wanted to play squash, you go to Trinity," says Helal. "And nobody really even mentioned any of the other schools. I was at my squash club and all of a sudden a girl from the gym came in and said, 'Amina, there's somebody on the phone for you.

She's got a funny accent, she's American.' Wendy sort of tracked me down."

"Oh yeah," says Bartlett, "I track these kids down everywhere. I just got off the phone with a girl from Bombay, India. She was on her cell phone, and the cars were beeping. She's gonna come next year. I love the phone calls. I really believe in that. You only can email for so long."

Bartlett first met Helal when she was sixteen years old, playing in the World Junior championships. "When Evan Dobell was here," says Bartlett, "he very much supported me going to England, to the World Juniors, things like that to watch players. We're not allowed to talk about Trinity. You know, we can't really be recruiting. But we can watch them play, and then contact them when we get back. It's just sort of ironic, I was over there watching a couple of other players from England who were interested, and they ended up not coming. But I had met Amina there. She impressed me because out of all the English girls, out of the whole English team, she was actually the nicest person. Always smiling, always a friendly wave."

Helal explains why coming to America to play squash and attend school is so attractive to many of the foreign-based players. "There's a huge pressure to go professional and play professionally," she says. But going pro and going to school is impossible. "They just don't mix. So it's really, really hard. My game would have plummeted. You'd lose your place on the performance line, and you'd lose your ranking 'cause you wouldn't be able to take time off from university to go compete, 'cause they just wouldn't understand. So the US offers a chance to do them together, and it makes more sense."

Helal is another player who entered Trinity in January, only to win the national singles championships in March. She first joined the team while they were in Amsterdam over the holiday break.

"We were training over in Amsterdam in January before classes started," explains Bartlett. "So instead of having Amina fly to the United States and then fly to Amsterdam with us, we just met her in Amsterdam. When Evan was president, he really encouraged us to take trips abroad with the team. So one year we went to England, we're allowed to go every two years, and our next trip was to Amsterdam. And you know, Paul and I would pick these cities according to how many courts they have, the competition level, a fun city."

Bartlett is also responsible for helping a South African men's team member learn about Trinity. The mother of a girl from South Africa, who grew close to Bartlett through the recruiting process, recommended Trinity to the young man, even though her daughter chose to stay home and attend a local university. The player, Nadeem Osman, told me, "I went on the Internet and saw that Trinity was number one, and I applied straightaway. And I met another guy in England, and he was coming to Trinity and he was a great player. And there was another guy from Botswana, he's a very big name in Botswana, and he was here. So I saw that."

Nadeem sent one email to Paul Assaiante, expressing his interest, and that's all it took. "Paul just kept it going, kept it going, kept replying to me," says Nadeem. "He said, 'We're going to try to make this work.'" Eventually, the coach did make it work, wooing Nadeem from Harvard, thanks partly to the January admission policy at Trinity.

Bernardo Samper, another member of Assaiante's last two championship teams, who was the intercollegiate singles champion in 2002 (he lost in the finals in 2003 to a Princeton freshman, Yasser El-Halaby, of Egypt), was recruited by the Trinity coach at the Pan American Games in Calgary, where Assaiante was coaching the US Team.

"It was funny because I met coach in a sauna," Samper says. "After a match, I went to the changing room, and I was in the sauna and coach came and basically that's where we actually started talking about Trinity. He told me about Trinity, that they were national champions, they had a really good program here, the team was really diverse. And so after we changed and everything, he gave me his card and I told him that I was gonna call him 'cause I was interested in studying here. But I told him first that I wanted one year off to do some English courses and go to Europe to play some tournaments, so I can practice my English and just get ready to come here. I didn't feel ready to come straightaway because of my English, and I was also thinking of one year off of school, training really hard, and playing tournaments. So then I got back to Columbia and I told my parents about this opportunity. They were really happy. I sent an email to coach that I was back home training, that I told my parents, that they were really happy, and then my father and Paul started talking on the phone. We started doing all the papers, I did all the exams, and that's basically how it went. I took the TOEFL and the SATs. Did all the application, the essays. Took the TOEFL twice, right after Pan Am games, and again after the year, and improved my score. We waited that year, and I got here in August 2001."

"Squash," says Bartlett, "is a small world. But you have the whole world. Everybody's playing."

For several years now, Bartlett has also had a strong connection to Zimbabwe. "About eight years ago a group of girl squash players made a tour of the United States," she recalls, "and they stopped here at Trinity. We still had the narrow hardball courts and everything. Sam Lewins, she was fourteen then, she fell in love with Trinity. After high school she applied to Trinity, and she started the whole Zimbabwe connection. She came, and she suggested Pam Saunders, and then Pam suggested Bronwyn Cooper. And next year, there's another girl from Zimbabwe coming. I think the word that gets out about Trinity is that we have so finely developed these international programs now, with so much support, and that's why I think the parents feel comfortable, particularly with their daughters, in sending them here. 'Cause they're not going slip through cracks, they're going to be really taken care of the moment they get off the plane. I take them to their room. We get the bank account opened. The girls from Zimbabwe don't have any warm clothes. I loan them down parkas, everything like that. Take them to the hospital when they need to go—everything from A to Z. It's a huge time commitment, but it's really so exciting and satisfying. I love it. It's added a whole new dimension onto coaching. And then the benefit is there are all these good players—great people, great students, great players—and they work so hard once they get into our system. I think the school just benefits so much from having them here, on the court and off the court."

But what about the American players, who have been displaced by the international stars? On the men's side, Assaiante carries twenty players, nine of whom can compete in any given match, and nine of whom, in 2003, were internationals. The lone American in that year's starting lineup was, in the words of Dartmouth coach, John Power, "a very, very good player. He played eight. I tried to recruit him as my number one recruit three years ago, and unfortunately he didn't get in. And they have other very good Americans who don't make the starting lineup."

"What happens is, I carry the bomb squaders," Assaiante explains. "What we do is when we recruit a youngster, we promise them that they will play in half of the varsity matches, no matter where they are in the line-up. So last year, Jay Boothby from Chestnut Hill, Pennsylvania, who's number eighteen, he played in eleven varsity matches. The number one player, Bernardo Samper, he played in seven. Bernardo's better off staying and practicing than going and playing against Colby. For Jay Boothby, that's a great thing. All twenty kids are mixed and matched, we have a ladder, we don't have a varsity and a jv, we treat them all equally, they all get national championship rings, they all go through the journey. And that's kind of a fun thing. It keeps everybody feeling like they're part of it. Economically, it's a smart thing to do because no matter what you say, in the end, this is business. This is a business we're running here at the college. And it relies on income, and it relies heavily on income from alums. Well, these international kids are probably not going to make a huge impact on the journey, so you've still got to keep the Americans happy and engaged. It's not a hard thing to do, they're lovely kids. But it's an important thing to do."

Assaiante, who recruits his international stars through intensive email communication, and by running into them and their parents at international competitions, had never made a home visit to recruit a player. But in early spring 2003, he did call on the family of a player who was headed to Trinity the following fall.

"We have a young man coming next year, Tom Wolfe. His father's the author," Assaiante told me, describing the visit. "I was in their house last Wednesday. And Tom is a delightful guy, so interesting, and what a dry sense of humor. You know, top hat, and to the floor all white, an amazing apartment in New York. Tommy is a big squash player. He's coming here next year. He's at Riverdale High. He's excited and we're excited. I went down, I was in New York, calling on Trinity alums, and I went over to meet with them to just make sure Tommy understood that what he could accomplish next year had to start now. If he waited 'til the fall, he wasn't gonna make the grade. Now is the time to catch up for lost time, because if you think you're working hard, you're gonna find out that you're not. And it was a really delightful visit, and the Wolfes were great."

Asked how he landed the younger Wolfe, Assaiante replied, "He chose Trinity because I did a good job recruiting him. He was deferred at Yale. He opted not to wait, and applied for second Early Decision here—and is very happy with the decision."

Why Yale would defer the son of Tom Wolfe, who earned a doctorate in American studies at the school before writing such best-selling books as *The Electric Kool-Aid Acid Test, The Right Stuff,* and *Bonfire of the Vanities* is a question only the Yale admission office can answer. But it illustrates the vagaries of the elite college admission process. If young Tom can play squash for Trinity, surely he can play for Yale, where there is a strong tradition and a stunning new facility. One can imagine Richard Levin, the Yale President, hunting for an admission officer's head. The elder Wolfe has earned a fortune, and now it's likely that some of it will wind up in Hartford, rather than in New Haven, Connecticut.

Putting the touch on Tom Wolfe on behalf of Trinity College will likely be Paul Assaiante himself. For the past several years, his other job at the school has been fundraising for Trinity's athletic department. "My role is to enhance and improve the athletic facilities," he explains, "and, in turn, the athletic experience." He raised the money to expand Trinity's handsome ten-court squash facility, with two, four-wall glass courts, offices, and a pyramid viewing gallery where two thousand people crammed in to watch the Princeton match in 2003. Fundraising is a natural fit for his personality, and it, too, began as the brainchild of Evan Dobell.

"He obviously saw some things in my skill set that would work," Assaiante says of his fundraising role. "I basically go in, hand out national championship shirts, or whatever, and there's always a conversation about *that*, and then it leads its way. And basically I'm calling on people who've had athletic exposure and experience to see if there's anything that resonates with them in the area of new bricks-and-mortar projects that we're building, or in endowment. One thing I find is very compelling right now is the women's athletic growth, how dynamic that it is, and particularly—you may have a guy, we have a guy who's the COO of Wrigley, a great guy who was a basketball star here in '74, and his daughter's a freshman here. So he's very into the giving for women's athletics. So I find that's a big thing. You also find the parent group very generous in a short window of opportunity, because they would like to enhance their child's time at the school. That's really what I do."

Looking back now, as he hits up Trinity grads for donations, Assaiante says, "Dobell was right. It makes them feel better knowing that their old alma mater is a winner. And that exudes confidence, and confidence is sexy, and so that's how it's worked. Hopefully, when they see me do my craft, they sense quickly that this guy loves the kids. But that's not what gets them excited when I walk into their office and they take me down the hallway to meet their partner who was a soccer player at Princeton, and they grind each other for a few minutes. That's not what gets them excited. But to me that's what's the driving force."

To this day, some college coaches and members of the squash elite on the cocktail circuit believe that the driving force behind the creation of the Trinity squash dynasty was actually Assaiante's idea, not Evan Dobell's—that the coach persuaded the president to make a commitment to excellence in the sport, rather than the other way around.

"That's a classic kind of rumor," he says. "It's just sour grapes. Why would I do that? Certainly no president—I mean, you can't convince the presidents of these schools of anything," he adds with a laugh. "And you know what? If that were true, I deserve a lot more credit than I'm giving myself. I would never have had that vision. It never would have even occurred to me to have that conversation. It's so out of line with everything that had been a part of my coaching experience to that point. This was an institutional mandate because we were trying to upgrade, trying to get our alumni excited, trying to raise money, trying to increase the profile of our student body's academic standards, so I wish that were true. I would feel pretty good about it. But it wasn't my idea."

"And in terms of my coaching abilities," he adds, "it's true that the jockey on the fastest horse wins the race. John Power knows as much or more about squash as I do. Satinder Bajwa at Harvard certainly knows as much or more than I do. Bobby Callahan at Princeton, Dave Talbott at Yale, these are great coaches. This hasn't been my doing. Yes, I've been very good at managing very high-maintenance, high-strung athletes and getting the centers of their respective universes to have a common goal. That I have been very good at. But this isn't my gig."

With the NESCAC presidents enacting new recruiting rules in 2003 that set a limit on the total number of "athletic factor" admits any school can make in a given year (meaning the number of recruits who may be admitted below a school's normal academic entrance criteria), Trinity's squash programs will now be limited to two "athletic factor" slots for the men, and to two "athletic factor" slots for the women on an annual basis. Prior to the changes, which were prompted by *The Game of Life*, Assaiante and Bartlett were given as many players as they needed. "It doesn't take a lot of numbers," says Assaiante. But it takes more than two a year to keep pace with Harvard, Princeton, and Yale, and not every great international player on the Trinity roster is also a standout student.

The year before the rule changes, Bartlett explains, she went to Admissions and said, "We need equity with the men. They had nine and we had five and that was inequitable, and we needed to correct that. And they agreed with me, and so they accepted four international students." All female, all top-flight squash players.

Now, those days are gone. Assaiante can see what's coming, and he is philosophical about what he calls, "his journey."

"This has been a really fun ride and a great journey and they won't take the banners down," he says, "but that's not the most important thing that we've done during these years. We've never had anybody go home yet. They stay, they graduate, and then ultimately, who knows where they'll end up. My guess is a goodly number will stay, make some professional impact in the world, and then go home."

As for Harvard and his other Ivy foes, who have anywhere from three to five slots a year for squash players, Assaiante says, "Soon it will turn, and soon the dominance will come back to the Ivy League. . . . This year [the class entering in the fall of 2003], Harvard had the best recruiting class of *anyone*. Next year, Harvard will probably be the number one team in the country. And, you know, my only comment on that is, 'Shame on you. Why did you let this go as long as you did?' Harvard just has to pay attention, for crissakes. So the coach flew out to the World Juniors in India, and scooped up four great players, and now they're off to the races. And that's great. That's good for the game.

"The top six kids at Princeton this year [2002–2003] were foreign players," he adds. "I mean these kids really are quite special. And the Harvard recruits are fabulous players."

He pauses for a moment to reflect on the bashing he and Trinity have endured for their championship efforts. "The thing that cracks me up is in two, three years, when we're four or five in the League again, I'll be Coach Assaiante, great guy, and we'll be Trinity College, cool school."

But the banners will stay, the life lessons will continue, and the glory days will be remembered with pride by Trinity alums for years to come.

Chapter Twelve

From Brown To Bates: Seeking Sanity In The NESCAC

"Well, I look at Williams and Middlebury. Those are good jobs. I'm talking to Mickey Heinecken [for many years the Middlebury football coach], and he's sailing on Sunday up at Lake Champlain. Christ, what am I doing? I'm in here all day looking at film, racing around. . . ."

John Lyons
Dartmouth College
Head Football Coach

In the summer of 2000, Peter Lasagna left Brown University and the Ivy League and stepped into a parallel universe at Bates College and the New England Small College Athletic Conference. He stopped trying to compete "in the middle of the pack" in Division I men's college lacrosse, recruiting nonstop against Ivy League rivals and scholarship schools, and moved to what he describes as "a great school, in a great setting, in an amazing league, that has a collection of the best academic institutions in Division III athletics." If the Ivy League has an academic and financial aid soul mate in collegiate sports, it is the NESCAC. The two athletic conferences share many of the same philosophical goals, but the manner in which they pursue and achieve those goals differs in some significant and telling ways. To some, Lasagna took a step down when he accepted the job at Bates and forsook Division I for Division III. To others, he took a step toward living a saner, more balanced life both on and off the field.

Lasagna took over a young program at Bates, where he says that, "the really tough groundwork had already been done by the two coaches, Web Harrison and Al Brown," who preceded him. "The school was building a brand new AstroTurf field," he adds, "which you really need in Maine during lacrosse season. The athletic director seemed very supportive of men's lacrosse and had sincere interest in trying to get me to look at the job. All the pieces were in place, and it seemed like it would be a really exciting time to be coming into the program to try to help build it."

He also liked the idea of living in Maine and being part of "a really interesting college that has a really interesting place in this community." And he felt the move would be good for his young family. "With an eight- and ten-year-old daughter and son, I could see that my wife and I were heading into this area where we had a very discreet number of years left with them, in the way that you have with your children at this age, and that you could really point to a day on the calendar when those days were going to be gone," he says. "And it seemed like, 'Here's a way for me to do what I love to do in a really uncomplicated way, where I don't have to deal with a lot of the other stuff. I don't have to raise $100,000 every year in order to run my program, and I'm not traveling all the time to recruit.' So it was just great, all those forces coming together in a really unexpected way. I thought I would die at Brown, and I would be buried somewhere on campus."

After twenty-four years at Brown, which he had entered as an eighteen-year-old freshman and left as a forty-two-year-old head coach, he began a new life. "Clearly," he says with a laugh, "change is not easy for me."

Given the changes taking place in Division I men's lacrosse, however, he knew that staying at his alma mater would be even harder. "It was not even a top three or four reason for me to make the move that I made, but it was a factor. In the Ivy League, in men's lacrosse, it's only ever going to get harder. Notre Dame has scholarships now. Ohio State is a major player now. The University of Denver is a player now. Georgetown and Duke didn't used to exist. I mean, their programs literally, in terms of competing for the best players, they didn't used to exist. So you have both these elite academic institutions with scholarships *and* these very powerful 'athletic factories' that are now getting into our sport, and I'm telling you, it was one thing to be competing with Princeton and knowing that if we're playing a national schedule and we're competing with Princeton for the Ivy Championship, we're doing pretty damn well. But I could see from many different factors, it was only going to just keep getting harder and harder and harder, where you're working so hard to be in the middle of the pack."

Welcome, Coach, to the NESCAC, a conference of eleven highly selective liberal arts colleges and universities that was founded in 1971 in the belief that "intercollegiate athletic programs should operate in harmony with the educational mission of each institution." Like the Ivy League, athletes are supposed to be representative of the student body as whole. And, like the Ivy League, the tenets of the Conference are generally more restrictive than those of the NCAA (in this case, Division III) with regard to season length, number of contests, post-season competition, out-of-season practices, and off-campus recruiting. But unlike the Ivy League, there are no paid official visits for recruits (all visits are unofficial, paid for by the prospective student and his or her family, except in rare cases of extreme financial need), and off-campus recruiting (a coach meeting with a player at his or her high school, after a contest, or in his or her home) is not allowed. NESCAC coaches are permitted to contact prospects by letter, email, and telephone, and most travel to watch players compete and evaluate athletic talent. But recruiting travel budgets in the NESCAC range anywhere from $200 to $700 a year, compared to annual Ivy recruiting travel budgets that range anywhere from $10,000 to "we have no set recruiting budget here at Harvard, and I've never been told I can't go see a kid" (as a few Crimson coaches told me).

"In my first two years of full recruiting seasons at Bates, I never even thought of turning in one receipt," says Lasagna. "The common understanding is that you are doing this out of your pocket. . . . I got an email last week from the woman who is sort of the business person in the athletic office and it said: 'For those of you that are doing talent evaluation, just know that you may want to get your trip reports in.' So I responded immediately and said, 'Jan, I never even thought of turning a receipt in. I've already taken five trips this spring, but I didn't save any receipts because I didn't expect to get that money back.' And she said, 'Well, I've set aside $200 for you, if you still have more talent evaluation to do.' So, that's your answer. The recruiting budget for men's lacrosse for 2003 is $200."

Doing what he loves in "a really uncomplicated way" has not been without some complications or challenges, however, for as is the case now in the Ivy League, admission spots in the NESCAC are more precious today than ever. As a result, the controversy and pressure surrounding the issue of athletic recruiting and admissions in this Division III "cousin conference" of the Ivies has grown intense in recent years (thanks, in large part, to Bill Bowen and his coauthors, who have been critical of the NESCAC for many of the same reasons they have been critical of the Ivy League). In reaction, the NESCAC presidents have enacted new rule changes to govern the admission process for athletes. Beginning with the class admitted in 2003, the NESCAC presidents, like their Ivy brethren, agreed to enforce limits on the number of athletic recruits who can be admitted to each school annually. Unlike the Ivy League, however, there is no Academic Index in the NESCAC (although some fear the adoption of an index is imminent), and there is no conference-wide academic floor.

"What NESCAC has done with athletes that is different," says Mike Schoenfeld, dean of enrollment planning at Middlebury, "is that we have defined through academic ratings [at each school] where a tip [for an athletic admit] is actually made, and we have agreed to limit the number of tips below a certain level of academic rating." In this respect, the NESCAC is quite different from the Ivy League, where the A.I. is applied as a universal standard.

But in many other respects, an overview of the NESCAC looks a good deal like an overview of the Ivy League. The eleven schools vary, sometimes dramatically, in their academic profile, in the degree of their elite status and national prestige, in the size of their endowment wealth, in their commitment to overall athletic excellence, in the scope and nature of their winning traditions, in the quality of their athletic facilities, in the attitude of their faculty to sports, and in the position of their presidents on this touchy issue. As in the Ivies, some schools are harder to get into than others (Amherst and Williams, for instance, are more selective than all the other institutions in the Conference, and more selective than a number of Ivies). As in the Ivies, financial aid is awarded solely on the basis of need. Six of the wealthier schools claim to be need-blind (Amherst, Bowdoin, Colby, Middlebury, Wesleyan, and Williams all say they admit students without considering an applicant's financial need), while the five remaining institutions (Bates, Connecticut College, Hamilton, Trinity, and Tufts) admit their students knowing exactly what each applicant's financial need will be. None of the schools offers merit scholarships of any kind, including athletic scholarships (which are banned in Division III). Athletes are treated the same as nonathletes (although, as we have seen, there are endowed scholarships at all of these elite schools that specify who is to receive them—whether it be an artist, a scientist, a student of color, an athlete, or another specified student).

Two of the NESCAC institutions, Tufts and Wesleyan, are universities with both undergraduate and graduate programs. Tufts, by far the largest school in the Conference, has 4,800 undergraduates and another 4,000 graduate students, while Wesleyan, the second largest school, has 2,700 undergrads and 150 graduate students. The nine smaller liberal arts colleges in the Conference range in enrollment from 1,650 students (Amherst and Bowdoin) to 2,350 (Middlebury). Like the Ivies, the schools each sponsor a large number of varsity programs for men and women (with an average of thirty), and they now compete for twenty-three conference championships (eleven for men, twelve for women). But a much higher percentage of students on a NESCAC campus play a varsity sport than on an Ivy League campus, thanks to the smaller student bodies of the schools. (At Williams, for instance, almost 40 percent of the students play a varsity sport, compared to a high in the Ivies of nearly 20 percent at Dartmouth and Princeton. At Colby, 52 percent of the males and 48 percent of the females on campus play a varsity sport.) Unlike Ivy rosters, NESCAC team rosters are heavily laden with athletes from New England, including a fair number from Maine, New Hampshire, and Vermont. These players grow up familiar with the schools, and they live close enough for coaches to hop in their cars and go evaluate them. But NESCAC coaches also recruit nationally (communicating with prospects via email and telephone, and evaluating their abilities by looking at videotapes and watching players compete at summer camps), and team rosters feature players from all around the country, from across Canada, and even a few from across the ocean.

On the national stage, the level of academic and athletic excellence in the Division III NESCAC parallels that of the Ivy League in Division I, albeit with some notable differences. Where Princeton has been named the best undergraduate liberal arts university by *U.S. News & World Report* several years in a row, Williams and Amherst have been named the best small liberal arts colleges for the past four years in row (and Williams has been tied for the top spot for thirteen consecutive years). But where Princeton has been ranked as high as twenty-fifth in the Division I Sears Directors Cup competition on one occasion (the only D-I nonscholarship school to ever break the top fifty in this National Association of Collegiate Directors of Athletics ranking), Williams has finished first in the annual Division III Sears Directors Cup competition for seven of the past eight years, including five consecutive first-place finishes between 1999 and 2003. Today, Williams is the best academic *and* athletic small college in America, an astounding accomplishment, given the high academic profile of their student body and the almost complete lack of recruiting regulations for the non-NESCAC schools in Division III, which has over 425 members. These other D-III schools can load their teams with practically anybody, in almost any way—even adding transfers in mid-season. "Division III is a much more wide-open mess than Division I is," says Middlebury Athletic Director, Russ Reilly. "It's what makes the success that NESCAC teams have had at the national level even more meaningful." And it's why, when Reilly speaks of the Division III national men's basketball championship that Williams captured in 2003, he says, "That thing is huge, absolutely huge."

Prior to this accomplishment, most of the national titles NESCAC schools have won since 1994, when the presidents lifted a ban on NCAA postseason competition, have been in the same niche sports where Ivy League teams also excel, not in sports such as basketball, which are played universally. For instance, Williams has won national crowns in men's and women's cross country, women's rowing, women's and men's tennis, and men's soccer. Middlebury has captured twenty national titles in the past decade, more than any other NESCAC school, in men's and women's lacrosse, men's and women's ice hockey, women's cross country, and women's field hockey. Trinity has won national championships in women's and men's squash, Colby won the women's crew title in 2003, and Amherst won the national championship in women's lacrosse in 2003.

This success has been a mixed blessing. No admission people had an input into the decision to enter NCAA postseason play, which in the view of Tom Parker, the longtime admission director at Williams and now dean of admission and financial aid at Amherst, "was a real big mistake. But I honestly believed that we would get out of NESCAC and get the crap beaten out of us. I really did. I thought we would go play Springfield College and get beaten, and go play Cortland State and schools in California like San Diego State, and I thought we'd get killed. I thought it would be a nonissue. And lo and behold, we do a lot better."

Parker laughs, but then turns serious regarding the fallout from that success. "As much fun as I've had with some of the national championship stuff here and at Williams, in retrospect I wish we hadn't done it because I think it did up the ante, and I think it really did intensify the kind of looking at one another. And I think with that has come a lot more, 'We've gotta regulate everything.'

"I think as we've become more formalized as a conference there probably has been a lessening in the amount of trust from one institution to another," agrees Russ Reilly of Middlebury. "If one institution gets too successful there may be the feeling out there that that institution is doing something wrong, and all of a sudden you've got people pointing fingers, and it's really kind of unfortunate. 'Cause I don't think there's anybody doing anything drastically wrong. I think everybody's doing what they feel in their hearts is best for their institution."

The NESCAC has witnessed the faults in the Ivy system and is now consciously trying to avoid many of them. (Whether it succeeds or not remains to be seen.) Thanks to their D-III status, NESCAC schools do not compete with scholarship schools for nearly every athlete, as the Ivies do. Even so, the high cost of attending one of these exclusive liberal arts schools often rivals the cost of attending an Ivy League school. While the monetary issue is a very real one for coaches, and for some recruits and their families, there are no prereads on financial aid given to athletes and their families in the NESCAC, (eliminating the associated "commitment quid pro quo" we heard about in the Ivies). Nor is there a league-wide bidding war under way for athletic talent in the NESCAC, as is the case in the Ivy League. There is no Princeton, raising the bar and increasing the stakes by eliminating student loans altogether, and thereby forcing other schools to find ways to combat a more generous aid policy. Certainly, applying to one of the need-blind NESCAC schools, as opposed to one of the need-based schools, can be an advantage, but no one in the Conference talked to me about getting outbid for football players by Williams or Amherst or Middlebury. No doubt this is related to a lack of pressure from scholarship school offers outside the Conference. But I suspect it also reflects the overall affluence of the student bodies and a recruiting game that is being played for slightly lower stakes.

"I hope it's legitimate to say that people aren't going to get fired because they don't win the NESCAC championship," says Harry Sheehy, the Williams athletic director. "You know, people get fired in the Ivy League, much more so than at our level."

That is certainly true, but today a NESCAC coach can indeed be fired for losing. As Russ Reilly points out, that truth was confirmed for everyone in the conference when Tufts fired its women's basketball coach in 2002 after she had led the team to a 9-14 record.

"Coaches feel tremendous pressure to be successful in one of the best Division III, highly publicized, very athletic conferences in the country," says Peter Gooding, the Amherst athletic director. "They feel they've got to do well in that, otherwise their job is in jeopardy. Now that profile is very little different than Division I, and there's some truth to that. It's much, much harder for athletic directors and coaches to ride the high ground and say, within reason, 'Do the best that you can. Let's not drop our standards hardly at all to field teams. We'll take our lumps, but you know, we'll hold our heads high.' Doesn't work anymore because we're trapped in this consumerism that these very affluent families, who populate 60–70 percent of our student bodies, have grown up expecting the best, wanting the best, and have been very involved in their child's welfare—and part of that is, they expect a very good team to play on."

Parents demanding success (and calling on athletic directors to fire coaches when teams don't win) is part of a larger societal trend, but they also reflect a specific NESCAC trend that has steadily increased since 1999, when conference championships began. Since that time, coaches, athletic directors, and admission deans have all seen a sharp increase in the competitive nature of the NESCAC. This has translated into pressure to find and admit the best players possible across all sports, for like the Ivy League, an effort is made to support recruits in every sport, not just the higher-profile sports.

A high percentage of these recruits are former prep school athletes. Their well-to-do parents can afford the steep tuition, and they qualify for the rigorous admission standards. (My Middlebury soccer and hockey teams in 1974–75 had three to four private school kids and twelve to fourteen public school kids; today, the ratio is almost the exact opposite.) One can argue that the NESCAC is even more of a rich player's league now than its elite D-I cousin, the Ivy League. Certainly there are players of high financial need on many rosters, but in the NESCAC recruiting game these days, money takes a far back seat to the mission of monitoring academic standards and regulating the new limits on athletic admits.

"What we're doing now is we're hoping to avoid the Ivy index," says Tom Parker, who heads a committee of NESCAC admission deans that has been charged by the Conference presidents with finding the best way to enact and oversee the new recruiting and admission rules. "Because I don't like it. And most of the people in the League don't like it. It works, but it's pretty darn crude. . . . Maybe we would be spared at the Division III level, but once you've got an index, the coaches learn it inside and out. And they start to say things like, 'Oh, don't take your three SAT IIs.' Or 'Why don't you drop calculus.' And they start mentoring their recruited athletes with the idea of getting the desired number."

Parker knows how the game is played in the Ivies, thanks to his years of experience at Williams, which, along with Amherst, will compete each year for potential Ivy athletes. A 1969 Williams graduate, Parker was the school's admission director for nineteen years and the architect of its highly successful athletic recruiting model. In 2000, he moved to arch-rival Amherst (a treasonous act to Williams coaches, who questioned his loyalty, and a highly suspicious act to Amherst coaches, who also questioned his loyalty!), and he is now instituting the Williams model all over again at his new school. In both places, he has witnessed the flaws in the Ivy League's A.I.

"We heard it at Williams, we hear it here," he says of Ivy coaches who advise kids on how to hit the A.I. number. "A kid will call up and say, 'Gee, I talked to the Penn coach, and he told me not to take the SAT IIs, and is that okay if I do it at Amherst?' I say, 'No, it's not okay.' And they go, 'Yeah, but Penn said we could do that.' I say, 'Well, that's a different world.' But more of it is just talking to my colleagues [at Ivy schools]."

Parker does not want to mention any names, but he will describe some of the problems his Ivy colleagues have shared over the years regarding the A.I. "Coaches begin," he explains, "in a crude way to make admission decisions. They say, 'I've got these five kids who meet the Index.' And then if an admission guy tries to argue with them, they say, 'Well, wait a minute. These are the rules.' So it leaves the admission director looking at one kid and saying, 'Geez, you know, if you read this folder, you don't want to take this kid. But yes, he does meet the Index.' And then they end up taking him. Or, in some cases, you know, there is a kid that just misses, but you read the file and you say, 'This is a fantastic kid.' What ends up is that the Index sort of supersedes the file.

"I will give you an example," he says, explaining how the numbers can overshadow the bigger picture. "When I was at Williams there was a football guy and, you know, the numbers looked good. But there wasn't a chance in hell that I was gonna admit the kid, when you read the file. You know, it was just underachievement, underachievement, underachievement. And that showed laziness, laziness, laziness. But, you know, he's a kid at an undistinguished public high school with 1380 scores who's cruisin'. He's not taking the AP courses that are available. He's got a B average. So it all conforms to the Index. But the fact of the matter is, you read the file, and my experience has been that if a kid is lazy in the classroom, they're also lazy on the field. You know, lazy people are truly lazy people. And the guy got into an Ivy. I just said to myself, 'Oh my heavens.' He's not going to be a distinguished student, but I'll betcha, once he's faced with a bigger challenge in football, he won't meet it.

"I followed him just because I was so curious about it," continues Parker. "At that time, the Ivies were taking thirty-five football players, so you've almost by definition got a minimum of twenty walk-offs. And he was one of them. So that's my objection to the Index."

Right now, instead of an index, each NESCAC school is creating its own individual academic ratings, based on test scores, class rank, or GPA and then determining within those individual ratings where exceptions are being made for athletes in the admission process. As Parker points out, "NESCAC's much more complex than the Ivy League. That's the other trouble with an index. Bates is SAT optional. Bowdoin is SAT optional. Middlebury is SAT I optional. I think Hamilton has got some kind of complicated thing . . . so how in the world you would superimpose an index on us, I just don't know. What we're trying to do is rely on our own internal reader ratings."

And then, at NESCAC meetings of the admission deans to review the data on incoming recruits, they are counting on honest accountings from every school. Parker explains, "We're sort of laughingly calling it and relying right now on public shaming. Meaning if Tufts comes in there with a whole bunch of jokers, we're just going to go, 'Wait a minute, don't tell us that that kid's an academic admit.' Or, if the kid really looks atrocious, gee, maybe the Tufts guy will say, 'You know, I'm gonna have to present this kid to my colleagues, and I'm gonna be kind of ashamed to do it.'

"This will evolve," says Parker of each school's heavy reliance on its own individual rating system. For instance, he points out that Middlebury "has sort of the murkiest sort of system" with nine rating variables, which can be applied in different ways on different parts of the application. "They're simply gonna have to come up with something a little more quantifiable, and I know that Mike [Schoenfeld, the dean of enrollment planning at Middlebury] is working with the provost there to do that." ("Murky" as the Middlebury system may be, it also illustrates the dangers of relying too heavily on a "quantifiable" numerical rating, based largely on test scores; the school's last two Rhodes Scholars were each admitted with board scores under 1200.)

Yet the ratings are critical to the new NESCAC system, which, beginning with the class admitted for the fall of 2003, imposes a limit on the number of "athletic factor" admits at each institution. (These are more commonly referred to as athletic "tips.") A few years prior to adopting the conference-wide limits, Williams, Amherst, and Wesleyan (known as the Little Three, the nation's oldest athletic "conference" with a rivalry extending over more than one hundred years) agreed to limit their total number of annual athletic admits to sixty-six. In the years prior to that agreement, Williams had been working under its own system, which limited athletic tips by essentially allotting quotas to each sport, based on its roster size and overall needs, while Amherst had been conducting its own internal review of its athletic admission process. When the NESCAC decided to institute limits throughout the league, the presidents turned to Parker to serve as the architect of the plan. After all, he had created the Williams model, and then he had successfully adapted it into the admission process at Amherst, where he trimmed athletic admits from ninety-four to seventy-five, and then to sixty-six in just a few years—all while boosting the overall success of the school's teams.

"We were told, essentially, by the presidents to figure out how to reduce the number of athletic admits," says Parker, of the NESCAC challenge. "I said, 'Well, what the heck, we did it at Amherst.' I couldn't really talk about the Williams model because it was so evolved. I said, 'Here's a place that changed pretty radically in a short period of time. Seems to have worked pretty well. Why don't we just do something mathematical?' And I said, 'We have x number of sports, x number of athletic admits, why don't we just work out a little simple algorithm.'"

Mike Schoenfeld explains how the formula works: "The maximum number of athletic factor admits varies at each school, depending on the number of varsity sports the school fields. . . . Middlebury's number is 74.5, which is the total you reach when you multiply our NESCAC varsity sports (excluding football) by two and our non-NESCAC sports (skiing and squash) by 2.5, and add fourteen for football."

The determination of how to distribute the athletic factor admits is left up to each NESCAC school to decide, and while some schools assign quotas by sport, others do not. At Middlebury, for instance, each sport does not automatically get two athletic factor admits a year, and football does not automatically get fourteen—the distribution varies year by year, and is determined by Admissions.

The question of how great an academic exception schools can make for an athlete is yet another touchy issue, and one that is still evolving. "A lot of the places were frankly in denial about what they were doing," says Parker. "Or they were obfuscating in all kinds of different ways. It's nobody's fault. I understand how these things happen."

Amherst and Williams use a banding system, he explains. "Meaning you can have x number from these academic ratings and x number from those other academic ratings. Our top academic admits are what we call a-bands, and then there's a middle group called b-bands, and then a bottom group called c-bands. And we have a definite floor that we cannot go below. We have a rating scale of one to seven, and we cannot take any sevens, under any circumstances . . . sixes are the lowest acceptable, they call 'em bogies. We will take maybe a couple there, then a limited number of our c-bands, which are our fives and sixes, and our b-bands, which are our threes and fours."

The ratings are based on SAT Is, SAT IIs, class rank, quality of the academic program, how students have done, teacher recommendations—in other words, the whole folder, not merely a mathematical formula. There are impact players at every Ivy League school who would not have been admissible at Williams and Amherst, where the academic numbers of incoming students are extremely similar, according to Parker. For instance, the average SAT score for a-band admits (the academic admits who comprise slightly more than 50 percent of the student bodies at both schools) was 1481 for the Amherst class entering in the fall of 2004. This places them in the top 1 percent of college bound students. For athletic factor admits at Amherst in the same year, the average SAT score was 1338, placing them in the top 7 percent of all students entering college (it's also one hundred points higher than the average for all students going to Denison or Kenyon). When combined with a 3.5 GPA, the 1338 score adds up to an Ivy League A.I. of 199, which is nearly 30 points above the floor of 171.

One of the keys to Parker's system is its complete transparency. He shares his athletic admission data with the Amherst faculty each year, just as he did at Williams. "We are very formal with the faculty," he explains. "They are aware of both the athletes' precollege academic data and how they perform at Amherst. They also have this data for legacies, students of color, 'special admits,' men, women, and any subgroup people are interested in, so athletes are not being singled out.

"In the Bowen and Shulman book they talk about underperformance of the GPA," Parker continues, delving into why he feels the transparency is so crucial. "I have a theory, for what it's worth, and this is worrisome to me as we go down this kind of very tricky path that we're going down. The kids at Williams did not get beaten up in the press or by the faculty. I think part of it was because it was so transparent.

"There's that phenomenon—it's mostly in reference to students of color—of stereotype threat," he explains. "And when you are subject to stereotype threat you tend to underperform. Certainly students of color do. Interestingly at Amherst, our [athletic admit] kids were underperforming. And it was not egregious, it's not kids who should have been A- who were

B-; it's much less than that. But our kids at Amherst were underperforming. And I think part of it was that they were subject to significantly more stereotype threat by professors than were the athletes at Williams. And I don't think it was, you know, prejudicial grading. I think it was kids who just said, 'I feel frightened here. I feel unwelcome here.' And one of the things I said right from the beginning is, 'Don't get mad at the athletes. We admitted them. Get mad at me, get mad at the board, get mad at the president, get mad at whomever else, but don't victimize the kid.'"

Another reason the Williams athletes were not under fire following the publication of *The Game of Life* is that the school has years of data on the performance of all its students, and the data proves unequivocally that the athletes perform exactly where they are predicted to perform—based on their entire admission folder, not on an academic index.

In Parker's experience, the greatest academic exceptions in athletic recruiting are usually made in football. "There are gonna be a couple, probably two, and those are with what I call the 'bogies.' What you will find across NESCAC is that it's football, men's hockey, in some cases women's hockey, and men's lacrosse at some places—but neither at Williams nor Amherst has that been a problematical sport. You know, people are always sort of surprised, and they'll say, 'Oh, the helmet sports.' And I'll say, 'Yes and no.' Our lacrosse kids seem to do real well. You know, we didn't get national championships, but . . ."

Middlebury certainly has, capturing three straight NCAA men's lacrosse titles in 2000, 2001, and 2002. Between 1995 and 1999, in men's hockey, another helmet sport, the Panthers won five straight national titles. (In March 2004, they won their sixth national title in ten years.) Russ Reilly, the Middlebury athletic director, makes no apologies for his school's athletic excellence.

"I'd like to think Middlebury has always believed that there's nothing wrong with being good in anything we do," he says, "whether it's athletics, academics, or any other co-curricular activity. I think we are very, very fortunate. We have absolutely fabulous facilities, which is a tremendous credo for the many benefactors who've helped the college upgrade our facilities to the point where, in my opinion, they are second to none. I think we're very fortunate in that we have a tremendously professional coaching staff, who not only teach the great lessons or skills of their particular sports, but also teach greater life lessons to the student-athletes that they work with. I think that we're very, very fortunate that as Middlebury's academic reputation has gone up, so has our athletic reputation. And we are attracting some truly remarkable young men and women who come here not only to get a great education, but also want to participate in a quality athletic program—and we've been successful, and I think success breeds success. And lastly, I think we have tremendous support of the college community, starting in the president's office, right on down, through all alumni and friends of the college. So it's a formula that when you put all four of those things together, you hope you do have success, and we've been very, very fortunate.

"I can't speak for other institutions," he continues, "but Middlebury College is not interested in that tip system. They're allocating a certain number of slots for this team, that team, or the other team. We've been told we can have x number of tips overall. We're not in the business of admissions. That's what Mike Schoenfeld does. Our job, our challenge, is to provide the admission people with the best students we can find, and kids who we also have an interest in athletically. I think that slot system is the biggest bunch of bunko there is, personally. And I don't mind going on record saying it. I think the job of admissions should be done by admission people, and I think it's up to each institution to look itself squarely in the face and decide who they are admitting. And if they're not admitting the right students for their institution, then they need to make changes. But I don't think Williams and Amherst should be telling Middlebury how to run their program, any more than we should tell Trinity, or Bates, or Bowdoin, or Colby how to run their programs. I think it's an institutional decision and each institution needs to know who it is, what it wants to be, and how it should get there. And as long as we can all look at ourselves in the mirror in the morning, we have no reason to apologize for anything."

Reilly points out that in the years prior to the publication of *The Game of Life* and the adoption of the tip system, "The presidents asked for information on selected sports. They would pick three, four, five, six sports a year, and share academic information on those kids. And it was always done in a confidential way, and in theory, done in a way where you wouldn't know which institution was which. I suppose everybody could identify themselves as they were going through the process. So they've been sharing on some level all along. But I think the level of detail that they're being asked to provide now is really tying the hands of admission officers around the Conference. I think they're turning down some young people at each of our institutions that would blend in well with the community, and because they happen to be an athlete, they're not going to be looked at with a limit of 74.5."

Given that NESCAC schools now sponsor an average of thirty varsity teams, "You're probably not going to be as good as you once were," Reilly points out. "And maybe that's the goal of some people. I just don't know why we have to apologize for being good in anything we do. It's mind-boggling to me."

For NESCAC coaches, the transition to two tips a year from as many as four, five, or six is mind-boggling. But there are ways around the new limits, and everyone tries to exploit them, as they try to bring in excellent athletes without necessarily using a tip in the process. The most obvious method is simply to find outstanding students who are also top athletes—the "academic admits."

"That's the premise behind this whole thing," says Parker. This approach has worked extremely well for Williams, and it is now being adapted successfully at Amherst, where the women's lacrosse team captured the national title in 2003. In recent years, as Middlebury's academic standing has climbed significantly, the Panther sports teams have benefited as well. As in the Ivy League, there is a NESCAC pecking order that tends to attract the best students and athletes to the schools with the best academic and athletic reputations. Coaches must overcome Williams and Middlebury in a number of sports, just as Ivy coaches must overcome the reputations of Princeton, Harvard, and Yale.

As in the Ivy League, the highly academic athletes in the NESCAC tend to cluster in certain sports: cross country, tennis, crew, squash, Nordic skiing, lacrosse, swimming, and soccer. Yet at Williams, the 2003 men's national championship basketball team featured a senior class consisting of two a-band players, one b-band recruit, and one c-band star. "It's not that hard to do," says Parker of his former school's NCAA title in basketball. "You have a squad of eighteen players, but you have seven or eight who really play."

Parker has proven the truth of this statement at Amherst, where he has helped the men's basketball team become a force as well. In December 2003, Amherst beat the defending Division III national champions from Williams just days after Williams had knocked off Holy Cross, a Division I scholarship school with an impressive record of success that included three straight Patriot League titles and three consecutive NCAA Division I tournament appearances.

Under the NESCAC system, there are other ways to recruit great players without being charged an athletic tip.

"Most, but not all of the NESCAC schools, use one rating to denote the academic qualifications of each applicant and a second rating to denote the personal qualifications [leadership, community service, artistic and athletic abilities, contributions to diversity on campus, legacy status, and development cases]," explains Mike Schoenfeld. "Having tried to quantify these personal qualities, the question then becomes at what point do we tip an admission decision based on nonacademic qualities versus academic qualities? In fact, we tip many, if not most, decisions based on some sort of factoring in of the nonacademic qualities.

"I don't believe that many, if any, NESCAC schools define their tips so precisely for any other group of applicants [besides athletes]," he adds. "Similarly, they are not defining an SAT/rank in class cutoff for a brilliant artist, musician, mathematician, or poet. Frankly, I would like to think we tip for everyone for some reason." (In fact, the athletic talent evaluation model is used across a number of other disciplines on every NESCAC campus. Professors are asked by Admissions to rate art portfolios, musical samples, dance and theater videos, and poetry and fiction submissions in the same way that Ivy League admission officers seek expert feedback on applicants with special talents.)

For athletic recruiting, these other "nonacademic" tip factors can mean that the soccer player who contributes to diversity, the lacrosse player who is a legacy, the basketball player with a record of outstanding community service, the hockey player who has demonstrated exceptional leadership on and off the ice, the football player whose family is in a position to donate a vast amount of time, resources, or money to the school are all athletes who may not count against a school's total limit of athletic admits under the NESCAC system—so long as their academic ratings are high enough to avoid a "public shaming" at league meetings of admission deans.

"This is where it gets a little bit confusing, and where we've tried to be very honest," says Tom Parker. "For example, in the last three years there have been some legacies who have been charged as athletic tips because they are legacies that would not have gotten in otherwise. And there have been a small number of students of color . . . I'm simplifying here. The danger of this is you start reducing people to a single dimension, and they're not. But the admission decision is a single dimension decision: it's a yes/no outcome. And so there have been some students of color who have been charged to the athletic department—an Asian-American swimmer, for example, where you say, had that person come through without any athletic support they would not have been admissible. But there are certainly some, where you say, 'Hey, Peter and Milt Gooding [the Amherst men's soccer coaches], thanks a million. These are great African-American males that you've turned up, and we're gonna admit them with bells on. They're terrific.' And no, we don't charge them an athletic tip for that.

"We've had very, very good luck recruiting students of color," he adds, "and that's why my hat really goes off to the coaches here. Because, again, the common wisdom was, 'Oh, we'll never get that kind of kid.' And you know, our teams are much more diverse than they were before, and I think that that's really important."

Another really important means of maximizing the limited number of athletic tips is to recruit athletes who play more than one sport. The NESCAC has a long and rich tradition of attracting superb two-sport athletes, and today it may be the last bastion of two-sport excellence in the country. Unlike the Ivy League, where out-of-season practices are now standard, in the NESCAC coaches are not allowed to conduct practices out-of-season. A football player is free to play baseball, a soccer player is able to play lacrosse, a field hockey player can run track, all without the Ivy League conflict of missing out-of-season practices.

"You can do some strength training on your own and you can basically play pickup," says Harry Sheehy, the Williams athletic director, of the NESCAC rules on out-of-season practice. "The captains can organize pickup. It can't be formal drills and things like that. What we want is kind of 'open gym,' and you know what happens more times than not, it's the basketball kids that show up. But I like looking out my back door and seeing six kids on the team with a few of the kids who aren't on the team playing, frankly."

"It gives the game back to the players," says Dave Saward, the Middlebury men's soccer coach, of spring pickup games organized by the team. "We are far too involved as coaches in this country, micromanaging everything. This lets them exercise their passion for the game without any interference from us."

It also lets players compete in another sport, which is a major lure for every NESCAC school. But two in particular use it to attract Ivy League–caliber athletes. "Within NESCAC, Williams and Amherst tend to be the only schools realistically that can compete with the Ivies for athletes," says Parker. "And the Ivies did Williams a big, big favor, and that was they made it virtually impossible for a kid to play two sports. They went in with spring football [and out-of-season practices in all sports]. I think the Ivies have gone really crazy. I just think they are pretending to be something that they're not.

"So we, at Williams, very consciously said, 'We can get a kid from Dartmouth.' They'll say, 'Okay, that's a comparable education.' But what we can say is, 'You can play football and lacrosse here.' Or, 'You can play hockey and baseball.' Or, 'You can play soccer and lacrosse.' When I left, I think there were 350 two-sport athletes at Williams, and over 100 three-sport athletes [many of whom competed in cross country, indoor track, and track and field]."

When coaches at Amherst say to Parker, "Oh geez, Hamilton can take these kids that we could never take," his response is, "Yeah, that's right, but you can get a two-sport kid away from Dartmouth, and Hamilton could never do that."

Ironically, when Parker arrived at Amherst, with a mandate to fix an athletic admission process that had gone awry and triggered an uproar from the powerful faculty (mainly because of exceptions made for the football team during the tenure of head coach Jack Siedlecki, who then moved on to Yale), a report had been issued by an Amherst committee investigating sports, which said, in effect, that the multisport athlete did not exist anymore, that specialization was killing it.

"I said, 'Oh boy, you're going down the wrong path,'" Parker recalls. "'This is our single biggest advantage.' We had kind of a bizarre system where we almost provided disincentives for coaches to go after two-sport athletes. The kind of game that might be played was: here's a rated kid in two sports. And instead of one of the coaches just claiming it, and the other guy gets it for free, they would say, 'Okay, my hope is that John will go for this lacrosse guy, and I won't get charged for it. And John will get charged for it, and that will affect John's numbers.' So there was almost a disincentive to communicate and to work together.

"And it was perverse, in a way. But the lacrosse guy thought the football guy would do it, the football guy thought the lacrosse guy would do it, neither one would do it, and then the kid would go to Williams or someplace else. So we've tried to replicate that thing, and we've done that with some success."

At Middlebury, two hundred athletes now play two varsity sports, but in the view of Russ Reilly, their days are numbered. "We live in an age of specialization. I know as much as we try to promote the multiple-sport athlete, it's very, very difficult to find kids today who are coming through the high schools or secondary school systems who are involved in multiple sports," he says. "The two- and three-sport athlete is rapidly becoming a dinosaur, even in NESCAC.

"Fortunately, because we promote it, I think we've been able to hold on to it a lot longer than most. A lot of institutions now are hiring single sport coaches, and when you hire a single sport coach, there's going to be some pressure on kids to be involved in just that sport. Whereas if you have a coach who's involved in a couple of different activities, they're much more understanding of the reason why a young person might want to be involved in more than one. There's definitely been a conscious decision on the part of some families for kids to specialize because they see that as their ticket to getting into a college or a university of their choice."

In the NESCAC that ticket is frequently punched in the early decision process, just as it is for athletes in the Ivy League. But today the premium on applying early is even greater, thanks to the new limits on athletic tips. With only one, two, or three tips a year, coaches may not have any influence left by the time the regular decision process rolls around. As a result, athletes who are on the borderline academically must now move early if they want a coach's support. Even so, the commitment game in the NESCAC is not played at the same level of intensity as it is in the Ivy League.

"I feel a little bit naïve, but also glad that I don't work in the Ivy League," says Tom Parker. "A lot of them have these summer camps now, and they invite recruits to the camps during the summer, they're allegedly open to everyone. . . . Some of our kids, who were interested in us, said, 'The [Ivy] coach said they really liked me during the camp, and that before I went home they would like a commitment from me, or not.' Again, I just say, 'Holy mackerel.'"

Yet with the new limits in NESCAC, the pressure to make a commitment will only increase and accelerate. It would be naïve to think otherwise. The pressure may occur at a summer camp held on campus, an increasingly common practice among NESCAC coaches in numerous sports. Coaches also work at camps held off campus, where they have additional exposure to players. A number of schools invite recruits to visit unofficially during the spring of the junior year, organizing an entire day for prospects and their parents. While many schools have been doing this for a long time, according to Harry Sheehy, Williams has been doing it for a limited number of sports for the past few years.

"It's a nice official way to get fifteen, twenty kids on campus, and have them get a sense of the place together," he says. "Sometimes friendships are made, or they find out they know kids. I've encouraged our coaches to try to work in that way. It's really efficient."

Sheehy describes a spring Saturday event in 2003, coordinated by the women's and men's soccer coaches. "I came in and spoke, I think the president might have come in and spoken. He was there. The director of admission came in and spoke. Basically, it's just a day of information, covering process and all those things. And then I'm sure the coaches talked individually with each kid about whatever it is that they're gonna talk about."

Increasingly, younger coaches are entering the Conference, and a number of them have held assistant or even head coaching jobs in Division I. They bring with them a new energy and commitment to the recruiting process, along with valuable recruiting contacts, knowledge, and experience. Peter Lasagna acknowledges that he is tapping into new regions for Bates lacrosse, including the hotbed Baltimore area, where he grew up and now works at summer lacrosse camps. Prior to that, he says, "One of my strategies was to get to places where I'm not competing with as many coaches, and where they might not know anything about Bates College. So I went to places like St. Louis and Texas," where he was paid to work at other coaches' camps.

Bill Beaney, the veteran men's hockey coach at Middlebury, laments the influx of what he views as Division I recruiting techniques in NESCAC, but when he is reminded that nearly twenty years ago he brought his own set of D-I recruiting contacts, skills, and commitment from the University of New Hampshire program, and built a national power by employing them, he admits his own guilt. For many years he would drive his own car to Burlington, where he would climb into a car driven by University of Vermont assistant, Roger Grillo, now the head men's hockey coach at Brown, and together the two coaches would head up into Quebec on recruiting trips. Beaney enjoyed a free ride and a free couch in a hotel room, while Grillo enjoyed having the company of a man who became "a big mentor."

When Beaney's teams won five straight national titles between 1995 and 1999, the Division I Ivies came courting. He was a front-runner for the Dartmouth job in 1997, but he pulled out after speaking with his friend, Bobby Clark, who was the Big Green men's soccer coach at the time.

"The admission process there was not like ours at Middlebury," says Beaney. "Here, they trust me and support my judgments on kids. We work together. I got the sense over there that the coach played a very distant role."

A few years later, Harvard tried to persuade Beaney to take over their hockey program. Reports in *The Boston Globe* gave readers the impression he was all set to accept the job. But, in the end, he says, "I couldn't picture myself in that environment, with the recruiting. It's so accelerated now, and the pressure on kids is just too much. I see Bobby Gaudet [the Dartmouth men's hockey coach] and ask him if he's gotten any high school sophomores to commit yet. And I'm only half kidding."

NESCAC athletes won't be asked for commitments at such a pace, but they will surely have to pick their school early if they want support, for as Tom Parker points out, "Our spots are probably more precious than the Ivies' because we don't have very much room for error."

In addition to Early Decision, for many years most of the NESCAC schools have also offered an Early Decision Two, or ED2, option (apply in mid-December, hear in mid-February). The timing of ED2 has been popular with some athletes who want to see where they stand with other schools before they commit to a NESCAC school, and for students who need a bit more time to make a decision. But under the new tip limits, the impact of ED2 on athletic admits is likely to diminish substantially, at least outside of sports such as football and ice hockey, where the senior year on the field and in the classroom can make or break a prospect's chances of being supported by a coach and getting in. In most sports, it is very likely that there simply will not be any tips left after the first round of early decisions is completed.

"We tried ED2 before my time for three years, mostly for athletic reasons and it was a fiasco," says Parker of his experience at Amherst. "It helped a little bit with athletes, but what we ended up with were a whole lot of bounce-backs from ED programs in the Ivies: 'Oh, shit. I didn't get into Harvard. I better apply ED2 to Amherst.' Then they didn't get into Amherst, either. It was just incredibly time consuming for very little return. But everybody in NESCAC does it, except Williams and us. You know, in a really kind of perverse way, we benefit by it because a kid will call up one of our coaches and say, 'The coach from college x in NESCAC told me that he or she could get me in ED2 if I applied, but couldn't make any promises later on. I want to go to Amherst.' And at that point the Amherst coach will come to me, and I'll say either 'yes,' 'no,' or 'maybe,' and then they're able to communicate that to the kid. So we end up getting a lot of kids sort of identifying us as a first choice without our even trying.

"It's the same thing in the Ivies for football and hockey," he says. "They virtually have a signing date of February 1 now. We would see the same thing at Williams that we see here. A kid will call us, and say, 'The coach from Dartmouth called me up. Today is Friday. I have to let him know by Monday. I want to go to Williams 'cause I want to play two sports.' Or maybe he'd say, 'I just want to go there.' But you just can set your watch by it—and at that point, again, we can say, 'yes, no, maybe.'"

There are coaches in the NESCAC who will call kids and tell them they'll be accepted if they commit to their school—but the offer always comes with a deadline. The kid must commit within the next twenty-four or forty-eight hours, sometimes before he or she has had a chance to hear from other schools. I know of a coach at Tufts who sprung such an offer on an athlete who had applied ED2 to Middlebury. In early February, when the player had still not heard from Middlebury, the Tufts coach called to invite the player down for a visit, during which he told the player (who had applied regular decision to Tufts in the fall) that he would be accepted to Tufts—but only if he committed to coming within the next two days. The offer was made in the admission office, where the player was handed an envelope containing the details of his financial award and told to call the coach within forty-eight hours or the offer would be rescinded. This was a top student, in honors courses, at an excellent public high school that sends at least a dozen graduates to Ivy and NESCAC schools each year. A two-sport captain and a capella singing group member with 1450 SATs, the player would not have counted as an athletic tip at either Tufts or Middlebury. And yet the Tufts coach was playing a game with the kid, preying on his fear of being rejected by Middlebury, and hoping to maneuver him into making a commitment before he had heard anything for certain from his first choice. Hanging over the decision was the threat of being turned down by Tufts if he decided to gamble and wait on Middlebury. (The player decided to wait, declined the Tufts offer, and was accepted at Middlebury two weeks later.) A similar scenario happened with a recruit at Amherst. This player had been deferred by an Ivy school in the early decision process, at which point the Amherst coach pounced, telling the player that Amherst could be a sure thing—but only if the player committed to coming within the next few days. (This player decided to take the certain acceptance and committed to Amherst.) Such scenarios are increasing in the NESCAC, where the commitment game is alive and well, just as it is in the Ivy League. Each year, kids are pressured to make decisions, often when they are most vulnerable.

"We had a kid recruited by Williams as a football kicker," says Bruce Bailey, the director of college counseling at the elite Lakeside School in Seattle. "And Williams obviously takes their sports pretty seriously. He was getting a huge squeeze about committing to all the schools that were interested, mainly Middlebury, Bowdoin, and Williams. He was getting all these promises, 'If you commit to us, we'll get you in.' And I know that those coaches don't sit on admission committees, but I also know that some have more influence than others. Anyway, I ended up calling the director of admission, Dick Nesbitt at Williams, and said, 'Look it, your coach is telling me if this kid commits to you, he's going to get in. And you're a

Division III school that's pretty competitive, and so I want you to tell me, what's the deal?' And he looked at the folder and said, 'Yeah, he's a good kid. It's official. He'll get in.' So I wrote that date, that quote, right down in my little notes. The family was saying, 'Is this really for real?' Because they didn't want to commit and have him not get in, and then lose the leverage he had at Bowdoin and Middlebury. It was interesting because as soon as he said he'd go to Williams, and told the coaches at all the schools, when the results came out from Middlebury and Bowdoin, he was wait-listed at both those places—which would be very typical. Because if somehow he flipped and wanted to go to Bowdoin or Middlebury, they hadn't used up a spot . . . but they still had him on a string, so to speak."

As in the Ivies, the NESCAC sport with the greatest number of tips by far is football. "It's the big white elephant sitting in the room that no one wants to talk about," says Mike Schoenfeld—the most problematical sport for the presidents because it uses up the greatest number of admission slots and because it requires some of the deepest academic exceptions.

"We cannot solve football," says Parker. "If somebody were to say, 'I want all the football kids to come out of the a-band category,' we can't do it. It's demonstrably impossible. So at that point, you say how much is football worth, which Swarthmore did, or can we play the game differently?"

Parker grew up playing football, and he played for a year at Williams. His father was a high school coach. He likes the Amherst coach a great deal. "I'm not one of these blindly anti-football people by any means," he says, "but the game has become so specialized. It's not as if there's an offensive team and a defensive team, but there's now a passing situation team, a short yardage team for offense, a short yardage team for defense. I've always said whatever happens in the NFL will be happening in NESCAC in three or four years, and that's exactly what's happened. To play the game as we're currently playing it just requires a whole lot of players."

Both Parker and Schoenfeld would like to see the NESCAC make a bold move: reduce the number of recruits by switching to one platoon football. "Frankly, a 285-pound guy in NESCAC can't play two ways," says Parker. "They're just not that good an athlete, and very often it's those big guys where you see your biggest scratches [academic exceptions]. I think if we play two ways, we wouldn't be playing with 285-pound guys who aren't very good athletes. I think our linemen would be 220-pound guys who were much better athletes. There was actually an article in *Sports Illustrated* about this. It was very interesting. Joe Paterno would be all for one platoon football."

He is quick to admit, however, that whatever Tom Parker and Mike Schoenfeld think about the issue doesn't make any difference. "But we can say to the presidents, 'You can only press us so hard on football. We can't fix it for you through admission means. You're gonna have to be imaginative, or you're gonna have to come up with something that goes beyond our control.' I can't walk over to Peter [Peter Gooding, the Amherst athletic director] and say, 'I want to play one platoon football,' any more than Mike can go over to Russ Reilly and say, 'Hey Russ, next year Admissions is gonna do x with the understanding that you're gonna play one platoon football.'"

The idea would be simple enough to institute, since NESCAC schools play their entire football schedules within the Conference. And it certainly would be a bold move on a national scale. "I think it would garner lots of incredibly positive attention," says Parker. "I'm convinced of it."

Many in the NESCAC are convinced that recruiting today is affected by powerful forces beyond the league's control.

"There are many who think we should be reverting back to the way athletics was in the '50s," says Reilly, "where there wasn't a lot of recruiting, and you survived with walk-on kids. There is no such thing as a walk-on anymore because the recruiting process is so sophisticated now. It's more prospective students and their families recruiting institutions, than institutions recruiting kids—especially at the NESCAC level."

Reilly says Middlebury coaches now spend between 40 and 60 percent of their time on recruiting, as opposed to 30 and 40 percent back when he coached fifteen years ago. The volume of inquiries from prospective students has skyrocketed, thanks to email, and parents are more involved than ever, spending considerable time, energy, and money on their children's sports and future.

"There are a lot of people spending an awful lot of money on video productions that never occurred when I started here twenty-five years ago," says Reilly. "It just didn't happen. And people realize that if they get their kid involved in summer camps, that it's going enhance their chances of getting into this kind of an institution. It might be sending their child off to a private school for a couple of years. They are looking for any edge they can to get their student into this type of an institution."

Sheehy estimates that half of the athletes at Williams initiate the first contact with a coach at the school. This is in sharp contrast with what happens at most Ivy League schools (the exception in my research being Princeton, which tends to recruit itself in many sports), where it is rare for an athlete who initiates contact to wind up on a coach's final list to Admissions. At the NESCAC level, players and their families set up appointments or stop by to see coaches, hoping to generate interest and improve their chances of getting in. But that self-promotion does not mean their son or daughter is being recruited.

"You see parents being a bit naïve and maybe a kid being a bit naïve about a kid's athletic ability," says Bruce Bailey. "Sometimes it's a little brutal reality. We had one kid this year, his parents were so out of it in terms of this kid's ability as a baseball player—which was very marginal—they just assumed that they were going to get into places like the University of Chicago and Pomona. No way was that the case. They just got snowed by a letter. These coaches are sending out computer-generated letters by the tons, early on, to juniors. They can buy these PSAT and SAT lists now and get scores, which gives them a pool to start with. I coached basketball here for twenty years, and that's the most out-of-control sport there is right now in terms of delusions of grandeur that a lot of parents have."

"I've heard kids say that they were recruited, who came into my office and sat on my couch after their admission interview," says Dave Saward, the Middlebury men's soccer coach. "They weren't recruited. They stopped in to see me. They weren't on my list to Admissions. If you ask fifteen people what recruiting means, you'll get fifteen different answers."

Ask a NESCAC admission dean what recruiting means and you'll hear this from Tom Parker: "To me this is not proathletic versus antiathletic. I think all the things that one learns from athletics that I did, that my kids learned, that's not what's at issue. I think what's at issue is, how representative of our students should our student-athletes be?"

"The sad thing is, I was just saying to our incoming president, it seems that everything in athletics now needs to be regulated. You know, the Ivy League might as well be the Big 10 now. And years ago, and I'm sounding like an old fogey here, but when I played, I think that a lot of stuff was, 'Oh, you just don't do that.' Or common sense tells you, 'You don't want to do that.' And now it seems that everything has to be regulated. What the coach will tell you is, 'Unless it's prohibited, it's okay.' So, we're headed that way in the NESCAC to a degree. I wish we didn't have to do some of these things, but I just think we have to. It's hard to compete, and I think it's the role of sport in culture. There are a lot of things that are beyond NESCAC's control."

Even so, athletics in the NESCAC looks a good deal saner and more balanced than in the Ivy League. Which is why, six years ago, one of the Ivy League presidents approached Jeff Orleans, and said, "I'm getting a lot of pressure from my faculty to consider moving to Division III. What do you think?"

Orleans says he talked to a lot of people, and then shared his answer. "One of the things I said was, the pressure to be nationally successful will be much more intense in D-III than it is in D-I. It's one thing for your team to lose in the first round of the NCAA basketball tournament to Michigan. But it's another thing to lose to Williams."

Or to Middlebury, Amherst, Trinity, Colby, Bates, or any other NESCAC school, in any number of other sports.

"I'm lucky that I got to learn a lot before I came here," says Peter Lasagna. "And now I figure I'm probably really hitting my stride now that I'm in this league. . . . It was a lucky coincidence that I got to Bates. We continue to be a school that truly puts forth student-athletes and gives them an opportunity to compete in the sport that they love, without making it a full-time job. I think that's part of what's really, really right in this league."

Chapter Thirteen

No End In Sight

"Recruiting is a never-ending process. It never ends, and there's never a break. And if you think there's a break, then you're falling behind."

Dave Roach
Brown University
Director of Athletics

It was mid-June 2003 and the summer college tours were underway. The Dartmouth Admissions waiting room, packed with high school students and their parents, was stifling hot. The head of a large standing fan rotated slowly in front of an open French door overlooking the college green, but the warm air it circulated only heightened the sense of tension and anxiety in the room. I was waiting to interview Karl Furstenberg as part of my research for this book. The others were waiting to take tours of the campus or to meet with an admission officer as part of their research for college. Parents looked at magazines, checked their watches, and stole furtive glances at each other's offspring, checking out the competition for their child's spot in the next freshman class. Was that girl in the corner a math whiz? Was the girl on the couch a legacy? Could that boy, working madly on his laptop, be a genius? Or was he a poseur? Some of the prospective students couldn't sit still, and kept rising from their chairs and couches to browse through the informational literature stacked in racks at the far end of the room. Others shifted in their chairs, unable to focus on the reading material in their laps. A few stared straight ahead, as if gazing into the future, wondering, 'Out of the ten candidates in this room, will I be the one who eventually gets accepted?' They were smart kids, weren't they? Accompanied by caring parents. Surely, they knew the odds. One out of ten would be accepted. One father leaned forward in his easy chair, looking very uneasy indeed, his elbows on his knees, an empty paper coffee cup crushed between his fingers, his eyes focused on the reception counter, as if by staring long and hard enough at the crown of the head of the student-intern seated there he could will his child's acceptance.

And then one girl rose from the couch where she was seated next to her mother, and strode confidently across the room to the reception counter. She looked fit, athletic, the sort of outdoor-oriented student you see around the Dartmouth campus. She placed one arm on the counter, leaned forward, and asked the receptionist for the name and phone number of the women's soccer coach.

The room grew silent. This girl had an edge.

The receptionist looked up at the girl, smiled, and said she'd look it up. She found the information and passed it along. Everyone in the room overheard her say: "It's Erica Walsh, and you can reach her at 646-3581 or by email at Erica-dot-Walsh-at-Dartmouth-dot-edu."

"Thank you very much," said the girl, writing it all down. She took her piece of paper and marched back across the room as every eye watched her, the whole room certain that she now possessed an advantage the others did not.

I found myself thinking, "If they only knew the truth. If they only knew how complicated it was."

Because the truth was as simple and as complicated as this. First, Erica Walsh was no longer the Dartmouth women's soccer coach. She had resigned five months earlier, back in January, to attend business school. Her assistant, Ben Landis, had been named her successor in April. The receptionist was clearly not a soccer fan (like me), or she would have known this. And second (and more importantly), any girl who had to ask an admission receptionist for a coach's name, while visiting the school unofficially on her own dime, was unlikely to ever gain an advantage in the admission process. If she had not yet received at least one letter from the soccer coach by June of her junior year, and if she had not completed and mailed back the enclosed questionnaire, the odds of her winding up on the coach's final, ranked list to Admissions were slim to none, at best. Not that Ben Landis would turn his back on finding a diamond in the rough (all Ivy coaches dream of such a scenario, especially one that rival coaches know nothing about), but it was extremely rare for a player to catch his, or any other Ivy coach's eye, in such a fashion.

I watched the girl take her seat, feeling badly for her, knowing her odds of being recruited were negligible. (To make matters worse, she was clearly pleased to have secured the wrong coach's name!) I admired her for seeking whatever advantage she could and for trying to play the cards she had. But the truth was she was not even in the game, and probably never would be.

And what a crazy game it is, shrouded in secrecy and filled with hypocrisy, based on a complex and confusing system, all of which makes it arguably the most challenging recruiting process in all of college sports. Looking inside Ivy League recruiting is like examining an intricate tapestry on a cloudy day. Each element (the A.I., financial aid, school size, location and curriculum, sport priority and tradition, league pecking order, football banding, facilities, budget, Likely Letters, admission support, total number of athletes allowed, even presidential involvement) is inextricably interwoven with every other element to create a distinct picture at each school. And then this picture is further refined within each institution, sport by sport. Alter one element in the tapestry, and the picture changes. Recruiting at Harvard differs from recruiting at Brown, just as recruiting wrestlers to Cornell differs from recruiting soccer players to Cornell. No wonder coaches coming from scholarship schools struggle to adapt to recruiting in the Ivy League. They come from an environment where NCAA academic minimums and athletic scholarships rule the game, and they enter the complex world of the A.I., need-based financial aid, some unethical applicants, and rival coaches who know how to play the Ivy recruiting game. They eventually master the A.I., only to find that financial aid considerations spoil the picture for a hot prospect. Or they recruit a kid whose academic numbers look good to Admissions throughout the prescreening process, only to watch helplessly as the player is rejected when Admissions hands down its final decision. Or they receive a verbal commitment from a player to attend their school, and arrange for a Likely Letter to be sent from Admissions, only to find out two weeks later that the player has lied and will be attending another school. Or they have sent a player their plane ticket to make an official visit, only to learn that an opposing Ivy coach has flown down to the student's home to make sure the recruit never gets on the plane. How much simpler the coaches had it at a scholarship school, where the NCAA minimum academic numbers are acceptable, athletic scholarships take care of financial aid, and players are bound by a written commitment! No wonder Tim Murphy, the Harvard football coach, says, "If you can recruit in the Ivy League, you can recruit anywhere." The complexity of the job undertaken by Ivy coaches is daunting. They have my respect for their efforts to do the job well.

The Academic Index, on the other hand, does not. The system is flawed, as we have seen, and so is the attitude of schools within the League that discourages coaches and administrators from talking about the A.I. Fran Dunphy, the Penn basketball coach dismissed my question about Penn's mean A.I., saying, "I don't have that information," as if such ignorance were remotely plausible, and he could ever manage to conduct his recruiting unaware of his school's, and his league's, boundaries. Julie Shackford, the Princeton women's soccer coach, was far more believable and forthright when she said, simply, "We're not supposed to talk about the A.I." Jeff Orleans, in the Ivy League office, would not share information on the mean A.I. of each school. One senses a league-wide policy has been put into effect to keep such information secret. This makes little sense, given that we know the overall mean A.I. standings, from top (Harvard) to bottom (Cornell). We know that Brown pays less attention to test scores than Dartmouth. We know that Yale and Princeton have mean A.I.s that are neck-in-neck, right behind Harvard's. We know that there is a gap between Dartmouth and the bottom four schools, Columbia, Penn, Brown, and Cornell. We can even surmise that Amherst, Williams, and Swarthmore have higher mean A.I.s than those bottom four Ivy schools, based simply on published average SAT scores of incoming freshmen. The Ivy League's public relations problem over recruited athletes, fueled by the books of Bill Bowen and his co-authors, will not vanish by adopting a secretive policy on the A.I. If you have a system, be transparent about it. Shutting down the flow of information only leads to skepticism.

Where on the A.I. scale, for instance, has Princeton been taking its athletes in sports that have not been regulated in the annual meetings of the Ivy admission deans? Up near Harvard, or down near Brown? We will never know. Jeff Orleans could not tell me. He just said it was a very good question.

The irony of the A.I. is that it creates as many problems as it solves. Take football, where "averaging" continues, despite the spin of league officials, who have renamed the process "banding." Each year, each Ivy football program admits thirty recruits. By the time these players are seniors, between one-half and two-thirds of the recruits will have stopped playing. Not held by athletic scholarships (a positive, in my view), many will quit. It's called "attrition" in the Ivy League. Others will suffer injuries. On average, then, only ten to twelve of these players will still be in uniform by their senior year. My question is: if admission spots are so precious and if recruited athletes are taking too many spots from the general pool, why not stop the A.I. averaging in football? Why not end the bands altogether, and have an A.I. floor above which coaches can take fifteen to twenty players a year, depending on their needs, injuries, and other factors?

rec.

The coaches will tell you that more of these players will still be on the roster as seniors. They may be high A.I. kids, they may be lower A.I. kids. But they will be kids who can play. Will they bring the school's academic standards down? The lower A.I. kids, according to every coach I interviewed, are the proven achievers. The higher A.I. kids, who "average" them out in the banding system, are far more prone to land in academic trouble. I find it ironic that these high A.I. kids are there to make the Ivies look good at admission time, but are usually the first ones to quit the team (negating the value of the spot they've taken), as well as the most likely to get into academic trouble. Bill Bowen's research on the academic underperformance of football players may actually be a reflection of his terribly flawed A.I. system. Banding is nothing more than averaging, and it should be eliminated, as averaging in men's basketball and ice hockey has been eliminated. The Ivy Group presidents are only fooling themselves (but few others) by maintaining it. A. Bartlett Giamatti was right: Ivy schools should not be told whom they can and cannot admit based on a mathematical formula. The art of admissions is diminished in the process. Eliminate the football bands but not a firm floor and you can add ten to fifteen spots a year to the general admission pool at each Ivy school. Everyone wins.

rec.
#1

But why treat football differently from other sports.

Since the Ivy presidents will probably never completely eliminate the A.I., especially while under fire from Bill Bowen (whose large Mellon Foundation grants may be compromising their decision making), they should focus instead on adopting the Letter of Ivy Intent, as I proposed in an earlier chapter. The Ivy League must find a way to make commitment a two-way street. It is unfair to ask Ivy coaches, who arguably have the hardest recruiting job in the country, to proceed without having the authority to ask a recruit for a written commitment. This is 2004, not 1954. Unfortunately, as Dartmouth football coach Pat O'Leary points out, "A verbal commitment means nothing today." Instituting a Letter of Ivy Intent would reinforce the Ivy League principles of honesty and integrity, of excellence in academics and in athletics, and of playing for passion, not for pay. It would eliminate the ugly lies and other negative actions that are all too common under the current one-way Likely Letter system. And it would stop coaches at schools outside the League from recruiting players who have made a verbal commitment to attend an Ivy League school but have not yet signed anything to confirm this intention. Such poaching is perfectly legal under NCAA rules, which recognize only written agreements, and it places even more pressure on coaches and players in the months between January and late April or early May, when every Ivy applicant must mail in his or her acceptance card. Having players sign a Letter of Ivy Intent should also free up a number of admission slots for the general pool, since coaches and admission deans would know for certain which athletes were coming. Again, everyone would win.

Eliminating sports to save money and add spaces to the general admission pool will not occur in the foreseeable future at an Ivy League institution. "No president wants to fall on that sword," says Karl Furstenberg of Dartmouth. Indeed, in 2003 Dartmouth President James Wright was wounded when he tried to eliminate the school's two swimming teams for budgetary reasons. Wright and Dartmouth Athletic Director Josie Harper found themselves in a battle with a bitter and determined army that included athletes on the team, alumni who were former swimmers, parents of team members, Dartmouth students (including non-swimmers) who protested outside Wright's office, and a local newspaper columnist who lent his support to the athletes' cause and kept the public pressure on Wright and Harper to reinstate the team. After months of intense public and private arguments, the Dartmouth administration reversed its decision when swimming alums and other supporters raised the money required to fund the program. Years before, Princeton faced a similar uproar when it tried to cut its wrestling team. The solution was similar, thanks to loyal wrestling alums who rescued the program financially. "I don't know that you have a God-given right to fence," says Marvin Bressler, the retired professor of sociology at Princeton, addressing the large number of varsity teams sponsored by Ivy League schools. Yet cutting a program seems to be taboo. For several of the lower-profile Ivy League sports, however, the need to make academic exceptions for athletes in the admission process occurs far less frequently than it does for athletes who play higher-profile sports such as football, hockey, and basketball. As Yale Athletic Director Tom Beckett points out, "Our coaches find a lot of outstanding students to come to Yale. They happen to be outstanding athletes as well. But 70 percent of our recruited athletes would be here anyway [given their academic credentials]."

When Fran Dunphy told me that he loses far more players during the recruiting process each year due to financial reasons than to academic reasons, I was surprised. But he was not the only person I interviewed who said they felt that the high cost of attending an Ivy school has made money the number one issue in Ivy recruiting. I see no solution here. Unfortunately, the Justice Department settlement (described in Chapter 8) prevents the Ivy presidents from doing anything about this. Even having a conversation to discuss some sort of mutually agreeable reform is illegal. Schools that can pony up more cash for financial aid now have a distinct advantage in the athletic recruiting process, especially when a large majority of Ivy athletes are weighing scholarship offers elsewhere. Dartmouth's resurgence in football in the fall of 2003 (when they finished tied for second place with a 5-2 league record after finishing last the year before) was predicted by many in the Big Green athletic department, who pointed to the school's increased financial aid pool as the saving grace of the program. The turnaround saved John Lyons his job, which to admirers was only just because he is one of the truly fine people in the League. That money should play such a huge role in a big-time college athletic conference is no surprise. That the endowments and wealth of individual schools should affect a team's ability to compete in the Ivy League is unnerving.

But that is the case: there is no financial equity in the League. The rich are getting richer, in terms of athletic success. Just look at the Princeton Tigers.

Equally disturbing is the fact that competing in the Ivy League is more and more an option for just rich kids and poor kids. The kids from middle-class families are increasingly being squeezed out, which is why Fran Dunphy and other Ivy coaches lose so many prospects to scholarship schools. As excellent as Ivy League schools are, they do not stand alone, and many of these other outstanding academic institutions in America offer athletic scholarships.

Even if no Ivy League school will ever offer athletic scholarships, the League can, and should, take a lesson from top academic institutions that do, including Duke, Stanford, Notre Dame, Southern Methodist University, and Michigan. That lesson is to stop being so conflicted about embracing excellence in the classroom as well as excellence on the athletic fields. Fred Hargadon of Princeton, with years of experience behind him, makes the point this way: "You know, when I was at Stanford, there wasn't any feeling, it seemed to me—certainly not expressed—that being a first-rate academic institution and also having first-rate athletics were mutually exclusive. They didn't have the sense that it was a zero-sum game—if you were good at this, you couldn't be good at that. And when I went to football games there, the entire row in front of me would be the biology department. And when I went to a basketball game, the entire section in front of me would be physics. They have kept that kind of balance. I mean, they're really in an enviable position." Instead of attacking its athletes, as Bill Bowen and his coauthors have done in their chapters that address the Ivy League, Stanford has celebrated them, embracing excellence in all its forms. As Hargadon points out, the Bowen-Shulman-Levin methodology for measuring the academic performance of athletes is flawed: "I would be interested to see how many students in an entire graduating class 'underperformed' using the Bowen-Shulman-Levin calculus for determining 'underperformance.' For instance, if we enrolled a freshman class comprised entirely of Academic 1 rated students, four years later at least half of them would graduate in the bottom half of the class, and at least a quarter of them in the bottom quarter."

Nearly everyone I spoke with believes that Bowen's description of Ivy athletes' underperformance in the classroom exaggerates the extent of the problem. While Ivy admission deans, athletic directors, and coaches acknowledged having concerns about the academic performance of some athletes, they also expressed their belief that the vast majority are hard-working, committed students, eager to make the most of their Ivy League education. In an article in the *Princeton Alumni Weekly*, Princeton President Shirley Tilghman noted "that Tiger athletes' underperformance amounts on average to a 3.2 GPA when comparably qualified students earn a 3.6—a B+ instead of an A-." If such differences equal underperformance for students who also train and compete at the highest levels of Division I, then Dr. Bowen and his supporters should reassess their judgment that a commitment to excellence in athletics jeopardizes a commitment to excellence in academics. For at the moment, Ivy athletes go on to grad school at the same rate as their nonathlete classmates, and they earn an average of 20 percent more over the course of their careers. Rather than being criticized, these students should be admired.

How much of the problem lies in stereotyping and in bias against athletes on campus? I was disturbed to hear that athletes at Ivy schools try to hide their athletic identity from professors, that student newspapers publish antiathlete editorials, and that some professors refuse to allow athletes to miss classes to compete (in the age of online class notes, and a willingness by student-athletes to meet with professors out of class). I question the value of such an environment for athletes. If these students had an exceptional talent they had worked hard to develop in music, painting, acting, or writing that helped them to gain admission, would they encounter the same kind of discrimination against them on campus? "They don't call them a student-writer, or student-artist, or student-musician," says Bill Cleary, the retired director of athletics at Harvard. "Why single out student-athletes? They are students first who are also athletes, just like other students who are also dancers or actors or editors of the student paper." It's unfortunate, but there does appear to be a zero-sum game between academics and athletics underway in the Ivy League—a belief that the institutions cannot achieve excellence in one endeavor without sacrificing excellence in the other. The presidents should end the game by making clear the distinction between academics and education.

Invaluable educational lessons are taught in the athletic arena that complement and enhance many of the invaluable academic lessons taught in the classroom. The lessons learned by athletes may sound trite by now, because they have been overstated and made into clichés, but for those who heed them, the lessons are very real indeed, and can be just as meaningful as their academic instruction. The cultivation of leadership; the development of character; the abilities to work within a team, to accept differences, and to overcome adversity; the fostering of self-discipline; the setting of goals; and the pursuit of excellence—these and other values are all an integral part of an athlete's experience as an undergraduate. As Mike Goldberger of Brown points out, students who participate in public service, the performing arts, the student newspaper, student government, and other co-curricular activities also learn invaluable lessons that are not specifically academic in nature. Of course, students engaged in academic pursuits can also learn many of the same lessons. For me, studying writing with professors at Middlebury, with authors at Bread Loaf, and in seminars and tutorials has been just as fruitful as competing on teams at Middlebury. Yet in my view, academics alone do not equal education, any more than education equals academics. I would no more encourage my sons to spend their lives reading books and writing papers at the exclusion of playing soccer or basketball than I would want them to play a sport at the expense of doing their academic work with care. Ultimately, the experiences athletes have on both the playing field and in the classroom do much to enhance their lives and their careers. Seeking the best of worlds—academics and athletics—these students arguably receive the best Ivy education of all.

"The issue we have to resolve before we can move forward," says Josie Harper, the Dartmouth athletic director, "is 'Do these kids matter? Are they valued?'" We know that admission deans value them, as do many faculty members and fellow students, athletic alumni, athletic directors, and coaches. Not surprisingly, employers and graduate school admission officers also value Ivy students who have played a sport; indeed in some cases former athletes are regarded more highly than classmates who did not compete at the varsity level, thanks in part to their proven ability to work within a team, to manage their time, and to perform under stress. Despite this record, the present controversy over the Ivy League's admission process for recruited athletes has been intense. Improvement is sorely needed.

My hope is that this account, based as it is on the words of participants, will help all those looking for solutions. In particular, I hope it will dispel many of the myths surrounding the recruiting process, encourage open discussion of the current system's pros and cons, and lead the presidents to reforms that serve the interests of both their schools and the students who are recruited to perform there.

In the meantime, Ivy athletic recruiting will continue as described in the preceding pages. The League cannot turn back the clock to a simpler time, much as some of its administrators might wish it could, and as Bill Bowen suggests it should. The Ivy Group is not a business consortium, an association of legal or medical professionals, or a collection of real estate holdings, as the name Ivy Group might imply. It is a Division I athletic conference, known by everyone outside its own inner circle as the Ivy League. Its executive director, Jeff Orleans, is an athletic conference commissioner. The corporate charter of the Ivy League is all about sports.

Which is why, as you read this, regardless of the time of day or the time of year, there are Ivy coaches off on recruiting trips, sending out letters and emails, or working their contacts on the phone—*right now*—looking for their next hot prospect. They are hoping that her A.I. is high, that her financial need can be met, and that Admissions will let her in.

The recruiting never ends, and if you think there's a break, then you're falling behind.

Acknowledgments

I want to thank Alex Kahan, the publisher of Nomad Press, for recruiting me to write this book—for entrusting me with his idea, for believing in my ability to handle the material, and for helping me to shape the final outcome. His insight, enthusiasm, good humor, and friendship have been invaluable.

I also owe a great debt to my editor, Susan Hale, whose patience, faith, and encouragement never wavered, and whose skill, attention to detail, and calm assurance helped to usher my initial proposal into a final manuscript. I cannot imagine having a kinder and more astute person to steer me through the process.

I want to thank others at Nomad Press for their friendship, support, and individual talents: Jeff McAllister for his handsome book design; Dave Morin for his striking cover; Mark Schiffman for his original cover photograph; Eric Goldwarg for his helpful feedback; Kate Carolan for her stellar work as publicity intern; Lauri Berkenkamp for her boundless energy as the book's publicity director; and Rachel Benoit for her good humor and attention to detail. The generosity of Team Nomad resonates through the pages of this book.

And so does the generosity of all the people who shared their stories and perspectives with me. I only wish time and space had allowed each of them to receive as much attention in the final manuscript as they deserved. To those who are absent entirely, please know that you played a more significant role than you may realize, by informing my overall view of the subject and by giving me a solid foundation from which to work.

Kathy Slattery, the sports information director at Dartmouth, was instrumental in helping me gain access to many people in the Ivy League. I would never have succeeded without her. My sincere thanks to her counterparts, Steve Conn of Yale and John Veneziano of Harvard; to Mike Noonan, who became an invaluable resource; and to Dave Faucher, Betsy Etchells, Mike Schoenfeld, Bill Cleary, Russ Reilly, and Dave Saward for their many referrals. The web of connections they provided made this book possible.

Without exception, everyone I interviewed was patient, forthcoming, and generous with their time. For sharing their stories, I am grateful to the athletes: Alai Nuualiitia, Alison Crocker, Beverly Moore, Carl Morris, Charles Harris, Chris Dodson, Chris Higgins, Hana Peljto, Jake McKenna, Mike Giles, Amina Helal, Rob Chisholm, Scott Turco, Alison Connolly, Julian Jordan, P.J. Scheufele, Pam Saunders, John Rusten, Bernardo Samper, Maura Bolger, and Nadeem Osman.

My heartfelt thanks to Jay Fiedler for contributing his Foreword.

My appreciation to all the coaches for their patience and insights: Jeff Cook, Jenny Graap, John Lyons, Bill Beaney, Peter Lasagna, Digit Murphy, Dave Saward, John Power, Pat O'Leary, Jack Siedlecki, Julie Shackford, Tim Taylor, Bobby Clark, Wendy Bartlett, Ruff Patterson, Tim Murphy, Dick Grossman, Scott Bradley, Glen Miller, James Jones, Dave Faucher, Mike Noonan, Fran Dunphy, Kathy Delaney-Smith, Roger Grillo, Paul Assaiante, Bryan Scales, Brian Roxborough, Keith Clark, and Scott Anderson.

My deep appreciation to athletic administrators Tom Beckett, Peter Gooding, Gary Walters, Josie Harper, Russ Reilly, Bob Scalise, Dave Roach, Harry Sheehy, Bob Ceplikas, and Bill Cleary; and to the admission deans, financial aid directors, and college placement officers: Karl Furstenberg, Tom Parker, Mike Goldberger, Bruce Bailey, Mike Schoenfeld, Don Betterton, and especially Fred Hargadon, who generously shared his insightful comments on the first draft and lent his support despite our differing views on certain issues.

My thanks as well to Dartmouth College President James Wright, and to recently retired Middlebury College President John McCardell, for making time to speak with me; to Jeff Orleans, Executive Director of the Ivy Group Council, for patiently answering my questions; to LaKesha Whitaker of the Ivy League office; and to Professors Marvin Bressler and Hal Scott for their time and insights.

Bruce Wood was extremely generous with his time, advice, support, and knowledge. Paul Witteman was magnanimous with his enthusiasm and editorial expertise. Jennifer Yokum did a superb job of transcribing many hours of taped interviews. Lee Currier was excellent as a second transcriber.

Margaret and Tom Fitzgerald, Wendy and Jack Marrinan, Carrie and Duncan Law, and Lynn and Mike McKenna were all generous with meals, lodging, and encouragement as I conducted research. I am also grateful for the support of Carol and John Clemency, Matt Freeman, Lisa and Jay Harvey, Charlie Woglom, Jim Keane, Andy Glover, Don Parsons, Sarah Barnes, Mark Klarich, Paul Glover, Tom Johnson, Eric Copenhaver, Paul Schleicher, Rob Connerty, and Dave Greeley. Thanks to my former Middlebury teammates who remain close friends and supporters; to my other Hanover pals; to my golfing buddies; and to my friends in the Upper Valley and points beyond who have encouraged me. To my friends at Golf Ski—especially Amy and Scott Peters and Ned Waters—thanks for accepting my passion for writing while providing me with steady work and income.

My heartfelt thanks to my family, who always back me no matter what I am working on: Peter and Peg; Brian, Robin, and Izzy; and the Peeler clan—the Judge and Barbara, Tater and Bill, Gail and Henry, Lee and Madelyn, Ray and Susie, and all the girls and one new lad. Nancy and Lee Stiles also blessed me with their support and generosity.

My father was instrumental in helping me improve the first draft, and I deeply appreciate his generous input and expert editorial work. My mother facilitated our collaboration with her computer expertise and usual good cheer. I can't thank them enough for fostering my love of sports and writing.

And I can't thank Cecy, Nolan, and Nick enough for their support during my immersion in this project. Nick, thanks for keeping me laughing and bringing the tray of tea and snacks out to my office at night. Nolan, thanks for reading each new chapter as it emerged and sharing your ideas and enthusiasm. And Peels, thanks for all the years of faith and love. It took a while, but here at last is the first published book . . . and to think it all started with that shooting star on Mount Olympus. Thanks for being here every step of the way.

Chris Lincoln
June 2004